MW01289082

Credits

Quotations from the spring/summer 2010 issue of *Learning Disabilities: A Multidisciplinary Journal*, a tribute to Sally Smith and the Lab School Methodology, used by the permission of the publication and the authors.

Quotations from "Who Are You, Elizabeth Benson (Ben) Booz?" by Ben Booz (*News and Views: The Quarterly Publication of the Geneva Monthly Meeting*, Geneva, Switzerland, Sept. 2013) used by permission of the author.

Quotations from *Land of Desire: Merchants, Power, and the Rise of a New American Culture* by William R. Leach (Vintage Books, New York © 1993) used by permission of Penguin Random House.

Quotation from *Model Woman: Eileen Ford and the Business of Beauty* by Robert Lacey of Harper, New York © 2015 used by permission of HarperCollins.

Quotations from *An Anthropology of Everyday Life: An Autobiography* by Edward T. Hall (Doubleday, New York © 1992) used by permission of Karin Berg Hall, trustee and executor of the Edward T. Hall estate.

Quotation from *How to Help Your Child in School* by Mary and Lawrence K. Frank (Viking Press, New York © 1950) used by permission of Penguin Random House.

Quotations and images from *A Child's Guide to a Parent's Mind* by Sally Liberman and Kiriki (New York, Henry Schuman © 1951) used by permission of HarperCollins.

Excerpts from the *Bennington Quadrille*, the *Bennington Weekly*, and the *Bennington Alumnae Quarterly* used by permission of Bennington College.

Quotation and cover image from *Nobody Said It's Easy* by Sally L. Smith (The MacMillan Company, New York © 1965) used by permission of Simon & Schuster.

Cover image of *No Easy Answers* by Sally L. Smith (Bantam Books, New York © 1995) used by permission of Penguin Random House.

Quotations and cover image from *Succeeding Against the Odds* by Sally L. Smith (Jeremy F. Tarcher Inc., Los Angeles © 1991) used with permission of Martha Casselman.

Quotations and cover images from *The Power of the Arts* by Sally L. Smith (Brookes Publishing, Baltimore ©) 2001) *Live It, Learn It* by Sally L. Smith (Brookes Publishing, Baltimore © 2005) by permission of Brookes Publishing.

Quotation from *Life, Animated* by Ron Suskind (Kingswell, New York, Los Angeles © 2014) used by permission of Kingswell.

Quotations and the cover image from *Different is Not Bad, Different is the World: A Book About Disabilities* by Sally L. Smith, illustrated by Ben Booz (Sopris West, Longmont, Colorado © 1994) used by permission of Scott McWhorter, Cambium Learning.

Cover photo © Terry Arthur, courtesy of the Lab School archives.

Photos from the personal archives of Sally Smith courtesy of her sons.

Photos from the *Bennington Quadrille* used by permission of Bennington College.

To Karen.

Thank you for the magic of your support in this and all things.

Chapters

One — The Clothes She *Didn't* Wear

"All the gaudy scarves, bright nail polish and lipstick, jangling earrings, and Giorgio perfume were part of who she was," said Gary Smith of his mother, Sally Smith. "They made her feel good. You always knew when she walked into a room that something great was going to happen. When I think about the outlandish clothes she wore, I also like to think about the clothes she *didn't* wear." Here Gary smiled slyly, allowing me to imagine a closet of zebra-patterned dresses, polka-dot vests, and ferret-headed boas.

Edward Behr, who taught in the early 1970s at the Lab School—the revolutionary school for students with learning disabilities that Sally founded in 1967—had an image in mind of Sally sitting on his desk in the front of his class, shoes off, legs swinging, engaging with ideas students threw out to her. A Bennington graduate himself, Behr imagined Sally acting just that way as a college student, a self-confident figure testing the norms of behavior for the late 1940s, as if she were the one in charge.

Growing up in school with Sally's oldest son, Randy, and her middle son, Nick, one grade behind us, I spent many hours in the Smiths' house in Washington. I remember watching Super Bowl III in Bob and Sally's bedroom, as flashy, goateed Joe Namath and the New York Jets ushered in a new era of the NFL by beating the staid Baltimore Colts and crew-cutted Johnny Unitas and Earl Morrall.

Though I didn't know Mrs. Smith (as I called her then) had been a dancer, I noticed her grace as she glided around her house, always with shoes off, with a spritely gait and a slip of the hip. She was full of life and—forgive me—sexy. She loved to laugh and smile. As she prepared for a social evening, she didn't mind evincing a hint of décolletage.

After some friends and I had bartended for one of her epic Christmas parties, she shared that one of our schoolmates' fathers, like mine an Episcopal minister, had put a note with his phone number in her hand. "He likes his women to call him," she said, with a wink and a smile.

"The parties included everyone she knew," said her longtime friend and editor Elizabeth Benson (Ben) Booz. "They came in waves, and she would stand at the door and greet us all. We older people would come early, and as we were leaving we'd see the younger ones coming in." Guests would enjoy the newest artwork, like the wood sculpture of a thunderstorm that doubled as a chandelier (her design), or a multicolored wooden bird. "My goodness, the colors she painted her walls," recalled Booz. "Orange in the dining room. Red in the kitchen. Purple in the halls." The character of the parties evolved over the years, from the dashing best-and-brightest couples of the Kennedy-Johnson era to a more eclectic mix of artists, musicians, writers, and politicians, with—during all eras—accents from around the world. My mother remembered watching Hubert Humphrey, then the vice president, circulate, chatting with every person present and somehow remembering every one of their names when it was time to leave.

The Smiths' home sat atop a ten-foot rise on leafy Cleveland Avenue, just a couple of blocks from the grounds of the National Cathedral. I loved its zebra rug, metal sculpture of a heron, pistachio nuts on the mantel, massive world map on the wall of the kitchen, and the countless board games in the living room cabinet. And I can always picture Sally in it. One day in 1999, several of our friends had adjourned to the Smiths' house after our twenty-fifth high school reunion. Though this was near the day of Sally's seventieth birthday, she hopped like a teenager onto her sofa, tucking her legs under her and leaning forward to hear the news about our classmates.

Then she told us of her recent adventure. She'd won a Woman of Distinction award from Birmingham Southern College in Alabama. It involved a trip in a private plane with Olivia de Havilland and Wendy Lee Gramm, an economist, member of the Reagan administration, and wife of former US Senator Phil Gramm, and a weekend with many remarkable women. Sally told us about the riotous fun they had, sharing stories, and finding endless commonalities. She said that de Havilland, the beloved Maid Marian of *Robin Hood* and Melanie Wilkes of *Gone with the Wind,* was down to earth and delightful. Gramm, though of a different political persuasion, was great fun. "That's exactly what it was like," confirmed Gramm from her home in Texas. "We bonded, no question."

In examining Sally's life, you get used to the fact that she never stopped attracting and befriending interesting people. Or perhaps she saw how each of us could be interesting with just a little support. Christine Chang, the Lab School's director of occupational therapy, remembers apologizing in her job interview for her eclectic resume, to which Sally responded, "We like eclectic around here!" All those she touched—educators, schoolchildren, friends, and colleagues—remember her encouraging words. I certainly do. I can think of three moments in particular.

One was especially undeserved. I had a dog I loved but, truth be told, was never able to properly housetrain. Nonetheless, when the Smiths got a dog—a black lab named Lucky—Sally referred to me in front of Randy, Nick, and Gary as an expert in training dogs.

A second kind remark came in my eighth-grade spring. I didn't know back then that Sally had felt herself to be too heavy in her youth, but I noticed she was always supportive as I wrestled with my girth. For the Flower Mart, a daylong fundraising carnival on the National Cathedral grounds, I fought my shyness and asked a girl to go with me. I dressed as sharply as I could manage, in brown pants and a matching shirt, and escorted her to the carousel, the mini-roller coaster, and the booth where you tossed ping pong balls to win a goldfish. "I saw you at the Flower Mart," Sally said later. "You looked great!"

A third encouragement came the summer after my tenth-grade year, when our school had introduced us to backpacking and camping. Sally hired me to assist one of her teachers in an outdoor program to take place on an island in the Potomac. She theorized that camping skills—making fires, paddling canoes, setting up tents—could help Lab School students grasp other concepts. When building a fire, for example, the tiniest twigs lead to small ones, which lead to bigger ones, and so on. These spatial relationships can be hard for children with learning disabilities. Similarly, the repetitive motion of paddling a canoe might be perfect for a hyperactive child who tended to perseverate—that is, do the same thing over and over.

One rainy day, the class retreated indoors to the Lab School basement and made a tent out of ponchos. I'm not sure what lesson we covered, but the focus of being contained under a tent was helpful. A few days later, Sally pulled her robin's-egg-blue Chevy station wagon up in front of our house, rolled down her window, leaned across the front seat, and said, "I heard you did great yesterday! Like a seasoned pro!" Undeserved, but inspiring all the same.

Strange how encouraging words stay with us. Or perhaps it's not strange at all. As much as encouraging words help every child, they are sips of water in the desert for children who struggle in traditional schools. That summer at the Lab School, I learned many things. One day the head of the program and I were looking at the children's paintings. One boy had drawn crows in the air cawing at him, a small figure on the ground, "You are stupid! You are nothing." My boss asked, "Do you see anything significant here?" He had to explain it to me: being mocked and teased was what the children experienced and expressed in their art.

In preparing to write about Sally, I met Gary for lunch at a Greek restaurant on upper Connecticut Avenue. At 53, he had survived leukemia. Throughout our conversation he surprised me with his ability to look back with objective distance and wit at the young man with behavior problems who ate his frustration and was thrown out of schools yet always had the self-awareness to know he was different and to feel the sting of teasing from other kids. "You go to the Lab School, huh?" one had said. "What are you, a lab rat?"

Gary still stings from the words of kids in his neighborhood and even his own schoolmates who suffered from the same challenges. Longtime Lab School art teacher Mark Jarvis wrote in a special 2010 issue of *Learning Disabilities: A Multidisciplinary Journal* on Sally and the Lab School Methodology, "Of all the concerns that Sally had for the child with learning disabilities possibly none is more important than self-esteem. She was eloquent in her description of what the interior life of this student is like: how fearful they are about being different, of being singled out as not being as capable as others." This is the same stigma felt by celebrities who had dyslexia—including Tom Cruise, Cher, Bruce Jenner, Magic Johnson, Robert Rauschenberg, and Henry Winkler, who have all been gracious enough to speak at Lab School galas over the years.

"Sally Smith made magic on a daily basis," wrote the issue's guest editor, Luanne Adams, Lab's longtime head of psychological services. "Children and adolescents with learning disabilities come to the Lab School in Washington or Baltimore and they have fun. They learn. They feel good about themselves. Adults with learning disabilities who did not get what they needed in school come to Sally's Night School and learn to read or write or to use a computer. Parents are reassured about their children's futures. Special education teachers feel effective because they are supported, inspired, and energized by their work.

"Sally developed a methodology for making magic upon which she built a large educational institution with three campuses[1] and an enrollment of nearly 500 students, Grades 1 through 12, intelligent students with moderate to severe learning disabilities. Sally trained legions of special education teachers . . . in the master's program in Special Education: Learning Disabilities she directed for decades at American University. . . . Sally expected every teacher in every classroom, whatever program level and whatever the subject matter, to be creative and use artistic principles to bring vivacity, interest value and engagement, clarity, and memorability to the subject matter."

Former American University students remembered the first day of many classes, when Sally would play loud music, flash the lights of the classroom on and off, write

---

[1] Including the Academy in Manayunk in Conshohocken, Pennsylvania, established in 2005 on the Lab School model.

unintelligible words on the blackboard, and create innumerable other distractions, explaining, "This is what the classroom environment is like for your learning-disabled children." Her training started with empathy and included the embrace of the odd. M. Sean Rozsics, the Lab School's longtime music maestro, wrote that at administrative meetings "Sally always had some unusual piece of art recently acquired that she would pass around as a stimulating conversation piece and often served some odd pastry or candy. She led with grace and humor and made every occurrence a colorful event in which everyone wanted to participate."

Sally's leadership, originality, and brilliance as an educator were sparked by necessity. She started the Lab School of Washington because Gary, her third son, needed a school that could address his severe dyslexia. She was indeed a devoted, determined mother who overcame the odds out of boundless love. The *Today* show got it right when it featured Sally and Gary on Mother's Day a few years ago.

Sally crafted the Academic Club Methodology out of her sons' themed birthday parties, when she saw how the kids became engaged in playing roles of characters in history—and how much they learned. When she launched the Lab School on twenty days' notice, she tapped artistic friends like the lanky Mary-Averett Seelye to teach dance, the stocky Ben Schmutzhart to teach sculpture, and the worldly painter Ben Booz to preside as the Cave Lady over the Cave Club, teaching the ascent of humanity by living it. "It was the material of what was later going to be fashioned into the Lab School system," said Ben. "The children were able to act parts and be completely enveloped and get into this total immersion. In dancing, one youngster who had trouble with the concept of time—of past, present, and future—was able to grasp it as he moved his body backward and forward. Back then it was highly creative people making it up as they went along. She collected all of these artists as teachers. Anyone who was around she just swept them in. It was Sally's genius."

Tracing the roots and many paths of this genius has been an inspiring and ever-surprising journey. Sally grew up in confined comfort on Park Avenue as the youngest daughter of a driven Lithuanian immigrant who came to New York at age thirteen, rose to wealth and success, and presided for decades over one of New York's great department stores. At Bennington College, Sally danced under Martha Hill, a close associate of Martha Graham, and studied psychology under Erich Fromm, the chief successor of Freud and Jung. Under Fromm's guidance, Sally's senior project became her first book, *A Child's Guide to an Adult's Mind*. While working for the World Health Organization in Paris, she met a rising diplomat, Bob Smith. They married, had three sons, and moved to Washington, where Bob joined John F. Kennedy's State Department. Sally and Bob Smith were smart and ambitious in the glamorous days of Camelot. Then the script changed. More than just starting a school, she found a calling and a passion.

Sally shared her methodologies and philosophies in speeches around the country, in articles, and in her books *No Easy Answers* (1978, with many versions and editions thereafter), *Succeeding Against the Odds: Strategies and Insights from the Learning Disabled* (1991), *Different is Not Bad, Different is the World: A Book About Disabilities* (1994), *The Power of the Arts: Creative Strategies for Teaching Exceptional Learners* (2001), and *Live It, Learn It: The Academic Club Methodology for Students with Learning Disabilities and ADHD* (2005).

The creative drive for those seminal works, with Booz as her amanuensis, will come as a surprise to none of her former teachers or students. "In the nineties," said Booz, "Sally had two weeks between the Lab School and her summer session at AU, so the last half of June and the first half of July was her creative time. She would announce when we would start."

Several years ago, when I drove north from Washington to meet Booz in her Quaker retirement community in Sandy Springs, Maryland, she was just shy of her ninetieth birthday. We talked at a table in the dining area. She had a yellow legal pad filled with notes about points she wanted to

make about Sally. With her twinkling brown eyes and short gray bob, Booz oozed energy and joie de vivre. She spoke with a bit of an English accent in a slightly conspiratorial tone, as if she were letting me in on a secret, which she often was. Booz told me she had first met Sally in 1954, when she and her husband, Paul, were stationed in Bangladesh[2] with the World Bank. Booz had been born in London in 1925 and educated at Vassar, Berkeley,

Ben Booz, in Sandy Springs, Maryland, in 2014

and the *Institut des Hautes Études*

---

[2] This nation was East Bengal when the Boozes met the Smiths, then became East Pakistan, then Bangladesh. For simplicity, we will call it Bangladesh. In the same way, Pakistan was West Pakistan when the Boozes lived there, but we shall refer to it as we know it today.

Internationales in Geneva. She met Paul when they were wielding pickaxes among the Swiss Brigades of postwar idealists building a railroad for Tito in Yugoslavia. Booz said she and Paul had lived a nomadic life of sorts as he was stationed in Lebanon, Jordan, Pakistan, Bangladesh, and then, after a few years in DC in the 1960s, Indonesia. Like a postcolonial Kipling heroine, she had borne five children, each in different foreign nation—four boys, then, in Indonesia, "a girl, at last." Booz found the Kipling reference apt. "In Karachi, Pakistan," she said, "We lived in Zamzama, the locale of *Kim*. Kipling is very much in me." After Paul died, Booz taught for four years in a remote province of China and wrote about the experience in *National Geographic*, where she worked for twenty years thereafter. Through it all, she kept a small pink house, an intended retirement home, in the idyllic French village of Yvoire on Lake Geneva, which she and Paul had bought for $3,000 in 1949. "Sally would come to Yvoire and we would go away to work," said Booz. "We'd go in my car. I'd pack nice picnics for the trip. Sally would book a five-star hotel. We knew each other so well. We went to Italy, Switzerland, France. She talked the book out, throwing out ideas, creating new ones. I caught the words and put them into paragraphs. I'd sit in the big wicker chair with my feet on a big footstool looking at the lake and she'd lie down on the bed and talk. Sally was extremely energetic and so brilliant. She knew she had something incredibly important to say and she did anything she could to get it out. She was like a volcano. If you've ever been inside a volcano and looked at the bubbling mud, it just comes up bubbling from inside."

Sally knew the power of ideas, and collected inspiring quotes that she used in her speeches. She liked to quote one of her heroes in the education field, John Dewey, who said, "The self is not something ready-made but something in continuous formation through choice of action."

Sally could see the potential in people, draw them in, and inspire them to do more than they knew they could. "There are so many people, including me, who went into the field because of her," says my older brother Stocky Clark, who started out as Gary's babysitter and counts Sally as the mentor of his life. "She made you see the impact you could have on so many lives." Kelly McVearry had been a commercial real estate broker on K Street when a high school lacrosse teammate teaching a summer Space Club asked her to paint a fourteen-foot-tall mural of an astronaut. Sally saw the mural, asked for McVearry's resume, and called her. "Kelly, it's Sally Smith," she said. "I really need to have you on staff." Sally offered her a 45 percent pay cut to teach plaster art and painting, adding that she would have to enroll in the AU master's program. "I felt the magic," says McVearry, who taught for five years at Lab, got her master's at AU and another at Harvard, then earned a PhD in interdisciplinary neuroscience at Georgetown. "Sally changed my life."

Sally, who believed in enjoying life, saved the Hans Selye quote "If you do what you like, you never really work. Your work is your play." She loved the words from

Sally L. Smith.   Photo courtesy of the Lab School of Washington.

Picasso: "Every child is born an artist. The problem is how to keep it that way." At the

base of it all, Sally believed in the power of artistic expression—that it can teach

children in ways that nothing else can. "The arts civilize us," she once said to the

winners of the annual Robert Rauschenberg Foundation awards for art teachers. "They

articulate the human experience—the wonder, the joy, the beauty, the excitement, the

sorrow, the anger. For children who feel badly about themselves, the arts offer a chance

to say, 'I made it. I did it. I can do it again.'"

Two — Gray Homburg and Spats—and a New Arrival—on West End
Avenue

On Sunday afternoons in the late 1920s, Isaac Liberman would don his gray spats and

matching homburg hat, pick up his wooden cane with a gold band around it, and usher

his wife, Bertha, and three daughters into their elevator at 272 West Ninetieth Street in

Manhattan. From the front of their building, they walked a few steps to the corner, where

Liberman turned and took the lead as they promenaded on West End Avenue, showing

off the family to the neighborhood. Ike, as he was called, a trim five-foot-four and

dapper, walked with a stride that was measured and determined. Bertha, barely five feet

and fuller of figure, struggled to keep up at the best of times. "My father and mother

never walked arm in arm," remembered Hazel Liberman Arnett, who trailed behind with

her older sisters, Ruth and Irene. Unlike the schoolgirls in the *Madeline* books, they did

not walk in a straight line. "It was more of a rotating formation," said Arnett.

This was the West Side of Manhattan in the last days of the Roaring Twenties. Just

a block to the west, fashionable figures like Babe Ruth, George Gershwin, and Damon

Runyon steered their roadsters along the tree-lined curves and rises of Riverside Drive,

which had been finished just nineteen years earlier but still felt like the modern world

come to life.

Sundays were the Libermans' family time. The rest of the week, including

Saturdays, Ike served on the board of New York's oldest retail store, Arnold Constable,

at Fifth Avenue and Fortieth Street, for the middle class and ran M. I. Stewart &

Company, the specialty store he had founded, serving upscale customers. "My father

was a workaholic," said Arnett. "We didn't see him, except on Sunday. He went to work before we got up and came home after we went to bed. On Sunday, we'd put on our coats and walk the neighborhood."

By any measure Ike Liberman had plenty to show off. Since 1901, when he had arrived as a thirteen-year-old at the Castle Garden pier from Lithuania, he had founded and built Stewart & Company into one of Manhattan's largest specialty stores, and in 1925 he had been asked to help with the management of Arnold Constable.

As the decade Lindy hopped toward its crescendo, Liberman was still on the rise, determined to build his fortune, burnish his name, and take his place in fashionable society. As with J. P. Morgan on Wall Street, the initials I. L. were identifier enough for Isaac Liberman in the retail world.

In 1928 he had supervised the creation of the inaugural gown for the wife of the newly elected governor of New York, Franklin Delano Roosevelt. The process of creating the gown included the input of Eleanor Roosevelt's mother-in-law, Sara Delano Roosevelt. "I had picked a group of dresses that made her look younger," said Liberman. "I had to show them to Mrs. Roosevelt's mother-in-law. She said, 'This is terrible.'" Liberman, being diplomatic, helped Eleanor and Sara settle on another style, although he knew it was not as flattering as the first group he had shown. Eleanor said to Liberman, "You know, you've been wonderful with my mother-in-law." Later, he said, "Eleanor realized she'd made a mistake."

It turned out to be the first of two inaugural gowns Liberman made for Roosevelt, who became a longtime friend and ally in philanthropic causes. At her behest, Liberman became an early and loyal supporter of the Wiltwyck School for Boys, which was located across the Hudson from the Roosevelts' home in Hyde Park and served the needs of emotionally disturbed "juvenile delinquent" African American teenagers.

In the spring of 1929, while Bertha was pregnant with their fourth child, Liberman was busy with another venture—joining his friend Sam Golding in starting the Sterling National Bank and Trust Company. As it happened, the bank opened on May 7, 1929, the same day Bertha gave birth to Sarah Bayer Liberman, named after Bertha's mother. Eddie Cantor, then starring in *Whoopee!* on Broadway, attended the bank's opening celebration. "We compared births," said Liberman. "Sally was my fourth daughter. Cantor said, 'I can top that—I have five.'" Sally's birth was long and painful: "The only one that had caused her such pain," Sally remembered her mother saying, "the only one to make it necessary for her to go to the hospital." As he had before the birth of Hazel, Liberman had strongly hoped for a boy to carry on his business, and he expressed his disappointment in Bertha for not producing the right gender.

"I do remember the day Sally was born," said Arnett. "I was in kindergarten downstairs in the building where we lived. There was this beautiful bassinette and inside there was this beautiful, fair-skinned baby. Later, in the summer, when we rented a hundred-acre estate in Dobbs Ferry, New York, I remember that beautiful bassinette next to my favorite tree, which I liked to climb."

"I was amazed about this fun little cherub," said cousin Abba Bayer, always called Abby, who was about the same age as Arnett.[3]

Thereafter, when the Libermans took their Sunday strolls on West End Avenue, the baby Sarah stayed back in the apartment with Anna MacDonald Fosdick, the Scottish

---

[3] At 90, Abba Bayer was still going to work each day as a coffee importer with J. W. Phyfe & Co.

nurse who had been with the family for eleven years. "She just took charge," says Arnett. "Our time was all with the nurse. It wasn't with our parents—just on Sunday."

Fosdick's influence on the household can be gauged by a switch she made soon after the baby's arrival. "Anna the nurse changed her name," says Hazel. "It's scandalous! She was named Sarah after her maternal grandmother, but Anna changed it to Sally because she had a sister named Sally."

That summer, Liberman's perspective as board member of a bank may have led him to take a close look at the surging stock market. Or perhaps he had a moment like that of Joseph P. Kennedy, who said he realized it was time to exit the market when taxi drivers offered him stock tips, the man shining his shoes gave him the latest financial news, and his cook had a brokerage account. Liberman may also have noticed the large numbers of his customers who were buying on credit. In fact, charge operations were making up 45 to 70 percent of his business, as they were in stores like Lord & Taylor, Best & Co., and Abraham & Strauss. Whatever Liberman's reasoning, he, like Joe Kennedy, sold short before Black Friday, October 29, 1929. In the aftermath of the crash, as Arnett put it, "He made a killing."

Although Liberman had been savvy enough to sell his own stocks, he couldn't save M. I. Stewart. In unfortunate timing, Liberman had built a new location at Fifth Avenue and Fifty-Sixth Street and opened it on October 16, 1929. An invitation to a luncheon preceding the inauguration ceremonies read, "signalizing through architecture and decoration a new era of art in fashion." After the crash, with Stewart customers unable to buy anything, Liberman closed the new store and sold it to Paul Bonwit, who had for some time been urging him to make a deal for the location. "They were on Thirty-Eighth

Street," Liberman remembered. "He said Bonwit Teller belongs uptown." Uptown it
went, and there it remained for fifty years or so until a young developer from Queens
tore the building down and erected a luxurious glass skyscraper that he named Trump
Tower after himself.

In the next phase of Liberman's business life, he took over as president of Arnold
Constable as it navigated the wreckage of the Great Depression. Part of his strategy
anticipated the rise of the suburbs. Under Liberman's leadership, Constable expanded
into New Rochelle in 1937, followed thereafter by the Long Island towns of Hempstead
and Manhasset; the New Jersey outposts Hackensack, Trenton, New Brunswick, and
West Orange; and Upper Darby in Pennsylvania.

In 1933, the Liberman family—Ike; Bertha; daughters Ruth, Irene, Hazel, and Sally;
and Anna Fosdick, the nurse—moved to the East Side and a twelve-room apartment at
1000 Park Avenue, at Eighty-Fourth Street. Ike, as driven as ever, spent little time with
the women at home. As his and Bertha's social profile grew, she was consumed with
raising money for Jewish charities and carrying out her role as a lady of New York
society. She ran her household with the help of a cadre of live-in help that, along with
Fosdick, included chambermaid and waitress Maria Sebek from Czechoslovakia; cook
Lou Michael from Germany; and chauffeur and butler Al Crain from Virginia, who served
the family for many years. This is not to mention the seamstresses and laundresses
who came in for the day.

The three older daughters went to Fieldston, the high school of the progressive
Ethical Culture Society, in a leafy section of the Bronx. "Despite I. L.'s sometimes
harshly competitive and Darwinian approach to life," said Jonathan Low, a grandson,

"he was a political liberal reformer, and Ethical Culture was an expression of that set of beliefs."

Sally, meanwhile, attended Public School No. 6, the Lillie D. Blake School at East Eighty-Fifth Street, named after suffragist Lillie Devereaux Blake. Each morning Fosdick walked Sally from their door on Park Avenue one block over to Madison Avenue and one block up to Blake, then walked her back when school let out. Sally loved her dearly.

Each winter Isaac and Bertha spent a month in Florida, leaving the children in Fosdick's care. "None of us traveled," said Hazel. "Here we are, rich kids. But we didn't feel rich. We didn't go to Bermuda. Other than camp in Maine in the summer, none of us went anyplace."

In this protected environment, "the baby" Sally spent most of her time at home alone with her dolls, her books, the games she made up, and Anna Fosdick. Sally's was a privileged Park Avenue childhood that contrasted dramatically with the remarkable coming-to-America stories of her father and mother, just a generation before.

Three — The Rise of Isaac Liberman

In 1899, a fire roared through the inventory of the yard-goods store owned by Isaac

Liberman's parents in the tiny rural shtetl of Ramygala, in northwest Lithuania, then still

a part of the Russian Empire. In the aftermath, the government-run insurance paid just

10 percent of what the fabrics had been worth. Liberman, then thirteen, looked around

at Ramygala (literally, "Quiet End"). Nestled in the highlands, it was remote from

everything— except, from time to time, the bootheels of the Czar's dragoons. Almost

half of Ramygala's 1,326 people were Jews, but

that didn't help when the pogroms came—or

maybe it made things worse.

    To one extent or another, waves of violence

against Jews were a recurring part of life in Czarist

Russia in the latter half of the nineteenth century. It

was said that things had been better in Lithuania's

capital city of Vilna, ninety miles to the southeast,

where Poles, Latvians, Estonians, Jews, Catholics,

Protestants, Germans, and Russians had lived

together in a cultural stew. But the Czar's soldiers

had seen to it that each pogrom was bloodier and

Isaac Liberman with his parents in Ramygala

more brutal than the last. Throughout the 1890s, Isaac's four older brothers and sister,

like thousands of Lithuanian Jews, had emigrated. His oldest two brothers, Udol and

Zalman, had gone to Israel. Philip, Meyer, and Rose had left for New York City. Their letters home from Manhattan described a city where they could make a living. As the old joke went, "America is paradise. We work only a half day: twelve hours."

Isaac had been born December 25, 1885. In later life he made it clear that he had no fond memories of the poverty and the injustice of having everything swept away in an instant. He didn't allow his daughters to go shoeless in their New York City apartment because it reminded him of the days of going without shoes. Nor would he allow them to wear head scarves, because they reminded him of the babushkas of the shtetl. His grandson Randy Smith once asked him, "Don't you ever want to go back?" Liberman paused and answered, "Why?"

Isaac's path of immigration likely took him through Poland and East Prussia to Hamburg, where steamers departed for America. Rose and Philip met him at the Castle Garden pier on the tip of Manhattan. It was 1901, and Isaac started working for Philip straight away. "My brother ran retail stores," said Liberman, "convenience stores." They sold dry goods, clothing, and notions. "His main store was on Eighth Avenue and Fortieth Street." The family lived above the first floor, and Liberman lived with them. "I was of considerable help to him," said Ike. "I didn't know what 'hours' meant. I'd work six in the morning until ten at night, Sunday night until twelve. We used to stay open on Sunday morning until twelve, twelve-thirty. In spring and summer the streetcars were five cents a ride, which was itself interesting. On Sunday afternoons I'd take a ride on the streetcar up to 110th Street, where they had a regular Coney Island up there."

Throughout his life, Liberman generally pronounced *v* as *w* and vice versa, as in "ewentually" and "vuz." The following sentence is rendered as spoken to provide a feeling for the way Liberman spoke. "My job ewentually vas to open up some of these stores and see that they were well stocked vith merchandise, at Canal Street and Broadvay and places like that. Eventually ve opened up a big one on Broadvay opposite City Hall. One of the big stores had occupied that corner. They moved further uptown and my brother took over that store."

Liberman remembered that Frank W. Woolworth had his offices on that corner. "Mr. Woolworth used to come in to the store, and he asked me some questions. He was very pleasant, very nice. Eventually, he put up the Woolworth building, one of the first skyscrapers."

One day in 1903 or thereabouts, Philip made Isaac an offer. "My brother said to me, 'I've just taken another store, and I'm going to make you a partner of mine in that store.' I was naturally delighted. I thought that was wonderful of my brother to have done. So we went down and saw where the store was, and he had laid out exactly what was happen to open the store, and he said to me, 'We're going to call it either Liberman Brothers or Philip & Isaac Liberman.' I couldn't sleep that night thinking that I would be in business with my brother. We opened up and it was very successful, we were doing business, but my name did not appear over the store, so I spoke to my brother. I said, 'I thought I was to be a partner of yours and we were going to call it Liberman Brothers or Philip and Isaac Liberman.' He said, 'I've thought it over, and I thought you were too young.' He thought that I ought to wait. 'Eventually,' he says, 'we'll do it. But you're too young yet.' So I was very disturbed about it. He was probably right, but youth doesn't understand that. [It] can't wait. I said, 'I hate to do it, but I can't put my efforts to the best if I'm thinking that my name wouldn't be up,' and I said I would like to step out of the business. He said, 'Well, that's all right, but I can't pay you out.' I said, 'I'll take one half of the merchandise, if you will permit me to keep it in the basement until I get myself located," and so it was. I must have been about seventeen."

This was Liberman's sanitized version of this episode, rendered with seven and a half decades of perspective. In fact, this parting of the ways was considerably more bitter. Philip later moved to Florida, where he started the first commercial bank in Miami Beach and his son Marcie served as mayor from 1947 to 1949. Liberman did not approve of Marcie because he was unpolished, was often quoted for his malapropisms, and reportedly socialized with mobsters. In later years, Liberman also broke off social relations with his older brother Meyer, even when Meyer was working for him at Arnold Constable. Liberman was self-disciplined and assiduous in his personal habits. He held everyone around him to his own lofty standards of behavior, appearance, and achievement. As apparent as these traits were in later years to Liberman's wife and children, they were also fully present when he was a teenager, beginning to build his business.

"My first store was on 1418 Broadway right opposite the Metropolitan Opera House," Liberman recalled. "It was an empty store and I took it. I went to the resources and they all welcomed me very nicely and they gave me credit, and I bought nice merchandise to add to what I had. Since that store was located next to the opera, in the middle of the block, and there was plenty of activity until about twelve o'clock, and so I stayed open until twelve o'clock. I was very envious of the papers, particularly the Sunday papers, and all the advertising there. I thought, "If I could only afford to spend some money on the advertising." I checked it out, and I thought it was too expensive. I went around to the newsstands and I asked them, if I was to print a circular, would they put it in the Sunday section of the papers. They wanted to know what I would pay, and I said, 'Whatever you say as a tryout, but you've got to be reasonable to start with,' and they said yes. The Sunday paper came out, it was the same size as the newspaper pages, and it was successful. That was my first experience in advertising, but it didn't last long. The newspapers put in a restriction because the loose flyers fell out of the papers and into the street.

"We were going along, the store was too small, and there was a store a block and a half away, near Forty-Second Street, opposite the Imperial Hotel and Broadway. The store was successful, doing good business. I was in that store for quite a few years. I operated under the name Stewart and Company because Liberman Brothers was taken."

His first Fifth Avenue store was between was between Thirty-Eighth and Thirty-Ninth. His next store, offering "Correct Apparel for Women & Misses," was at Fifth Avenue and Thirty-Seventh Street.

Around this time, Liberman helped organize the Fifth Avenue Association, which shaped the future of that storied commercial district. "Between 1913 and 1920," writes William Leach in *Land of Desire*, "streets were widened, trees planted, public space freed—to the 'extent that it was possible'—of 'riff-raff,' as the association's notes reported. 'Isles of safety' for pedestrians were created on the streets and garish billboards were demolished. At the urging of the association, the city adopted new subway stations and rerouted bus service to serve the retail district better."

At that point, Liberman decided to take a buying trip to Europe, "particularly to France." He and his two closest friends, a lawyer and an engineer, started out in Paris.

"We made an arrangement with the commission there, had everything lined up so we can place orders. So it was." Next they took the train to Venice, because Isaac wanted to see what Venice looked like. "I didn't know if there was anything I was interested in purchasing in Venice, and I just couldn't take the smell of the canals." His friends said he was too fussy. "I may be too fussy," he told them. "But I can't breathe. I can't fall asleep." So they adjourned to the Adriatic oceanfront at Lido Beach. "It was beautiful," Liberman recalled. "It was a great place for schoolteachers, and"—a memory that plainly endured— "they used to bathe nude." Then, said Liberman, "a Sunday morning came along and there was an extra: Austria had declared war against Serbia. 'Oh my God,' I says. 'What's that going to mean?' We were supposed to leave on Monday morning to Trieste." They asked Cook's travel bureau what they should do. "They said, 'Oh, don't pay attention to that *Austria Declares War*. They're going to walk in and that will be the end of it. Go ahead.' And that's exactly what we did."

The three Americans found that their original itinerary would take them into the war zone. They were told that a big inland city, Vienna, would be safer. They ended up stuck in Vienna for three or four months. Fortunately, the manager of their hotel had managed the Imperial Hotel across the street from Liberman's store in New York. Liberman and his friends had to obtain passports from the American embassy because up until that time, as he said, "you didn't need 'em." Eventually they made their way back to Paris, hoping to pick up some merchandise, but with nothing available they went on to England and home. "I was a different person when I stepped off the boat," said Liberman. True to that statement, for the rest of his life, he never again left the United States.

A Match Is Made

By 1916, Liberman had established himself as a successful entrepreneur and a respected civic leader. "So it was time for him to find a wife," said Hazel Arnett. In line with the culture of the day, his introduction to twenty-two-year-old Bertha Bayer was probably the work of a matchmaker.

If the matchmaker was not named Dolly Levi, no matter. We can still picture Barbra Streisand at Luchow's arranging to bring Isaac Liberman and Bertha Bayer together.

To Bertha, the matchmaker might have said, "So what if he's nine years older? He owns his own store. He's full of energy. Everybody who tries to keep up with him at Stewart & Company knows that. He doesn't drink or smoke. He's fit and trim—never touches dessert. He even has good teeth—never had a cavity in his life. Let's face it, Miss Bayer, a person could do worse!"

To Ike, Mrs. Levi might have cooed, "Miss Bayer is pretty and young—plenty of time for lots of children. She comes from a good Lithuanian family. Good businessmen. They're devout, very orthodox. She was born in this country, even. [She wasn't, but coming over at eighteen months is close enough.] Remember, Mr. Liberman, you're no spring chicken."

To properly express his intentions, I.L. would have been introduced to Bertha's father, Samuel Bayer, at 54 an owner of Bayer Brothers, a thriving textile business with offices at 53 Fifth Avenue and a mill across the Hudson in Paterson, New Jersey. Bayer was a dignified gentleman, with a white moustache and goatee, his white hair swept back, with the piercing eyes of a man who, like Liberman, had made his way in New

York business and thrived on his hard work and savvy. In fact, when Liberman called upon Bayer in his apartment at 2 West Ninety-Fourth Street, he met a man whose journey from Lithuania to America had much in common with his own.

Four — Meet the Bayers; Ike and Bertha's Life Together

In the year 1900, Eldridge Street between Canal and Division was crowded with pushcarts, fruit and vegetable vendors, and horse-drawn wagons. It was a hub of life for thousands of Eastern European Jews on the Lower East Side, much of it focused around the massive, ornate façade of the Eldridge Street Synagogue, at No. 12. Two doors down toward Division Street, at No. 8, stood a typical tenement house. Among its twenty-four tenants were Samuel and Sarah Bayer, their six children—Annie, fourteen; Henry, eleven; Alexander, ten; Mortimer, nine; and twins Bertha and Isidor, four—and Samuel's younger brother Jack, who had come over from Vilna the year before. Samuel himself had emigrated in 1894. Sarah and the children, including the twins who were then only eighteen months old, had followed in 1897.

On a Saturday morning, the family might have walked the two doors up to the synagogue. Samuel and Jack would have settled in with the men downstairs. Sarah and the children would have climbed the wooden staircase to sit in the balconies. In the records of the congregation, the Bayers are not listed among its members. There were hundreds of synagogues in the neighborhood where they might have felt more comfortable or where Samuel's older brother, Phil, and his family might have chosen to worship.

The Bayers had been textile merchants back in Vilna, selling undyed cotton, or what was known as gray goods. When Phil had come over in the early 1880s, he had transplanted the business and encouraged Samuel to join him. As Samuel prospered, he joined many Jewish and Italian immigrants in moving his family to Harlem, first to 251 West 112th Street, two blocks north of Central Park. By 1910, they lived at 187

West 118th Street, where they were doing well enough to employ a Polish maid.[4] As Samuel prospered more, he moved the family to 2 West 94th Street, on the corner of Central Park West. In time, he was a founder and first president of the uptown Talmud Torah. He was also a founder and president of the West Side Jewish Center at 131 West Eighty-Sixth Street.

Samuel Bayer

When Ike Liberman started looking for a bride, the Bayers' oldest daughter, Annie, was still living at home. She eventually married her uncle Phil—not exactly ideal, but sometimes things happen that way. Henry, Al, Moe, and Iz were working for Bayer Brothers. When the United States joined the Great War, Moe registered for the draft, became a doughboy, and showed off the portrait in his uniform for the rest of his life.

The Covenant of Marriage at the Astor Hotel

In later life Ike Liberman said, "I met my lady at one of the functions. I don't remember which one it was. She appealed to me. I was around 31 years old, and she was about 22. So it was I asked her, and she was foolish enough to say yes." At other times he told a story, almost certainly apocryphal and having the ring of a line from a vaudeville routine, about meeting Bertha when she fell off a bicycle. "I helped her," he would say from time to time, "and her father made me marry her."

---

[4] The Bayer Brothers firm was eventually sold to Cannon Mills in 1938.

If the marriage was the work of a matchmaker, she earned her fee. Isaac and Bertha were married on February 25, 1917, in the Grand Ballroom of the Astor Hotel. The service was performed by M. Hyamson and Rabbi Oraih Chaim Congoly.

The witnesses were Gus Nathansoly and Wolf Kufeld.

From the certificate of the day:

This Certificate Witnesseth

That on the First day of the week, the Third day of the month Adul in the year 5677, A.M., corresponding to the 25th of February 1917 the holy Covenant of Marriage was entered into at New York between the Bridegroom Isaac Liberman and his Bride Bertha Bayer.

The said bridegroom made the following declaration to his bride:

"Be thou my wife according to the law of Moses and of Israel. I faithfully promise that I will be a true husband unto thee. I will honor and cherish thee, and will provide all that is necessary for thy due sustenance, even as it beseemeth a Jewish husband to do. I also take upon myself all such further obligations for thy maintenance, during thy life-time, as are prescribed by our religious statute."

And the said bride has plighted her troth unto him, in affection and in sincerity, and has thus taken upon herself the fulfillment of all the duties incumbent upon a Jewish wife.

This Covenant of Marriage was duly executed and witnessed this day, according to the usage of Israel.

The commemorative photo, by Drucker & Co. NY, shows guests in formal attire, mostly white tie, seated around some twenty-one round tables in the grand ballroom, with six chandeliers and twelve Beaux Arts statues on each of the decorative supports leading to the domed ceiling. The bride and groom, with the latter in a top hat, are standing to the left and back in the photo, at a table with Sarah and Samuel Bayer (also in a top hat), a rabbi, and the rest of the Bayer children.

Isaac and Bertha set up housekeeping in an apartment at 135 West Eighty-Ninth Street, between Amsterdam and Columbus, with a French maid and a Bohemian cook who knew how to keep kosher. Bert, as Isaac called her, pious and observant, went to an Orthodox synagogue on West Eighty-Sixth Street. When daughter Ruth arrived on January 7, 1918, the Libermans hired Anna Fosdick, then fresh off the boat from Scotland, to take care of her.

The next year Liberman was part of a group of merchants, led by Percy Straus of Macy's, who founded the School of Retailing, which later became the Institute of Retail Management, at New York University. "Retailing in New York had a problem," said Liberman. "No one was doing anything to develop any people in the retail field. None of the colleges had a retail course. We had to bring in some young people and train them, which takes years, before they could be of importance. We thought some of the colleges would be interested in developing a retail course so that people can go and be taught retailing in a year, year and a half, and have some talent."

As described by William Leach, "the first start-up meetings were held at the Strauses' private offices at Macy's and in the Mandarin Room at Lord & Taylor's on Thirty-seventh Street and Fifth Avenue. More than twenty merchants from stores in Newark, Manhattan, and Brooklyn attended these meetings, along with people from the New York City Board of Education and New York University." Liberman found himself lecturing at NYU along with colleagues like Straus and Samuel Reyburn, head of Lord & Taylor and Associated Dry Goods Corporation.

After Irene was born March 1, 1920, and Hazel on December 14, 1922, the family moved to the larger apartment at West End Avenue and Ninetieth Street. "We lived in a fourth-floor duplex," Hazel Arnett remembered. "The address has since changed to 610 West End Avenue, even though the front door is still on Ninetieth Street. The apartment had a room-sized foyer, living room, kitchen, maids' rooms, dining room, and parlor on the first floor. We had a huge icebox in the pantry, so the iceman cometh. On the second floor was our parents' room and dressing room, a room where our two older sisters slept, and a room for the nurse, the baby, and me."

In the middle of the Roaring Twenties, Arnold Constable & Co., established in 1825 and the oldest department store in New York, was having management problems. "Arnold Constable was being run by an advertising man," said Liberman. "He knew nothing about retail. Our attorney, as it happened, represented the Chase Bank, which held 50 percent interest in Arnold Constable. My lawyer, George Haight, asked, 'Are you having lunch in the same spot, at the Waldorf?' He said, 'Give me some figures. What kind of a deal would you like?' I said, 'It seems to me that it's kind of a deal where we ought to make a merger—Stewart & Co. merges with Arnold Constable.' He said, 'You are in that business. It seems to me that you ought to be able to work up a deal whereby we could merge and make a success.' Within 24 hours they had it all written up and I accepted, just as they had written it."

That was 1925. "It took a few months to reorganize," said Liberman, who led from his position on the new board. As the stock market soared and the economy boomed, Stewart & Company—serving the upper crust of New York society—and Arnold Constable—catering to the middle-class market—prospered together.

In 1928 Liberman helped found the Hundred-Year Club, an organization of New York companies in continuous existence for at least a century. It was a promotional effort that ended up with more than 400 members. It took considerable effort for Liberman to get Cornelius Vanderbilt and the New York Central Railroad to take part. "I'm only the president," Vanderbilt told Liberman. "The vice president, he'll work with you."

On May 9, 1929, came the birth of Sally and the Sterling National Bank, followed by the Crash and the demise of Stewart & Company.

Although Liberman had exited the stock market, his in-laws had not. "They lost everything," said Hazel Arnett. "The tables were turned." The Bayers, who had previously been considered the more established family, now needed Liberman's help to get back on their feet. His annoyance at this burden was evident to Sally. She saw it as a source of tension between her mother and father, whose relationship was chilly and distant at best. In 1932, Liberman got his nephew Merwin Bayer, just seventeen, a job at Arnold Constable. He was successful enough that in 1938 a *New York Times* story announced that he was part of an "executive committee" of younger employees who would "take over merchandising during the store's 113th anniversary celebration." The team reported to Liberman's brother Meyer, who was then the vice president and treasurer.

In 1945, a young Eileen Ford was hired in Constable's advertising department, reporting directly to Liberman as a stylist and working on some of America's first story catalogues. "'They were pages—whole sections in the catalogue—that had a running theme with an editorial feel,'" she recalled in Robert Lacey's biography *Model Woman: Eileen Ford and the Business of Beauty.* "'And it was at Arnold Constable that I learned about accessorizing: what goes with what when you're styling photographs and presenting clothes.'"

Most of all, Ford recounted, she dived deeper into the modeling business. "'It was my job to hire all the models for Constable's advertising campaigns and catalogues. So I was on the telephone a lot. I got to know how all the different agencies worked, and I made good friends with a lot of the models. I learned a big lesson when Mr. Isaac

Liberman saw what I was paying for some models per hour. He was not happy, and he let me know it. So we had to work much quicker in the photo studio.'"

Lacey writes, "Negotiating with photographers and modeling agencies, arranging photo shoots, and devising the marketing campaigns for one of the city's most eminent department stores, she rapidly made a name for herself as she bustled around the high-pressure world of New York City's fashion business. Lively, self-confident, and efficient, Ford was clearly a rising talent, and it was not long before the headhunters came calling."

"'I made a terrible mistake,'" recalled Ford. "'I let a recruitment agency, a lady called Betty Corwin, talk me into leaving Arnold Constable. It was partly the money, but also the idea that, in fashion terms, Arnold Constable was getting a bit homely and had become out of date.'" Nonetheless, the lessons she learned from Liberman at Constable came in handy when she started her own modeling agency.

In the early fifties, Liberman, as president, replaced Meyer as chairman and took over the job himself, one of many instances over the years when he grew impatient with his less polished older brothers for not living up to his high standards. Amid the Roaring Twenties, Liberman's older brother Philip and his son Marcie had started a chain of clothing stores in Wilkes-Barre, Pennsylvania. In 1929, they moved to Miami Beach, where Marcie, a rotund, lovable bachelor, became a liquor wholesaler. In 1931 Philip, as his brother had two years before, started a bank. It was the Mercantile National, Miami Beach's first commercial bank. When Philip died in 1937, the bank went to Marcie and his sister, Bertha Miller, back in New York.

As mayor of Miami Beach from 1947 to 1949, Marcie Liberman was known for his malapropisms. When he was named mayor, he said he had reached "the pinochle of success." Sometimes he fell asleep during long city council deliberations, then woke up and said, "I move that we abdicate for today. I got work to do." His obituary in *The Miami News* notes, "He admitted that he sometimes dreamed up other assaults on the language to break the tension at council sessions. 'If I can get those guys laughing, they may forget what they were arguing about.'"

"Marcie was quite a character," said his second cousin Jon Low. "Ike apparently despised him because he was so wild and ostentatious. He always took Mom and Dad [Irene and Jerome Low] to showy restaurants, then out to clubs. He consorted with Mafiosi, show girls, etc. He was a high liver and a great guy. Never let anyone pick up a bill."

Marcie lived for twenty years at the Albion Hotel, where friends could always find him in the lobby or in the barbershop across the street. "He was a shrewd businessman, a millionaire, and one of the area's most generous philanthropists," reads his obituary. He and his father helped build the Beth Jacob Orthodox Congregation at the beach, and he "without publicity, contributed fortunes to Miami Sinai Hospital, the University of Miami, and many other institutions."

Perhaps a less driven, less perfectionist Liberman could have been more forgiving of his relatives. In the years to come, he amplified the prestige of his role as president of Arnold Constable by continuing his charitable and civic activities. He was a founder of the Businessmen's Council of the Federation of Jewish Philanthropies and a longtime executive board member of the New York chapter of the Boy Scouts. In 1947 he and

Bertha established the Bertha and Isaac Liberman Foundation, which supports worthy causes, many of them in the arts, to the present day. Liberman ended up supporting Eleanor Roosevelt not only in the Wiltwyck School for Boys, but also in the American Association for the United Nations when she assumed her role with the American delegation to the UN.

While Ike and Bertie, as they were known, cemented their reputation in New York society, young Sally Liberman gave deep consideration to the way they acted as parents and carried out their roles in society. As a psychology student in college, she explored her feelings about her Park Avenue childhood and her immigrant parents' drive for perfection. [5]

---

[5] Isaac Liberman remained president of Arnold Constable until 1963 and retired as chairman in 1970. He died at 97 on August 2, 1983.

Five — Young Years on Park Avenue

"For the first eleven years of my life," wrote Sally, "I only saw my mother on Wednesdays [when the nurse was off] or when there was company around. . . . I never knew my father until I was around ten years of age. I felt he was cold and aloof—too wrapped up in his business life—and yet there was some affection between us."

Left to play mostly alone in her early years, Sally's response was to invent imaginative games with her dolls and inhabit her books. As she wrote in an autobiographical prose poem,

> She did as she was told.
> But expressed her
> Real feelings through play.

As Anna Fosdick was the main figure in Sally's daily life, Sally loved her deeply.

When Sally was nine, the Libermans decided to get rid of Fosdick, who by that time had been with the family for twenty years. "They fired her and gave her a one-way ticket to Scotland," said Hazel Arnett. As to the reason, she said, "I would love to know that."*

After that, Sally had a series of French governesses whom she disliked.

Said Arnett, "It was difficult at times."

On June 28, 1940, Sally earned a special praise card for "General Excellence – Loyal Cooperation" from Principal Emily Nosworthy and Louise H. Rosenthal, teacher of class 6A at Lillie D. Blake School.

Reading Sally's descriptions of her childhood, self-doubts, and difficult family relationships will surprise those who knew her later. In her prose poem, Sally wrote

> ...she knew she was
> Dumb, and her sisters
> Were bright

Even Arnett, hearing these words many years later, had a hard time imagining that her radiant younger sister could have felt herself to be anything but brilliant and the apple of their father's eye. "No, no," said Arnett. "She was always bright, and the golden girl."

With her sisters being seven to twelve years older, Sally had relatively few interactions with them, especially as they left for college and started their own lives. "My sisters and I have never had too good a relationship," Sally wrote. "I have many too many memories of their ridiculing me, their playing hostile tricks (such as filling my Christmas stocking with ashes and rotten vegetables; their helping me to feel dumb because I did not understand the things they were studying or act old enough to be good company to them)."

Family systems studies tell us that "afterthought" siblings— that is, those born more than five years later than the others—share traits of both youngest siblings and only children. As the youngest of six with a span of eight to fourteen years between me and my older siblings, I can attest to this.

As an afterthought sibling, I can also offer some thoughts about the otherwise inexplicable idea of Sally seeing herself as dumb. When you are that much younger, you see your older siblings doing things when you can do nothing, as Sally describes to some extent in her parenthetical note above. Your older siblings are doing their homework, playing sports, practicing their instruments, going on dates—when all "the baby" can do is watch. In the swirl of activity and culture of my childhood, I had the idea in my mind that my older brothers strumming folk songs actually *were* the Kingston Trio. And what was I? As I entered school, I brought this lack of confidence with me, and I can understand how young Sally did the same. Her prose-poem reflects that this

underlying feeling is hard to shake, even when you begin to measure up to your peers:

> At school, the better she did
> The harder it was,
> For now the stigma was
> "grind". The parents
> Were proud and lauded the child.
> But sisters brought laughs
> And jeers,
> Staining each inch of pride.
> When the "A" grades flowed in,
> The centers of teasing
> Became her shape and her hair.
> For the child was the only one
> Blonde- and with figure chubby
> And round. Feeling different
> From them
> Brought dreams of adoption,
> An unwanted part of the whole.

Sally wrote alongside the words above that her dreams of having been adopted

"lasted for at least four years." It is significant for her development that, as a college

psychology major, she put these experiences on the table. Out of her analysis emerged

not only her first book, A Child's Guide to a Parent's Mind, but also a commitment to

examining complex problems and developing positive original solutions. In her college

paper, she was hard on her parents, but over time she came to better understand them

and their path as striving immigrants determined to ascend and make a mark in

American business, philanthropy, and society.

In a reflective moment, Sally's son Randy and I talked about the legacy of his

driven, determined, disciplined grandfather. The Czar's pogroms and the grinding

poverty of Ramygala lurked in Ike Liberman's mind and fueled his hard work and

commitment to excellence. No surprise, perhaps, that he passed along this drive to

Sally, who passed it on in turn.

"I felt it," said Randy. He had to be the first in his class, and usually was. As a schoolmate I could see, though I never understood, the pressure. "I don't want that for my daughter," he said. "I love being a lawyer because it is like a game, a very demanding game that draws on both sides of the brain, and because I do like helping others. I don't care about making a lot of money. I want to have friends, enjoy life, and help people." This follows the pattern of the third generation and allows us to understand the patterns of the first.

"[My father] was strict and degraded me a great deal," wrote Sally. "I was not to speak unless I could think straight and make myself readily understood—I was always too heavy—I was spoiled because my parents were too good to me. But he was honest with me, and he was consistent and still is in his behavior. . . . My father has been demanding of me in terms of achievements . . . [but] he will listen to what I have to say, and at times has shown consideration and understanding towards me."

Sally and Her Sisters

The four Liberman daughters responded to their home environment in different ways.

"Ruth and Irene were very predictable in the way they acted socially," said their cousin Abba Bayer. "They didn't make waves. Hazel made waves. And Sally was pretty much a wave-maker herself."

"Sally's two oldest sisters were always very fashionable and very different from her," remembered Ruth Lyford Sussler, a college friend of Sally's. Ruth Liberman went to NYU, Irene to Cornell. Both married promising attorneys, one from Harvard Law School, one from Yale, and each had two sons.

As her mother had done, Ruth married a man nine years her senior—Seymour M. Klein, a native of Manhattan who had graduated from City College Phi Beta Kappa and then from Harvard Law. He served in the 1930s in the US Attorney's office in Manhattan under Thomas Dewey and prosecuted gangsters. A famous case involved John Torrio and Count Victor Lustig (real name Robert V. Miller), a master counterfeiter and swindler who had previously been arrested thirty-seven times over five years but never convicted. Klein went on to work at several New York law firms, ending up at the politically powerful Shea & Gould. One of the partners was William Shea, for whom Shea Stadium was named, and the other was Milton Gould, a famous trial attorney. He and Ruth belonged to the prestigious Sunningdale Country Club in Westchester, around which their social life revolved. For many years Klein served as his father-in-law's outside counsel. Like Liberman, Klein was active in philanthropic and cultural activities, serving in various capacities with the Metropolitan Museum of Art, the Museum of Modern Art, and the New York Public Library. He and Ruth were noted collectors of contemporary art and helped discover many now-famous artists when Soho was still an inexpensive artists' colony. They also pioneered some of the galleries in Chelsea. Klein was a president and chairman of the iconic 92nd Street Y and a trustee of the Federation of Jewish Philanthropies. As a board member of the Robert Wood Johnson Charitable Trust, he steered $500,000 toward the Whitney Museum of American Art in their efforts to keep the Alexander Calder work *Circus*. Like the Libermans, they left a philanthropic legacy, in the Ruth and Seymour Klein Foundation.

At Cornell, Irene Liberman majored in art history and studio art. She also played field hockey and basketball, serving as team captain of the latter. Later, as a nurse's aide during World War II, she would take the subway to the Brooklyn Piers at 2:00 a.m. and ride in ambulances ferrying the wounded to hospitals in the region. "She said the ships always docked late at night so the citizenry would not see the vast numbers of the wounded and the horror of their injuries," said her son, Jonathan Low. Irene studied at the Art Students' League in New York and produced her own sculpture, tapestry, and paintings. She went on to co-found a studio in Briarcliff Manor, New York, where she and her husband, Jerome Howard Low, lived for many years. He had gone to Dartmouth College and Yale Law School, and worked for his father-in-law for many years as Arnold Constable's treasurer and general counsel.

Hazel Liberman Arnett, who lives in Cambridge, Massachusetts, is open about her role as the black sheep. "I was unwanted," she said, echoing Sally. "When I had the nerve to come out female, that was a disappointment. I don't know if I was supposed to be a sort of surrogate heir when my father strangely chose Stewart for my middle name. Well, I say this because it seems I'd been named after his store at the time, Stewart & Company." I chuckled a little. "You laugh," she said. "But it wasn't funny. In fact, I felt so ashamed of having a boy's name that whenever I was asked what the S stood for, I invariably lied, answering, 'Susan.'

"Not only was I not forgiven for not being the wished-for male heir, but also for not having my siblings' light skin. My father, for some odd reason, overlooked the fact that my dark skin had come from him! As a result of being made to feel different, my image of myself was that of an ugly duckling Yet there were those who saw me through another lens, like Sally's Bennington buddy Ruth Lyford, who said, 'Hazel was absolutely gorgeous and so different from the older sisters. She did things her way.'

"Yes, I was the maverick in the family. I was the rebellious one. Although Sally was less so, I knew there were times when she looked up to me. Contrary to her memory, however, she was strongly supported emotionally by our parents. She was what you might call their golden girl. Whatever—putting perceptions aside, I am enormously proud of my sister, who left a giant footprint in the field of teaching children with learning differences."

Other aspects made Hazel different from her sisters. As she admitted, "I was a loner and a culture vulture, which I still am. I would often spend Saturday afternoons at a museum by myself. Or, sit in the last row of the balcony to see a Broadway show, would you believe, for just fifty cents!"

With high hopes of becoming an opera singer, Hazel started her training at the Cincinnati Conservatory of Music while enrolled as a liberal arts student at the University of Cincinnati. "Unfortunately," says Hazel, "the conservatory was not at all good." So, she returned to New York, where she entered the BS degree program at the Juilliard School of Music as a voice major. Although the basic music program was superb, the voice department was not, forcing her to change her major. "I soon discovered the vocal faculty had always been notoriously weak, and when the outside teacher I eventually chose heard me sing he exclaimed, 'Oh, another Juilliard wreck!' That he took me on was incredible considering he had produced such stars as Todd Duncan, the first Porgy, and one of the Metropolitan's greatest baritones, Leonard Warren."

With tuition having been paid by her parents, it fell to Hazel to pay for the lessons. This meant getting a job. At first she found part-time work at Columbia University tabulating true-false exam scores. After a year she was hired to do research for a music-loving advertising executive who had contracts for a monthly music page in *Good Housekeeping* and articles for the programs handed out at the Met. "To my shock and amazement," she told me, "this man also expected me to become his ghostwriter! Who? Inexperienced me? In all honesty, I had never considered writing my strong suit, but somehow I rose to the challenge and managed to muddle through. Since part of my job was to conduct interviews behind the curtain, I got my first taste of backstage life. Although thrilling at first, it soon became quite the tutorial on the less glamorous side of stardom.

"As time passed, plus the unpredictable vicissitudes of life, I was to switch gears and, with the help of many kind folks, was able to gain a footing in my new trade. Early on I racked up credits as a radio music continuity writer in New York and for a show produced by the Marshall Plan in Paris starring film actor Jean-Pierre Aumont." Following that, Hazel scripted another show for the Marshall Plan called *The International Women's Program*, which was in essence an exchange of inspirational ideas beamed to four other European countries.

Back in the States, Hazel worked as a TV writer and producer for two years at CBS crafting scripts for Mike Wallace and three years at NBC working for Hugh Downs and Arlene Francis. Later she wrote and produced industrial films for AT&T and Dow Chemical.

Hazel also enjoyed a magazine career. While in Paris she worked as a reporter for

Line, an American start-up publication created for Seventh Avenue fashion houses that

couldn't afford to view haute couture shows in person. There, Hazel's beat was to cover

runway shows, as well as culling boutiques for newsworthy items to copy. Years later

she was to edit *Sew Fashionable,* a sewing magazine. After that she spent two years as

Fashion Editor of *Woman's Day,* landing next at *Family Weekly* as its manuscript editor.

Her final stop for five years was as executive editor of *Science Digest.*

Hazel has published two books: *I Hear America Singing: Great Folk Songs from the*

Revolution to Rock (1975) and *Converso* (2005), a three-generational novel tracing the

legacy of the Inquisition that created Portugal's "hidden" Jews.

As mentioned earlier, Hazel did things her way and, as was her wont, she set her

course in another way. Whereas all her sisters had had huge Jewish weddings, Hazel

said, "I eloped with Russell Arnett, a non-Jew, and we

promptly moved to France for him to learn filmmaking at

the prestigious Institut des Hautes Études

Cinématographique."

Toward the end of his studies at IDHEC, Russell

served an apprenticeship with motion picture producer Alexander Salkind on two

features, one made in Spain, the other in France. On

Hazel and Russell Arnett

returning to the United States, he was employed as an assistant director on the Army's

Signal Corps training films. From there he became assistant director of the Guy

Lombardo TV series for two years before moving on to feature films. Among several

well-known directors he assisted were Bud Yorkin and Peter Bogdanovich. As a director, his specialties were TV commercials and industrial films. His major clients for industrials were Lederle Laboratories and Singer Sewing Machines; for commercials, the production company Screen Gems.

After fourteen years of marriage, Hazel and Russell had her parents' only granddaughter, Hayley. Approximately six years later the couple divorced.

In 1984 Hazel moved to Saint Louis to head the media arm of a famous institute. Within a year she met her second husband, Wayner Swenson, a successful contractor and realtor. After seventeen years, the very happy union of two culture vultures suddenly came to an end when Swenson died in 2001.

Hazel, now in her nineties, remains very active. She recently submitted a different ten-minute play to two playwriting festivals and is hard at work on an original feature film treatment.

Learning by Doing at Lincoln School

Sally went to high school at the progressive Lincoln School, at 425 West 123rd Street, at the north end of Morningside Park. It was small, with some twenty students in the elementary school grades and not many more in the upper grades. Some students arrived by bus or subway. Many walked. Some, like Sally, had drivers. The mission of the school dictated that the student body included the children not only of Columbia faculty members and well-to-do families but also of middle- and lower-income families.

It is significant for Sally's later life that Lincoln School had been founded in 1917 as the lab school of Columbia University's Teachers College and that it was an environment in which children with various learning styles could thrive. The original grant from the Rockefeller-funded General Education Board called for "a pioneer experimental school for newer educational methods." Specifically, Lincoln was to promote the progressive child-centered theories of John Dewey.

Betsy Clark McIsaac was two years behind Sally at Lincoln. Her father, John Roscoe Clark, was a Teachers College faculty member, the principal of Lincoln School, and a Dewey disciple. "It was all based on learning by doing," said McIsaac. "We were very hands-on at all stages. It wasn't all rote memorization. We had to understand, do, and see. In our Pioneer Unit in third grade, I had to make a bow and arrow in shop and shoot a rabbit and skin it. All boys and girls took both shop and cooking. In seventh grade we learned the curve of normal distribution. We had come in to class and report our father's income and put it on a graph, which showed the curve of normal distribution. Can you imagine asking that today?

"The basic concepts were taught by involving yourself in the process of doing, seeing, and acting. As it turned out, it was also a great place for kids with learning disabilities. The hands-on approach allowed kids with learning disabilities to use the right-hemisphere creative strengths that they have. Success is perhaps the primary ingredient of future success.

"Nelson Rockefeller went to Lincoln and he was very, very dyslexic. So was I. My specific form of dyslexia didn't affect my reading, but I still don't know my times tables and I couldn't spell. But when I drew whales in the ocean for a social studies assignment, the teachers thought I was adorable. My father and eight heads of other progressive schools had an agreement with many colleges that they could admit students based only on headmaster recommendations and not on the basis of test scores or marks. My father had Nelson Rockefeller in geometry class. He was very bright, but he had a strange little problem with reading and numbers: he read and wrote backward. My father talked to Dartmouth and said that he'd do fine if he had a reader to help him. And his family was well able to afford it."

Sally did well in her academic subjects at Lincoln, while still harboring feelings of inadequacy. It was in music, art, and dance that she began to build an enduring foundation of confidence and expression.

She heard about Bennington College from Hazel, when she had wanted to transfer there from the University of Cincinnati because she had heard that you could pursue the arts there. Bennington had been founded in 1932 as the first college to include the visual and performing arts as full-fledged elements of the liberal arts curriculum. In the dance world, Bennington's summer programs directed by Martha Graham between 1934 and 1942 had become synonymous with innovation and freedom of expression.

"I applied to Bennington," said Hazel, "but my parents said they wouldn't pay for it." Instead, Hazel returned to New York to study voice at Juilliard. "I was a thorn in their side," she says, "so they said no. Sally was the golden girl, so it was OK."

Six — Modern Dance and Erich Fromm at Bennington

On a December morning in 1947, the members of Martha Hill's Dance Group assembled in the Bennington parking lot, a flock of camel's hair coats huddled against the Green Mountain chill. Since they were about to drive to New York City, most of the girls wore the obligatory kilts, cashmere sweaters, and saddle shoes. "There was a sort of kilt madness at the time," said Ruth Lyford Sussler, then a sophomore. "There were six different plaids." She remembered that Sally and another classmate, Allegra Fuller (later Allegra Fuller Snyder), both New Yorkers, tended toward darker, more urbane fashions like those found in Greenwich Village coffee houses. The dancers piled into cars and headed south to perform their workshop dances in three evenings inside the YMHA at Ninety-Second Street and Lexington Avenue.

Among the workshop dances that year, Sally, Sussler, and three other girls enacted a social ritual in "New in Town." In it, wrote *Beacon* reviewer Barbara Ushkow, "the shy girl's tentative efforts to get into the group and the leader's friendly relationship to her played against the lively group movement. . . . The dance . . . is completed as the shy girl takes the leader off, having been accepted in the group."

Sally and Sussler had met in a freshman class. "I was very taken with her forthrightness and her courage, which I lacked," said Sussler, who is now retired in New London, Connecticut, after a career as a painter of New England harbors and landscapes. "She spoke up so well. I was a country bumpkin, from a small town and a public high school [Westport, Connecticut, and Staples High, respectively]. Sally was an incredibly articulate young person.

Ruth Lyford Sussler, in her New London, Connecticut, home, in 2016

"We took a few dance technique classes together. I was torn between a dance major and a visual arts major. Dance was very important to Sally. We went to the dance choreography workshop. She had the ability to create choreography. I didn't.

"We were each of us exotic to each other. Here she was, a big city girl, living in a very fine Park Avenue suite. I was shopping at second-hand shops and sewing my own clothes. She was so gorgeous, with her blonde hair—helped along with beauty products, but very skillfully done. She sort of took me under her wing. She taught me to be less scared about this stimulating atmosphere."

The dance group's annual expeditions to the 92nd Street Y gave Sally the opportunity to introduce Sussler to her family. "I visited their home on Park Avenue," said Sussler. "I knew they were Jewish, but I didn't realize what it meant to be a kosher home. I was hungry at night and I went to their refrigerator and got something. Sally was horrified and frightened that I had used the wrong dish. I quickly learned what went together in a kosher meal and what didn't. I asked for butter for the baked potato once, and I didn't ask again.

"When we ate dinner together, it was Sally on one side of the table, me on the other. It was normally a very functional dinner table talk. I thought Bertha was the most beautiful elderly woman I had ever seen. She was so fashionable in her bearing, so stylish in her dress. She had such lovely manners. She was very gentle and very tolerant of Sally. She was lovely in every way. Sally's two older sisters were always very fashionable and very different from her. Hazel was absolutely gorgeous and so different from the older sisters. She did things her way. She was very theatrical. Her hair was

Sally Liberman

very dark, shiny, pewter, smooth, combed back in the Martha Graham style, in a bun."

In the workshop performance, Sally danced a duet, "Recess," that she had composed with classmate Gail Greig. Reviewer Ushkow praised "a fine full use of the stage" and the essence of the situation "well expressed in the quick, light movements, fast pace and clear devices used for the dramatization of the idea. The two dancers made full use of their dual roles and friends and antagonists. The dance ended when both victor and vanquished simply left the stage."

Allegra Fuller composed and danced "Suite," set to a Purcell suite. "The effectiveness of the satire on ballet was enhanced by the total expression of the dancer," wrote Ushkow, "considering not only her super-sober demeanor but also the expressive furbelow use of her hands. The movement, too (slow movement against a fast beat in the music; using a slight off-beat during quickened movement; her serious preparatory waltzing between beats) was fundamental to the drollness of the dance.

Before coming to Bennington, Fuller had danced professionally with the School of American Ballet, the first company of New York City Ballet, which gave her plenty of material for her satire.

Sally performs in "Election Night," a parody of "modern, modern dance" she composed with Allegra Fuller.

"I realized ballet was limited in terms of its vision," says Allegra Fuller Snyder, now professor emerita of dance ethnology at UCLA, "although George Balanchine was inspiring and creative. After two years, I decided to go to Bennington."

In the second half of the program at the Y, the entire group danced in senior Tish Evans's project, "Where the Two Came to Their Father," based on a Navajo hero myth. Snyder said, "Tish had spent a great deal of time in New Mexico and had personal contact with the Navajo, but the dance was specifically inspired by Joseph Campbell's book *Where the Two Came to Their Father.* Jean Erdman, Joe Campbell's wife, was an early Graham dancer and had been at the Bennington Summer School of the Dance, so Martha Hill knew them both very well."

Evans had spent her time with the Navajos under the guidance of Bennington anthropology professor Edward T. Hall, a lanky Missourian who had done fieldwork with the Navajos and Hopis in the 1930s and took students to nonresident terms on Native American reservations. "Bennington was noted for its training in modern dance under the expert and dedicated tutorship of Martha Hill," wrote Ned Hall in *An Anthropology of Everyday Life: An Autobiography.* "Mostly because of students who came to me each week for counseling, it wasn't long before I found myself involved with the dance classes. The students' problems with dance (they were constantly having to create new dances) seemed to center on three problems, the most common of which was a tendency to indulge themselves in overly complex statements—a failure to simplify their dances. A girl would come into my office, collapse into a chair, sigh, and say, 'I'm having trouble with my dance.' 'What is your dance about?' I would ask. 'It's about Negro/white relations.' 'Isn't that a bit complex for one dance? How about cutting it

Ned Hall on site in the pueblo country

down to something more manageable, like, the relations between a black man and a white woman?' I would suggest."

Hall went on to become a pioneer and prolific author in nonverbal and intercultural communication, and he credited his work with the modern dancers in opening his mind to later discoveries in the field of communication. "Both the dancers and I saw the dance as a system of communication that was capable, in the hands of a trained and talented practitioner, of transmitting some rather complex ideas and situations to an audience. Without this experience with the dance students I am sure that later discoveries in the field of communication would have come to me much more slowly." But at Bennington he was just one of a remarkable group of innovative thinkers whose commitment to the synergies of interdisciplinary studies infused students with a vibrant, energetic vision of what education was all about.

"Sally had a really powerful understanding of the essential importance of creativity for the mind as well as body in every aspect of learning," said Snyder. "Sally understood that experience is the great teacher, that experiencing things through oneself is the essence of understanding and motivation. That is very much what the Lab School is all about."

Snyder went on to pioneer the field of dance ethnology, focusing her research on dances among American Indian tribes, particularly the Yaqui, and on dance among ethnic groups in Africa and Asia. In a sense, her passion was also the product of Bennington's mixture of disciplines. "I was doing a piece of choreography using the Library of Congress's recordings of Georgia Sea Island children's songs and games," Snyder remembered. "I became more and more frustrated that I could find no solid research not only on this but also on children's songs and games, and their anthropological context in general. I was taking a class from Hall, and I asked if there was a need to study dance anthropologically, and his answer was yes."

As Hall wrote in his autobiography, "One of the advantages of a college like Bennington was that it was possible to integrate the material presented in one class with that of other classes, so the entire curriculum, instead of being fragmented, could be a more or less coherent whole. In fact, the college had been founded on the idea that the curriculum should be comprehensive and in many ways it was."

Dance at Bennington helped Sally build her sense of self and purpose, and foreshadows the formation of her insights into roles that artistic expression, movement, and emotion can play in education. "Martha Hill was an incredible mentor," remembered Snyder. "She allowed us to grow in different directions, in choreography. I saw the need in film for dance. It was a critical time for that. Martha enabled me to spend a year in New York to work at the National Film Foundation on a fellowship for the study of dance and culture there."

Near the end of her Bennington career, Sally assessed her feelings of self-confidence that her college experience had instilled in her. Not coincidentally, she described these feelings in the language of dance:

The pulse of life beats a new rhythm,
A rhythm that's free.
A rhythm that's rising with knowledge
And stirring great joy within me.

Sally Liberman in a dance at Bennington.

The love [or warmth I'm [feeling is] unbending, expresses
A rhythm that's free—
A rhythm splashing on foams of love
Embracing new strength waves in me.

The straightened tides of thought, expresses
A rhythm that's free—
A rhythm stroking unbounded depths
Fingering ebbs of reason in me.

The swelling flow of days, expresses
A rhythm that's free
A rhythm unbridled from despair
Riding the surge of life within me.

The pulse of life beats a new rhythm
A rhythm that's free
A rhythm that's full with activity
Greeting one force—it is me.*

Sally Liberman in a parody of modern dance.

"Sally was deeply involved with everything that was going on in the dance department," said Snyder, "more in the area of production." During summer vacation after her freshman year, Sally painted props for the Clare Tree Major Children's Theatre Company in New York. "All I remember is Sally's presence," said Snyder. "She was darn funny. She had a lot of concern and passion. It was a small college. We were all families. The departments were families, involved together in various ways."

Ned Hall's best friend at Bennington was another of Sally's favorite professors and key influences—Erich Fromm, the oft-published successor to Freud and Jung in the field of psychotherapy, who had taught at Bennington since 1942. "No matter how often we met," wrote Hall, "I never lost a sense of awe at his ability to formulate problems in his head, evaluate them, and come up with a well-reasoned judgment."

Hall remembered that Fromm taught on Mondays, left town on Tuesdays to practice psychoanalysis in various cities, then flew up from New York on Fridays "with a satchel full of gourmet edibles he had bought in delicatessens." A college car would drive him

from the airport for late dinners either with friends at his home on Murphy Road or in the

Halls' house in the orchard on Bennington's grounds. In Martha Graham's rare free time

during her summer sessions, she had socialized with Fromm and his wife, Henny,

"perhaps," suggested dance critic Debra Jowitt, "eager for insights into dreams and fairy

tales that he could give her." *

Hall ended up volunteering to drive Fromm to and from the airport. "The

trip took about an hour and would give us an extra two hours a week for

our discussions," wrote Hall, who also treasured his hours trading ideas

with Allegra Fuller's father, Buckminster Fuller, the architect and visionary

who had built one of his early geodesic domes on the Bennington campus

in 1945. Fuller served on Bennington's board, and frequently lectured

there. "Comprehensive thinking [was] a favorite phrase of [his]," Hall

remembered. "When we first met, Bucky was not yet famous. I found him

to be gregarious, loquacious, rotund, and energetic. . . . He was not only

fun to be with, but he also stimulated students' minds."

Hall and his wife, Mildred, also attended parties and dinners at the large

Victorian home of English professor and blues scholar Stanley Edgar

Hyman and his wife, the writer Shirley Jackson, best known for her chilling

1948 *New Yorker* story "The Lottery," in which the people of a New England town draw

lots each year to see who is to be stoned to death. Hyman and Jackson "seemed to

thrive on controversy," wrote Hall. Their get-togethers often included Ralph Ellison, a

frequent houseguest from New York, who wrote much of *Invisible Man* during prolonged visits in an upstairs room reserved for him in their home. Jackson acknowledged that she had the idyllic town of Bennington in mind as the setting for "The Lottery." Hall posed, only half in jest, that perhaps Jackson's chilling story owed more to Bennington than just its setting. "All that talent in a tiny isolated community made Bennington a complex place to be," wrote Hall. "What was possibly most unsettling was its profligate treatment of talent. Every semester, it seemed, someone had to be sacrificed, either a faculty member or a student. None of us figured out how this informal system worked, though Shirley Jackson obviously had it in mind when she wrote 'The Lottery.'"

"Ned Hall was influential and a very good force," said Sussler. "I was a complete scholarship student. When I was having dark thoughts about losing my scholarship, Sally said, 'You've got to talk to Ned Hall.'"

While serving in the Army Corps of Engineers during World War II, Hall had commanded a black regiment in Europe and the Philippines. This, along with his work on the reservations, gave him sensitivities to racial discrimination ahead of his time. At one point, Sally went to Hall when she heard about an incident involving two African American students. "One of them was a beautiful singer," remembered Sussler. "Someone stuck hate letters in their mailboxes—saying you shouldn't be here, that sort of thing. Sally picked up on this. She was very conscious of the injustice of society. She suspected two beautiful, popular southern girls. They were from Mississippi, I think. You wouldn't think Bennington would have had such problems. In her friendship with Ned Hall, Sally may have mitigated this somewhat, but without success. The black girls weren't up to the harassment and left."

Fromm's "congenial and scholarly manner," as biographer Lawrence J. Friedman described it, was as popular with his students as it was with the faculty. The class of 1948 even paid him the rare honor of choosing him as their commencement speaker. This caused Fromm to worry to Bennington President Lewis Webster Jones that his conviviality may have made his students "'less engaged with the substantive course materials.'" Nonsense, Jones replied: Fromm's students "'mastered far more than their required assignments. He had cultivated a love in most of them for rigorous reasoning and the life of the mind.'"

None more so than Sally Liberman. "When I had decided on my art major, we had some discussions about what we should take," recalls Ruth Sussler. "Sally, being a psychology major, thought I should take some psychology. Erich Fromm was holding forth in those days. I said, 'No, I like to get my psychology out of Shakespeare.'"

Sally's Bennington journey—even in her dance themes and choreography—was an exploration of relationships and the complicated ways that humans do and don't communicate, very much under the guidance and inspiration of her mentors Fromm and Hall. "At Bennington," says Fuller, "Sally was taking a very important and unique path."

Fromm's course "Human Nature and Character Structure" dealt mainly with the questions of ethics in the tradition of Aristotle and Spinoza, but also with the connection between human nature and character structure and with the symbolic language of the unconscious. These lectures provided the basis for much of *Man for Himself* (1947) and at least some of *The Forgotten Language* (1951). And, wrote Friedman, "The class prompted Fromm to expand his reading list and to convey more of his appreciable background in social psychology and psychoanalysis to his students."

During Sally's freshman work-study period, January through March 1947, she was an assistant teacher at the City and Country Day School in Greenwich Village. The next winter, January through March 1948, she took advantage of an internship program set up especially for Bennington students at the United Nations, then in Flushing Meadows, where Sally worked in the Social Affairs Department. This glimpse into the workings of the U.N. paid off after Bennington in Sally's work with the World Health Organization.

During her sophomore year Sally, in her words, "realized things were bothering me and upsetting me but I could not communicate them to anyone." She talked with William Cabell Smith, an African American psychologist known fondly to all as Smitty, who taught courses in social work and family dynamics, and counseled students about personal issues. In Sally's "Family Biography," written two years later for Smith's course "The Family," she explored relationships and psychology and implications in the larger world, giving considerable thought to the relationships and psychology of her own family. In later years, she told Ben Booz about a conversation with her father. "While she was at Bennington," Booz said, "her father always dictated his letters and had his secretary type them up. One day, during her vacation, she confronted him and asked why he couldn't take the time to write a letter himself to his own daughter. He put her off, but she persisted until finally he broke down and admitted that he did not know how to write letters. She greatly regretted how she had hurt him by pushing him to the point of having to admit this. It was one of the big regrets of her life that she had wounded her father so much. Had she known, she wouldn't have done that, and she never let people know."

That summer Sally taught modern dance at a summer camp. In her junior year

work-study term, December 1948 through March 1949, she worked as an assistant to

Catherine Mackenzie, the "Parent and Child" editor of *The New York Times.*

In the spring semester, Sally's psychological explorations and her work with Hall

and with Henny Fromm caught the attention of the *Times* education writer Leonard

Buder, who reported on her study of cigarette butts and pipe cleaners as indicators of

personality under the headline, "Snuffed Cigarette Butts Disclose Human Traits in

College Tests: Figures Made From Pipe Cleaners Also Used in Two Psychological

Experiments on Bennington College students."

> BENNINGTON, Vt., June 27 — Pipe cleaners and cigarette butts may help psychologists discover hidden personality traits, if two experiments now under way on the Bennington College campus prove successful.
>
> One project, by student Sally Liberman of New York City, has as its goal the development of projective tests which would use pipe cleaners for the detection of basic emotions. The other experiment, conducted by Mrs. Eric (sic) Fromm, wife of the noted psychologist who teaches here, is trying to determine whether an individual's personality has anything to do with the way he snuffs out a cigarette.
>
> ### 25 Students Assist in Test
>
> Miss Liberman asked twenty-five students, who were selected at random, to make five simple stick figures, using three pipe cleaners for each figure. The figures were to express different emotions—sadness, happiness, relaxation, anger and embarrassment and self-consciousness.
>
> Most figures from a particular group were similar. Ninety percent of the figures portraying sadness featured a bent or drooping head. Of those expressing comfort and relaxation, two-thirds were lying down. However, certain deviations appeared and it is these discrepancies, Miss Liberman said, that may provide a clue to personality.
>
> One student, six feet tall, made her "self-conscious" figure show a very tall person. For her picture of "happiness" she evolved a very small person in a sitting position. This was in contrast to other figures in the category; most of those portraying "happiness" were leaping, running, jumping or standing.

This would seem to indicate, Miss Liberman explained, that the tall girl was quite self-conscious about her height and was happiest when in a position whereby her size was not apparent.

Beware of Butt Mashers

Analyzing Mrs. Fromm's findings on the cigarette habits, Dr. Edward T. Hall, anthropologist and cultural psychologist at the college, held that a person who mashes his butt "apparently is holding back a great deal of hostility."

A person who permits his cigarette to burn out usually is the kind of individual who has concern for no people after their usefulness is over.

If a smoker tosses his cigarette on the floor, it is not necessarily a sign of improper upbringing, Dr. Hall explained. It denotes, more, some inward defiance.

Likewise, a confused person who is being "torn apart inside" may take it out on his cigarette by shredding the tobacco while smoking.

But the "lowest form" of cigarette smoker, Dr. Hall declared, is the one that puts butts in coffee cups.

"This person has nothing but contempt for himself and for everyone else," he observed, "and he really wants to mess things up. He's the kind that would pollute a spring after taking a drink from it."

That summer, Sally and Ruthie Sussler took a trip in Sally's two-door gray Dodge sedan. "The car was understated," said Sussler. "Sally was very careful not to be too showy. She was quite aware of the symbols of wealth. We went to Newport, Rhode Island, where my cousin Elaine Lorillard lived. Several years later she and her husband, Louis, who were great jazz fans, founded the Newport Jazz Festival. We went to Gloucester, Massachusetts, and stayed with a Bennington friend. Then we went to my family's summer camp on Mount Desert Island, Maine, where my mother grew up. I had not warned Sally that there was no indoor plumbing, a wood stove, and an outhouse. We stopped there for a few days. It was quite an event for her. It was pretty rugged for someone who was not used to it."

Sally returned to New York for six weeks assisting occupational therapists in the psychiatric ward of Grasslands Hospital in Westchester County.

Ruth said, "Our senior year, we saved a little money when three of us shared a double room. We put all three beds in one room and used the other room as a living area. It was a suitable arrangement. Judy Kanin was the other roommate. Sally was a night owl and I was a morning person. At six thirty or seven a.m., I got up for breakfast. Lots of interesting things went on because of that. She was always fighting her weight problem. She would go on a diet of grapefruit and steak."

That fall, Sally served on a committee that had been set up, reported the Beacon, to make the non-resident term a more effective and integral part of the curriculum. To explain the non-resident term to freshmen, the NRT Committee held freshmen meetings at which Kay Brown discussed the policy of the NRT; Sue Knight, evaluation of the NRT; and Sally Liberman, job procedure." At the 92nd Street Y in December, Sally performed "I Can Mystify and Terrify," a dance she composed, tapping her special brand of humor and based on the William Stieg *New Yorker* cartoon, to Peggy Lee's "Simalau."

In Sally's senior nonresident term, January through March 1950, she worked in the editorial department of *Parents* magazine. That spring she choreographed two dances. One, "Calypso," was built on Caribbean rhythms that were gaining in popularity. The other, "Goodnight, Irene," was a nod to social-justice-minded Pete Seeger and the Weavers, who had just released their version of the Leadbelly song. "My sometime roommate Chickie Chapple was very good friends with the Weavers," remembered Allegra Fuller Snyder. Chapple had arranged for the Weavers to perform at Bennington and, said Snyder, introduced them to Sally.

That spring Sally took her second class from Fromm, "Education in the Art of Living," on the dynamics of interpersonal relations. She also took William Smith's course, "The Family." In her paper for that course, "Family Biography," she explored her own family's dynamics, beliefs, relationship with wealth and money, and ideas about Jews and Gentiles, along with ideas about parental love and the emotional needs of parents as they raise their children. These feelings inspired Sally to embark on her senior project.

Then as now, guides for parents about children abounded. In 1946 Benjamin Spock had published what became the Bible of the upcoming baby boom, *The Common Sense Book of Baby and Child Care.* In 1949, Catherine Mackenzie had come out with her book *Parent and Child.* And in 1950 the Columbia human development scholar Lawrence Frank and his wife, Mary, were finishing up their book *How to Help Your Child in School,* to come out in September.

Sally turned the formula around: why not create a guide for children about parents? To that end, she gathered friends and classmates (age seventeen to twenty-five) and asked for questions they had about their parents. As she wrote in the preface to *A Child's Guide to a Parent's Mind,* the groups discussed "how they could create a better world for their children, with more satisfying human relationships. They were concerned with the kind of parents they will be, the mistakes they will make, how they can understand their parents so as to avoid making the same mistakes, how they can understand the responsibilities of a parent."

Many of the questions that emerged coincided with topics on Sally's radar, notably—

- Why must children always have to live up to someone or something?

- Why do parents force extracurricular activities on their children which the children do not want? (piano lessons, acrobatics, violin, tap dancing)
- Why can't parents accept their children for what they are instead of what parents want them to be?
- Why are parents so concerned with what other people think of their children's every action?
- Why are parents so competitive about everything, even including their children?
- Why do parents want their children to be successful at everything?

Drawing from dozens of such puzzlers, Sally set out to explain the mysteries of why parents do what they do. In her prose-poem style, with children as the audience, she wrote in her preface

> Some books on child-care
> and parent-care
> give you
> their home-cooked recipes
> to follow.
> We offer no ready-made solutions,
> No magic formulas.

Sally's jump of originality was to create her roadmap to a parent's mind in practical statements about parents, coupled with scenarios showing—in a mostly gentle, witty way—parents' troubles, insecurities, and hang-ups. For example, she wrote, "Some parents ration their love like cookies." The drawing that eventually appeared on the opposite page shows a mother reaching into a cookie jar labeled "Love." The caption: They behaved very well with the company today.

This reflects a beef that Sally wrote in her paper for "The Family" about her mother— that Bertha rewarded Sally with material things and was overly concerned with what others thought.

Fromm, her project advisor, recognized the originality and potential of Sally's vision and—prolific author that he was—suggested that she turn it into a book. He made a call to his publisher, and Sally set about turning her senior project into her first book.

Sally created *A Child's Guide to a Parent's Mind* by means of scenarios, which needed illustrations. To render them, Sally was directed to a classmate, Kiriki de Diego (now Kiriki Newmark Metzo). "I was in the art department," remembered Metzo, who in her late eighties still teaches an exercise class in her West Village building. "Sally asked me if I would do some drawings, and I said I would. We hadn't really known each other before the book, but we got to know each other very well in the years that followed.

Seven — Kiriki and *A Child's Guide to a Parent's Mind*

On a rainy New York City April afternoon, after a Saturday matinee of *Fun Home*, my wife, Karen, and I had arranged to visit Kiriki de Diego Newmark Metzo at her apartment in the West Village. "Get on the Eighth Avenue line," she advised. "Get to the front of the train. Get off at Fourteenth Street and head to the river." We made our way through the maze of streets, stopped to pick up a couple of bottles of wine, and arrived at the Bethune Street entrance of the former Bell Telephone Building, also bordered by West and Washington Streets, which was long ago turned into the Westbeth Artists Community, an affordable residence for painters, sculptors, actors, and musicians. "She's waiting for you," said the man at the front desk, smiling.

We got off the elevator at the third floor, made our way down the long linoleum hallway, and saw Kiriki standing in front of her door. She is slender. She wears her gray hair long, straight, and parted in the middle, in the manner of the Greenwich Village art types and folk singers of her era. Her apartment has tall ceilings and walls covered with paintings—surrealistic works by her father, Spanish artist Julio de Diego, by herself, and by other friends. One, on a far wall, is an oversize oil portrait of herself as a young artist, with wine glass in hand, seated beside a window of her apartment looking out over the West Side Highway and the Hudson River—the same view we were looking at now.

If you miss the vibrant mind of Sally Smith and the nonstop flow of creative

connections between events of the day and disparate concepts and ideas, then sitting

down to wine and crab dip with her first collaborator is a powerful tonic. *The New York*

Times was open on the back of a chair to a David Brooks op-ed that had mentioned

East Tennessee, where we live. "I read it and I thought of you," she said. *The New*

Yorker and *Atlantic* were sitting on tables close by. When she is not teaching an

aerobics class in her building, Kiriki works as a guide at the Merchant's House Museum

on East Fourth Street between Lafayette Street and the Bowery. Built in 1832 and once

known as the Seabury Tredwell House, it is the only nineteenth-century family home in

New York City preserved intact—both inside and out.

"Did you like *Fun Home*?" she asked. "I hear it's very good." It's a remarkable

musical about a cartoon artist with a complicated but loving family life. One good reason

to be an artistic New Yorker is that, in your late eighties, you can keep up with

Broadway hits.

"It's performed in the round," Karen answered. "The singing is remarkable."

We sat down, wine glasses in hand, and Kiriki told us about meeting Sally in their

senior year at Bennington: "We had lived on opposite sides of the campus and not really

interacted before that, but we got to know each other very well in the years that

followed."

We ask about a surrealist painting above the sofa. "That's Julio's," she says. Kiriki

tells us that she spent her early years in Chicago with her father, Julio, and her mother,

Rosalita, until they visited Spain for a summer and Rosalita decided to stay there. When

her parents divorced in 1932, Julio moved to New York and Kiriki became a member, as a ward, of the large family of Julio's friend Paul G. Hoffman, the longtime president of Studebaker, based in South Bend, Indiana. Hoffman became "Daddy" to Kiriki, and his wife, Dorothy, who had hired Julio to paint a mural for the children's room in their home in South Bend, became "Mommy." In the late forties the Truman administration called on Paul Hoffman to serve as administrator of the Marshall Plan. Based on that success, he was asked in the fifties to head up the Ford Foundation. During Kiriki's last two years of high school, she boarded at the Putney School, a few miles east of Bennington in southern Vermont. After high school, Kiriki moved to New York to try to make it as an artist.

Around this time, Julio became the third husband of the burlesque queen Gypsy Rose Lee. "I was there when they met," remembered Kiriki. "It was in 1946, at a party in Gypsy's house at 163 East Sixty-Third Street between Lexington and Third. She was a wonderful woman." The couple married in 1948 and traveled together with the Royal American Shows, where she worked as a performer while he created posing performance art, with elaborate painted backgrounds, where people sat naked but could not move. "The narration was very Freudian," said Kiriki. "Julio and Gypsy divorced in 1955. They were very good friends, but with those two massive egos, they just couldn't be in same room at the same time. He was a very individual painter. He was European, after all."

When Kiriki decided to put off her New York aspirations and go to college, Bennington, with its arts focus, was a natural choice. In February of her senior year, she married Ben Newmark, who had graduated from Williams College in December. "We got married in Gypsy's house," said Kiriki. "She wasn't there. She had a gig in Havana."

They moved back to Bennington for Kiriki's last semester, when she created most of the drawings for *A Child's Guide to a Parent's Mind*. "A lot of the book was done before we graduated," says Kiriki. "Sally was determined," said Kiriki. "She really had a feeling of what she wanted to do."

Sally and Kiriki bonded during this creative experience, finding new insights as they worked, with the art taking inspiration from the words and vice versa. The book's statements about parents and matching scenarios are forgiving, insightful, and as fresh in their perspective today as they were in 1950. Kiriki told us, "Sally had a way of seeing the problem from a different point of view."

One page reads:

> Many times,
> parents feel a child is a BOTHER
> because
> IT is unbothered,
> and
> THEY would like to be unbothered.

In Kiriki's illustration on the opposite page, a mother looks disapprovingly at a child in a sandbox. Caption: "Why must she act like a child?"

Another page reads:

> Some parents seem to be more concerned with the proper "techniques" and proceedings than they are with their child and his needs and feelings.

The caption on the opposite page: Does he need more milk?

The words on page 52 are

> Parents feel a child's accomplishments
> speak for them,
> so they tune him up
> when
> company is around.

Kiriki's illustration on page 53 shows two parents and a child looking on as a child bows an oversized violin in front of two other parents. The father is saying, "They say he may be another Heifetz." This theme comes up again and again in Sally's written words—her annoyance at parents pressuring children to learn to play piano or violin, even if they didn't want to. It may have been later in life that Sally resolved some of these feelings and allowed her parents some credit for instilling both a love of and commitment to the arts in their four daughters and being significant arts benefactors themselves. But these ironies were less evident to the young woman—confident on the outside, still carving out her sense of self on the inside.

In conceiving *A Child's Guide to a Parent's Mind*, Sally had gotten significant input and guidance from *Times* columnist Catherine Mackenzie, for whom she had interned in 1949. This was around the time that Mackenzie published her book *Parent and Child*. Sadly, Mackenzie died in October of 1949, and Sally dedicated *A Child's Guide* to her mentor "who gave so much."

The year before, Mackenzie had been co-recipient, with Lawrence K. Frank, of the Albert and Mary Lasker Foundation Award for contributions to adult education on mental illness issues. Frank—whose book *Personality and Culture: The Psychocultural Approach* had come out that year—was director of the Caroline Zachry Institute of Human Development at Columbia University. His next book, co-authored with his wife, Mary, *How to Help Your Child in School*, won the *Parents* magazine award for outstanding book of 1950, the same year Sally had interned at *Parents*.

As Sally prepared *A Child's Guide* for publication, she reached out to the Franks,

who became her special mentors and contributed a three-page postscript, including the

following paragraph, echoing the book's forgiving tone:

> "In the questions for the young men and women which were the bases for this
> book, we detect a rather striking plea for just plain, ordinary humanity—in parents.
> "Why not," it seems to imply, "look at us as persons like yourselves? We make
> mistakes and so do you. We detect doubt, upset, unhappiness, anxiety in your tone
> of voice as you do in ours. What is so wrong with being human and making
> mistakes?"

In some spots, the Franks' book parallels Sally's approach to parent-child

relationships. For example, the back cover of the Franks' dust jacket lists seventeen

questions like "Why does your discipline work sometimes and not others?" and "What

are the 'new methods' of teaching that seem so different from the ones you remember?"

Students of Sally's later educational methodologies might take special note of a

section of *How to Help Your Child in School* titled "Music, Rhythms, and the Arts."

> Music and the arts are no longer considered extra bits tacked on to a school
> program. They are part of almost every dramatic production, part of discussions
> and storytelling. . . . More and more we are beginning to realize that the child's
> expression of his feelings, in music and art, is a valid statement of his developing
> self. He combines his intellectual ideas and his feelings in color and in rhythmical
> sound.*

After her Bennington graduation, Sally returned to New York to get *A Child's Guide*

ready for publication and to prepare for her next steps. Ruth Sussler also headed to

New York. "Sally was dating now and then," Ruth recalls. "I would stay with her when I

was job hunting. I heard about a job in a fashion house. It was a factory. I went to the

interview without scissors. They asked how I could come in without scissors, since

that's what everyone did all day—cut fabrics. I went home and the next day there was

this little velvet box from Sally. Inside was a pair of scissors. It was a very unexpected, very nice gesture, and I appreciated it." Ruth worked on windows displays at Altman's

on lower Fifth Avenue. She painted scenes from fairy tales, had gigs at other firms, and

ended up as a freelancer on Eighth Street and Greenwich Avenue.

Kiriki and Ben Newmark, meanwhile, decided to see the country. Ben, slated to

start a graduate program at Columbia University that fall, had rented them an apartment

on West Eleventh Street in Manhattan. That summer,

they climbed into their convertible — "a Studebaker,

naturally," said Kiriki — and embarked on a car trip.

"We drove to Washington, DC, and visited Daddy,"

who was by that time at work on the task of rebuilding

Western Europe. "We drove to New Orleans, Texas,

Mexico, and ended up in California," she

remembered. In Pasadena they stayed with her sister

Barbara Hoffman and traded in the Studebaker for a

smaller, sportier Austin. "Ben felt that, living in New

York, we needed a smaller car," said Kiriki. "We

cracked up in Wyoming. He was killed, and in the hospital I was delirious. I kept

repeating Sycamore six, eight-four, eight-four. One of the nurses recognized it as a

Pasadena number and called it. My mother [Dorothy Hoffman] and sister Barbara, and

brother Lathrop [Hoffman], and Julio all arrived. They took me back to Pasadena. There,

in a body cast and a sling, I continued doing the drawings for the book."

One of the last illustrations went with the statement: "Some parents want their

children to be just like them because . . ." and the caption "My child is an extension of myself." Kiriki drew a dad wearing a Nehru jacket and a medallion—"It was fashionable then," she explained—with the child growing out of his outstretched arm, wearing the same trendy uniform.

When she was able to travel, Kiriki returned to New York. "I moved back to our apartment on West Eleventh Street. Sally had been taking care of it. She was very helpful to me. That was when we really became friends." Up through December, Sally worked on rewriting her book and Kiriki put the final touches on the drawings. "Because [Sally] was very interested in psychology and had a background in dance, there was a strong feeling on her part of being involved in the arts. She loved food and cooking and enjoyed having a good time. One dish she loved was rib lamb chops. Sally was a constant comfort to me," says Kiriki. "I was still healing and feeling the devastating loss.

a child's guide

to a

parent's mind

by sally liberman

illustrated by kiriki

with a postscript by mary and lawrence k. frank

new york: henry schuman

In January 1951 Sally started her master's degree at NYU's Centre for Human Relations Studies with the course "Human Relations: Educating for Democracy." That month she also started teaching six-year-olds at the Reece School. Foreshadowing the Lab School, Reece served children with certain learning difficulties, centering its curriculum on dance, music, and the arts. At one point, one of Sally's pupils kicked her in the leg, leaving a bruise that created a blood clot. At the publishing party for *A Child's Guide* (published by Henry Schuman Company in April), Sally was under doctor's orders to say off her feet. "So she held court sitting down," Kiriki recalled. On April 25

she and Sally returned to Bennington for a book-signing tea, where they sold twenty-two

copies. A *Bennington Weekly* story summarized the book as follows:

> Written from a child's-eye view of parenthood, this witty and amusing series of
> cartoons has something to teach mother and father for a change, rather than
> junior who is there because he started it all. Every section very neatly
> emphasizes that peculiar aspect of child development that is different from what
> the parents expect they must cope with. This subtlety points out, I think, that the
> parents' need to grow up more than the kids who have some problems that can't
> all be answered by parental affection and all-knowing advice. The beauty of this
> book lies in the simplicity and humor with which our Bennington authoress and
> illustrator have combined to give a true-to-life picture of the baffling and
> challenging task of child raising. Each page is a question for the parent to answer
> for himself, if he can; and Sally and Kiriki seem to think he can—if he tries. The
> section by Mary and Lawrence Frank summarizes the purpose of the book and
> the research from which the girls gathered their amazing material. Her research
> was talking to friends about problems and pressures that were put on them as
> kids.

Later, Sally and Kiriki adapted *A Child's Guide* for filmstrips produced by the National

Association for Mental Health. Lawrence and Mary Frank contributed a discussion

guide, and the filmstrips were shown at PTA meetings, child study groups, and some

colleges.

Working with her literary agent, John Schaffner, Sally shopped story ideas to

magazines. Schaffner had been an editor at *Collier's* and *Good Housekeeping* before

starting his own firm. One of Sally's stories, "Subversary in the Nursery" played off the

anti-Communist rhetoric in the headlines: "In your home at this very minute, a

subversive is probably at work. He is plotting, fervently plotting, against the existing

order." In August 1951, she wrote a series of articles for the *New York Post* reporting on

the World Assembly of Youth, held in Ithaca, New York. Kiriki went along, remembering

it as "a political trip" and noting, "She got me into that."

With the older girls gone from the household, the Libermans downsized to an apartment at 875 Fifth Avenue. "It was two bedrooms," said Hazel Arnett, "a dining room and a living room plus a maid's room, on the eighteenth floor, with a view of Central Park." Sally took the next step toward her MA—independent study with the World Health Organization in Paris on the social conditions and social welfare activities that determined the meaning of mental health in different areas of the world.

Eight — Paris and Bob Smith

Sometimes you have to be nice, thought Bob Smith. He hadn't meant to blow off the Bennington girl from the World Health Organization, but each time they had set up an appointment, something came up and he had to cancel. This time, the third time, he told her he'd make it up to her. He'd buy her dinner and she could get her interview while they ate. She said she was researching the state of mental health around the world. She said she'd gone to Lincoln, five years behind him, and remembered him lifeguarding at the pool. As he sat waiting at a corner table on the second floor of Lapérouse, Bob had a view across the Quai des Grands-Augustins of the Seine, the Pont Neuf, the buildings of Île de la Cité, and the towers of Notre Dame Cathedral off in the distance. A New York City girl, he thought to himself, can write home to her parents about dining in a place like this, established in 1766, filled with luxurious red-cushioned furniture and Beaux Arts paintings. Sometimes you have to be nice.

When a curvy twenty-two-year-old blond glided into that room with her dancer's

impertinent grace, she took Smith by surprise. She extended her hand with unusual confidence. Her striking dark eyes met his. Smiling her magnetic smile rimmed with cardinal red lipstick, she said, "Sally Liberman. Thanks for meeting with me." She glowed with vivaciousness, intelligence, and energy. She had indeed remembered Bob at the Lincoln pool—that he had cut a dashing figure, with his wavy blond hair, chiseled features, and blue-gray eyes. He had been a top student, president of the student body, and star swimmer.

Sally was a little surprised, too, by the man who sat amid the crimson velvet

banquettes, rococo mirrors, and Romantic art in Lapérouse. At twenty-eight, Smith—

who had been a little full of himself as a high school lifeguard—now combined a

polished Ivy League demeanor with the confident authority of an ex-Navy officer and the

worldly intelligence of a budding diplomat. And, yes, there were those blue-gray eyes

and that wavy blond hair.

Sparks flew. They never got around to the interview.

As they chatted, Sally and Bob established that, in addition to having both gone to

Lincoln, their parents lived just thirteen blocks from each other on Fifth Avenue— hers

at Sixty-Ninth Street; his between Eighty-Second and Eighty-Third, across from the

Metropolitan Museum of Art. Sally found out that the chiseled lifeguard had gone from

Lincoln to Yale in 1942 but joined the Navy and served as a lieutenant in the Pacific.

After the war, he had returned to Yale. He was on the swim team, sang in the Glee

Club, helped found the National Student Association, and graduated in 1947. He went

on to Harvard's School of Government. In 1948, he had served as a member of the

executive board of the United States Commission to UN Educational, Scientific, and

Cultural Organization. He received his master's in government in 1949 and completed

the coursework for his PhD before moving to Paris as deputy to the permanent delegate

to UNESCO.

In her college paper about her family, Sally had bristled at her parents for

demanding "that I date boys with good social backgrounds from fine families who are

Jewish; I have not been able to get them to understand that I don't care about the

background, but about the person—the kind of person I am dating." But here she was, enthralled with someone who was not just suitable, but pretty much tailor-made to meet her parents' proscriptions. The more they talked, the more Bob and Sally realized how much their lives and families had in common. For one thing, Bob—like Sally—had a grandfather who had left Eastern Europe in the late 1800s and carved out a New York City success story.

Robert Simon Smith (1864–1923)

"Two hands upon the breast and labor is past," were words the peasants of the small village of Groidla, near Kiev, Russia, used to describe death. Bob Smith's grandfather and partial namesake, Robert Simon Smith, was born in Groidla on January 16, 1864. Before he was ten, Robert's family fled the oppression in Russia and moved to a small town in Austria. At fifteen, with nothing but the proverbial clothes on his back, he set out to immigrate to America. As recounted in a printed memorial, "He made his first business deal on the waterfront of Hamburg. He saw one steamship office crowded, a more remote office empty. He made a quick deal with the latter office. His passage was promised if he could bring them four customers. He brought them five—all enticed from the busy office; and the result was a ticket to New York and a few marks." With those marks Smith bought a supply of cigars, which he sold aboard the ship. He stepped ashore through the portal of the Castle Garden pier with $4.50, bought the stock of a pushcart peddler—shoe laces and other notions—and commenced his business career. "He possessed . . . innate initiative, pluck and courage which dynamically acclimated him to this new country," read the tribute.

During Smith's first two years in New York, he sent money home to his family. "After twenty-four months, I had seventy dollars in reserve," he told the *New York Sun*.* Around 1881, Smith met a manufacturer named Bloom at 51 Water Street. Watching the workmen cutting up cloth and making coats, he figured out how to make plush coats with a cutter and sewer. Within a year his business was worth a thousand dollars. Within three years he employed five hundred people; within five years, a thousand. He moved his business to Fourteenth Street, lost $5,000 the first six months and profited $50,000 in the next six. "Twenty-eight years ago [1894], I had the pleasure of making up more fur and seal into coats and cloaks than any other six houses in the United States."

In 1901, Smith made the "daring purchase," as the tribute called it, of the northwest corner of Thirty-Fourth Street and Broadway from Alfred Duane Pell for the sum of $375,000. "Some of his friends stood aghast at his courage, others shuddered at what they believed was his folly; but Robert S. Smith saw the future of that section before others had even grasped its possibilities." Even Isidor Straus of Macy's said Smith was paying $175,000 too much "for this little corner," as Smith put it, "around which R. H. Macy & Co. have since built their wonderful business emporium."

With Isidore Wise, Smith organized the firm of Wise, Smith & Co. in Hartford. At the time, it was the biggest department store in New England outside of Boston. Smith then established and built up the large R. Smith & Co. Department Store at 52 West Fourteenth Street in Manhattan, acquiring parcel after parcel of real estate as the demands of the growing business required. In 1904, said Smith, "when the uptown movement accelerated, I bought and sold $14 million worth of real estate in the block where the Waldorf-Astoria is situated. Yet what difference does the money make? We can't take it along with us."

Smith's memorial book emphasized that, when the US Government needed to buy property as part of its mobilization for the Great War, Smith was proud to sell it for no more than a fair price.

Like Sally, Smith kept sayings. Under "Gathered under His Wisdom," his son (and Bob's father) Solwin W. Smith wrote, "I have gathered some bits of his philosophy which, in veneration and affection, I feel happy in placing in the hands of his friends." Some examples:

- "If we would only stop and think, we would live a better life in a better world."
- "We all make our own lives. We get one hundred percent of what is coming to us. The world owes nothing to anybody."
- "Get the habit of smiling. Many of the seeming troubles of life can be smiled away."
- "Mistakes corrected make life sweet."
- "Wealthy parents are often the cause of misfortune to their children; the rich children know not the sufferings of life; they get everything prepared for them, and very often they are fed and kept on all luxury, and forced to go to college, whereas they would have accomplished much more at work."
- "It is a mistake to send children to private schools. It makes them conceited and selfish."
- "A man may make a mistake and suffer a loss, but money loss means nothing. Reputation is above money. Money cannot make a success. Reputation can.

Give me a poor man with a good reputation and I will give him anything he requires, but a man with money but without reputation—goodbye."

After the World War I, Robert Smith turned his attention to the beachfront at Far Rockaway and invested in it. His *In Memorium* portrait described him as "affable, approachable, democratic almost to a fault," and "a faithful, devout Jew." It also provided the following portrait:

> Sitting in a heavy carved armchair before the great table in his private office, Robert Smith today, as he signs the checks and vouchers piled a foot high before him, gives directions by long distance telephone to his New England employees or adjusts some trivial detail on the appeal of a particular customer, might not be taken for the typical New York business man. He seems too little in a hurry and too much without nerves. He is ready to give his time to the woman buying a $20 suit as well as to the woman interested in expensive furs. There is softness in his manner and voice. There is the physical bulk of 200 pounds as well to support the direct assertions of his earnest movements.

Not long after Robert S. Smith died, on December 17, 1923, a photo in the *New York Post* showed his grandson Robert, then four, with his bulldog. The caption explained that he "fell heir to the property of 34th St. and Broadway when his grandfather died recently, arrived in New York yesterday aboard the *Majestic*, to be with his parents, Solwin and Florenne Smith."

Bob Smith's mother, Florenne, was a Christian Scientist. Her family had come to the United States from the Alsace-Lorraine region of France in the 1830s, and some members had fought in the Civil War. Her parents, Jeanne and Paul Elkin, had moved from Chicago to Philadelphia, where Paul ran shoe factories. Solwin worked for his father's various enterprises.

Bob Smith grew up at 239 Central Park West. Like the Libermans of Park Avenue, the Smiths of Central Park West had live-in help—including in their case Maria Lappon, a French cook, and Maria Deutchle, a German nurse.

Like Ilsa Lund and Rick Blaine in *Casablanca*, Sally Liberman and Bob Smith quickly fell in love amid the sights of Paris. At some point, he took her on a trip to Rome, adding a touch of naughtiness to the romance. Amid the courtship, they realized that their families shared not only parallel biographies but also a commitment to achievement, philanthropy, and service to the world. Both of them driven and articulate, Sally and Bob became a formidable team. "He said the timing was right," their son Randy recalls. "He was getting toward thirty, and he was beginning to get some pressure from his family and from the expectation that every rising diplomat have a charming, presentable wife."

On April 18, 1952, Sally Liberman ascended from Hoboken Pier 5 to the *SS Veendam*. Her room was No. 338 on Deck C. She spent three days (May 8–11) in Oxford, two weeks (May 14–28) in Paris, three weeks (May 28–June 20) in Madrid, and three days (June 20–23) in Geneva. In her notes, she wrote, "Walk around city— bicycles ever present. Healthy, contented-looking people. A somewhat static utopia. Banks, watch stores + hotels everywhere. City of shopkeepers. Cultivated every bit of land, prosperous. Precision of transportation, gadgets for every convenience. Dinner with Henri and Jane Jacques [Bob's cousins]." Between June 23 and September 12, she traveled from Paris to Toulouse, Prudes, Nice, Paris again, Stockholm, Olso,

Copenhagen, Hamburg, Berlin, Frankfurt, Cologne, Dusseldorf, and Brussels. "Bob—

wonderful evening dinner at Lapérouse, red plush cushions." She was in Paris August

12–20 and described a "wonderful evening dinner" on the 12th with a friend n the Porte

Jaune in the Bois des Vincennes, where she and Bob heard about their friend's trip to

the Middle East, notably about Syria and the Muslim world. On August 14 they saw

Marcel Marceau— "really fine stuff, expertly enacted." From Paris, it was on to London,

Edinburgh, London again, and back to Paris September 5–12. She made a note of

Bob's address and title: Bob Smith Asst Counsel, UNESCO, American Embassy, 6 Rue

des Bausches, Paris 16.

That fall, Sally returned to NYU for courses in Child Development, Programs for

Child Development, and Case Studies in Propaganda.

She and Bob were married March 12, 1953, in the Jade Room of the Waldorf-

Astoria Hotel. The ceremony was

performed by the Rev. Dr. Julius Mark.

As reported in the announcement in

The New York Times, the bride wore a

gown of ivory Italian poult-de-soie,

made with an off-the-shoulder neckline,

long sleeves and a full skirt. One

wedding picture shows her sitting

playfully on his lap, both of them

laughing.

Kiriki Newmark was matron of honor. "I didn't realize I had the title," she remembered. "I was feeling bereaved still, kind of mourning. Sally's friendship was an incredible thing to have." Lois Klopfer, another Bennington friend, was maid of honor. Dr. Robert C. Ascher, Bob's best friend from Lincoln School and a prominent psychiatrist, was best man. The ushers included Sally's favorite cousin, Abba Bayer; and Bob's uncle Paul Elkin.

They sailed on the *Queen Mary* to, as the *Times* noted, "make their home in Paris, where he is a permanent delegate to the United Nations Educational, Scientific and Cultural Organization." They set up their home at 5 Rue Schoelcher, in the Montparnasse section of Paris, near the Jardin du Luxembourg.

That August, Sally taught a seminar for nine days in West Berlin on "The Psychological Factors of Prejudice," held under the auspices of the American Friends Service Committee. The participants were around thirty-five young people (sixteen to twenty-one) primarily from Germany, but also from Austria, England, India and the US.

Around that time, Bob learned that his position had been cut out of the budget in a Congressional slash of international missions. The newlyweds decided on an adventurous plan: They would set out on October 1 for a nine-month, fourteen-nation journey, on which Bob would collect material for his PhD thesis and Sally would research a treatise to be presented at the World Federation of Mental Health Annual Conference to be held in Toronto August 15–21, 1954.

In a letter to her literary agent, John Schuman, dated July 22, 1953, she outlined the ambitious itinerary:

> On October 1, we will set out by car to Yugoslavia, where we will spend two weeks, then we will drive on to Greece where we will spend two weeks, then

drive on to Turkey for 2½ weeks, then on to Lebanon and Syria for a week or so and then to Egypt for three weeks. Somewhere in that area we will sell the car and go on by boat, train, or plane. After three weeks in Egypt, we shall try and pull a bit of gimmickry (thru the Israeli Ambassador here) and fly to Cyprus which will take us into Israel for three weeks. Then we hope to go to Pakistan for 3½ weeks, from there to India for over a month, two weeks in Thailand, a week in Singapore (possibly Hong Kong), three weeks in the Philippines, and then three weeks in Japan. We will then take a boat back to the US and land there in the better part of June.

I will be looking into all possible work being done in the field of child development; what progress has been made, what kind of education exists, what kind of clinics are operating, and more important, what the needs of the various countries are.

Bob's thesis is on the role of cultural relations in foreign policy; specifically, he intends to look into the way in which several 'new nations' of the Middle East and Asia conduct their foreign cultural relations—how much they make use of UNESCO membership, how much they do on a national basis. Because of his work over here for the past few years he has all sorts of "ins" with the top educational and cultural people. Besides that, the British Council will have a person in each country looking after him, and the American Embassy has offered the same; then his work for UNESCO will bring him into contact with all international teams in that part of the world. His contract work for UNESCO will be checking on the Exchange of Persons Program—interviewing about 50 to 75 people for UNESCO—and generally writing an evaluation for them on the work they have or have not accomplished. He shall also be studying the effectiveness of Technical Assistance Projects, particularly the Fundamental Education Centers which UNESCO has set-up in Egypt, India, Thailand and he may have to go to Ceylon.

It was to be a honeymoon appropriate for both a rising diplomat in the tumultuous

era of new nations and an astute observer of relationships and mental health in Third

World cultures.

Nine — Honeymoon Across the Middle East and Asia

On October 1, 1953, Bob and Sally Smith left their building on Rue Schoelcher, tossed their bags into the boot of a small English Hillman, slid into the seats, and waved adieu as they set out across the French countryside toward Switzerland. On arriving in Geneva, they checked in to the Hotel Bristol on Rue de Montblanc, saw some friends, and dined at Café de Midi on the Square de Bergues. In the coming days, they received general briefings from members of UN agencies.

In his thesis, Bob wrote, "Preparation for the research trip, which began from Paris, where I had been serving as Assistant United States Representative to the United Nations Educational, Scientific and Cultural Organization, included arranging for letters of introduction to persons in all of the countries on the route my wife and I were to take. One set came from UNESCO to the secretaries of UNESCO national commissions. Another set was from the United States State Department to American cultural attachés and information officers. A third set was from the chairman of the British Council to the Council's representatives in the countries we were to visit. I also had several letters from the executive secretary of the International Association of Universities, the executive secretary of the International Commission for the Scientific and Cultural History of Mankind and from various friends and advisors. In addition, based on my international work, I had personal acquaintances and friends to see in every country on the route."

They drove for two months in the Hillman—two weeks in Yugoslavia, two weeks in Greece, two weeks in Turkey, and a total of two weeks in Syria, Jordan and Lebanon.

They then continued by ship from Beirut to Egypt. After a month in Egypt, they sold the Hillman, flew to Jordan and walked across the Mandelbaum Gate into Israel, where they spent a month. Sally met up with her father's oldest brothers, Udol and Zalman Liberman. When her devout uncles asked if their youngest brother worked on Saturdays, Sally told a white lie. "Oh, no," she said. "He has a Shabbos goy." (That is, a gentile who handled the business on the Sabbath.) In a way, she was telling the truth: the vice president of Arnold Constable was James Dingavan, a conservative Catholic.

In his thesis, Bob noted that he had lived abroad for three and a half years before going to the Middle East and Asia, so the transition to vastly different cultures "was not so marked as it would have been if I had come directly from the United States. Nonetheless, my wife and I found that we had to reserve at least a couple of days at the beginning of our visit in each country just to walk around by ourselves—and often take an organized sight-seeing trip. Only after that did I begin interviewing. As we moved from culture to culture, thirteen in all, and the time went by, we took longer and longer to become acclimated to each country."

"While Bob was exploring the political scenes of the countries and the cultural affairs," Sally wrote, "I was looking into the social conditions, social welfare work and meeting those interested in mental health work. I was sending reports to the Director of the World Federation for Mental Health, Dr. J. R. Rees in London."

In one of Bob's many nods of respect to Sally's research acumen, he noted, "At the same time my wife was engaged in a study of mental health and social welfare activities. Her observations and interviews helped to provide a valuable perspective for my findings." Sally provides a feel for their daily itinerary in a diary:

Oct 2, appt at WHO with Dr. Ronald Hargreaves of WHO.

Oct 10 left Padua for Trieste.

Oct 15—Zagreb—stop for lunch—old farmer who said all people were alike by showing fingers and saying 'We all have these' or some similar phrase in his language. Belgrade Oct 21—Bob's tummy out of order Bob to bed."

Oct 22 saw Mr. Buch of FA0 [the UN Food and Agriculture Organization], then taken to State and Cooperative Farms beyond Zemun, suburb of Belgrade.

Oct 31 - Athens.

Nov. 10 Bob went to see Mr. Mantoudia, Gen Secy Ntl Commission for UNESCO, 11:30 Bob met King Bradow, WSSF Secy

12 saw Weld again

12 saw Miss Alexandralai of Ministry of Wlefar for 1½ hours

Visited Acropolis, Parthenon, Erechgteum   Saw corny but swell "Merry Widow"

Nov. 1 saw lovely, white ruins of the Temple of Poseidon, where Byron carved initials

Read Time Mag. To keep alert on current events

Nov. 2, Mon., Bob went to USIS offices at 9. Met with Robert Speer, acting Pub Affairs Officer. Made application for Egyptian visas. Bob saw Mr. Erstein, USIS radio officer

Meetings all days

Nov. 5, Bob saw Weld at 9, for summing up 10:30 saw Mantoudis again, to discuss work of Nat Cms 12:15 finally saw Minister to Prime Minister, Sifnaious for interesting hour 1:15, King Bradow, WSSF came for lunch, took Bob to Daphni—

Nov. 9 boarded Barletta—"Athens complaint"—reached Istanbul at 9 pm Nov. 10

Nov. 16 Bob went to see Bob Kerwin, Public Affairs Officer of Embassy

Nov. 25—Jordan—Hotel Orient House men at desk horrid

Nov. 26—Mt of Olives

Nov. 29 to Beirut—Met with Ravets [cousins, perhaps?]

Dec. 4 Alexandria

Dec. 9 Bob to cultural department for talks with Mohammed Fathy, former GM of Egyptian broadcasting

Dec. 15 train to Luxor

Dec. 22 in Cairo—Sally went to St. Girgis' [George's] School Health Clinic—child guidance clinic in horrible rickety building in old quarter near Citadel

Wed., Dec. 23 Sally had appt with Robert Bogue, WHO Health Educator advising on Kalion Demonstration Project—then met Bob at Cairo University

Dec. 24, Thurs., Bob at Ministry talking with Manfaluti regarding UNESCO Ntl. Commission in Egypt

At the end of January 1954, the Smiths flew from Israel to Pakistan, where they researched for six weeks. In the coastal port of Chittagong, Bangadesh,[6] known since the reign of the Moguls and through the centuries of the British Empire as the gateway to the region of Bengal, Bob and Sally met Paul and Ben Booz (pronounced "bose" because of its linguistic roots in an area of the Netherlands and North Germany). Paul, a straight-talking Kansan, had previously been stationed with the Harvard Group, also known as the Institute of International Development, for two- to three-year stints in Jordan, Lebanon, and West Pakistan. He had come to Bangladesh with the World Bank. The Boozes took Sally and Bob on a boat trip to view the Bay of Bengal coast and the growing industrial activity along the Karnaphuli River.

While Paul and Bob talked international development, Sally got to know Ben. In her gentle English accent, Ben told Sally that she had been born in London, where her American father represented a Boston bank. Ben and her older sister had been brought up as English children in the 1920s. Their strict nanny ruled the day and night nursery at the top of their house in South Kensington, with meals arriving by dumbwaiter from the kitchen two floors below. They did not eat with their parents until they had learned proper table manners at age five or six, and then only for Sunday breakfast. "This life

---

[6] As noted earlier, this nation was then East Bengal and later became East Pakistan before becoming Bangladesh. For the sake of simplicity, I will refer to it as Bangladesh.

mercifully ended in 1932," said Ben, "when the Depression threatened my father's bank. He bought a house with a big garden near East Grinstead in Sussex and took the train to London every morning." In Sussex Ben and her sister had more freedom. After two younger sisters were born, Ben, was packed off to boarding school at the age of nine. Her older sister was homesick, but Ben found boarding school much more interesting than home. In those five years, she learned the life skills of how to get around senseless rules and maintain a goody-goody public life while enjoying a lot of private naughtiness. She learned how to lie convincingly and to be obedient whenever necessary.

In the summer of 1939, Ben's family was preparing to move to Switzerland, where her father was to join an international bank. "This was considered a good time for visiting America," said Ben, "to meet our many relatives in New England. But one week before we were to sail home, Hitler invaded Poland and England declared war. My father returned to Switzerland and the rest of us waited in America, always expecting the war to be over in six months. In fact, we stayed for six years. I went to boarding school in New Hampshire, college at Vassar, and graduated with a master's degree in history from the University of California at Berkeley." By that time, Ben was a firmly convinced socialist. When her father moved back to America after the war, the socialist and capitalist argued ferociously. Ben wanted to continue her studies in Europe, so her father urged her to study economics, believing that it might help her learn to argue sensibly. He enrolled her at the Institut des Hautes Études Internationales in Geneva, under the care of his friend William Rappard.

"I was gloriously happy in Geneva," said Ben. "My courses at the Institut, all in French, were challenging but engrossing. Students in Europe took themselves much more seriously than their counterparts in America. We young socialists really believed that the future of postwar Europe depended upon us. We were deadly earnest about our chosen role in history and we were determined to do it right this time."

In 1947 Marshal Tito invited youth brigades worldwide to help the youth of war-blasted Yugoslavia to build a railway, mostly by hand, from Sarajevo to the main rail line in Serbia, with a seaside holiday in Dalmatia at the end in return for five weeks of hard work. Ben eagerly joined the Swiss brigade with a chance to do a real proletarian job. "We were ninety strong in the Swiss brigades," said Ben, "and we met brigades from more than twenty other countries. Very few of us had ever wielded a pickax or a stick of dynamite before, but we learned fast and worked hard. For two weeks we were moved to a small valley in Bosnia to help demolish the spur of a mountain. To my amazement I found an American conscientious objector from Kansas attached to a Serbian brigade in the valley. He was thirty-two-year-old Paul, who worked for the United Nations Relief and Rehabilitation Administration in Belgrade, lending a hand on the railway during his vacation.

"Our brigade was collectively awarded a labor medal before we left Yugoslavia, and the Swiss became known for having the cleanest, tidiest camp along the whole railway. I had only two disappointments. There were no brigades from either the USSR or the USA. And the sanitary, germ-free Swiss had no immunity to withstand dysentery, so we spent our last week languishing in quarantine instead of swimming on the Dalmatian coast.

"My experiences in Yugoslavia and meeting Paul changed the direction of my life. Paul returned to America and I returned to the Institut in Geneva, but a mysterious lung ailment—not tuberculosis—confined me to a sanitarium in Leysin for six months. Paul

sent me many books, and I had ample time to think. My old socialist obsessions now

seemed narrowly intellectual and abstract, so I lost interest in politics. I wanted to stop

talking, pursue social justice, and address real human needs the way Paul was doing.

"The next year, Paul moved to Geneva with the UN Relief for Palestine Refugees

and doubled as my tutor, helping me pass my final exams at the Institut. We were

married in Geneva in May 1949 and bought a small pink house for $3,000 in the

desperately poor fishing village of Yvoire across the lake in France." As fishing gave

way to tourism in the ensuing decades, the Boozes kept the pink house as their family

home, even as their world travels continued.

"In 1950 we followed the UN Relief and Works Agency for Palestine Refugees in

the Near East to Beirut and began a nomadic life across Asia," she said. Paul worked

for the UN in the Middle East, then for Harvard University, which placed economists in

the long-term planning commissions of countries that requested them. Paul and Ben

lived for two years in Jordan, where they made friends with a couple who worked

tirelessly with refugees and introduced them to Quakerism. They spent two years in

West Pakistan and then on to Bangladesh. They had four boys, all born in different

countries. "It has been a wonderfully interesting life," said Ben. "Paul loves his work.

The boys learn local languages and attend various international schools where I am

sometimes called upon to teach, too. I paint a lot. I've written and illustrated children's

books published in America."

Like Kiriki and Ruth, Ben was an artist. Like Sally, she had published books,

rebelled as a young girl against a sterile upper-class upbringing, learned to craft her arguments with a strong-willed father, and married a Harvard man committed to making

a difference in the world. Perhaps most appealing of all—for the Sally who loved

adventurous souls—Ben and Paul had actually wielded pickaxes to create a postwar

nation. Ben the mother of four and Sally the newlywed made a strong connection.

From Chittagong, the Smiths journeyed to India for about two months, then to

Thailand for two weeks, Hong Kong for a week, Japan for three and a half weeks, and

back to the US in June.

In Sally's story "Some Observations on the Role of Mental Health in the Middle

East and Asia" in the *Bennington Alumnae Quarterly*, excerpted below, her descriptions

of life in these nations in many cases remind us how little certain parts of the world have

changed in the intervening sixty years:

> Before we started, we read a little about the countries we were to visit and talked with acquaintances who came from or had visited the countries on our route. We were fortunate also to have friends and acquaintances as well as many letters of introduction in every country we visited.

> Since we felt that a foreign visitor to the United States who sees only New York City leaves with a very limited view, on our trip through the Middle East and Asia we spent a good bit of time in the small towns and villages as well as the big cities. After we gave up our car, we were fortunate in being able to borrow cars or go via donkey to the outskirts of main cities. We had such experiences as spending a day with the tribesmen in the Khyber Pass bordering Afghanistan and Pakistan,

The Smiths in an Indian village not far from New Delhi. The woman in white scarf and the man next to her are "village-level workers" who are trying to raise the living standards of the villagers through improved agricultural methods, certain health precautions, and recreation (to slow down procreation).
A photo from a story in the Bennington Alumnae Quarterly.

attending pre-wedding ceremonies in an Indian village, joining an anthropologist (Mr. Lucien Hanks, on leave of absence from Bennington College) for a full day's work in a village in Thailand, living with a Japanese shopkeeper and his family for a day, and accompanying a public health doctor on a visit to the houses of prostitution in the poorer sections of Bangkok. I mention these very few experiences to give you some idea of my approach to learning about social conditions in the countries we visited. I felt it was important to have as much contact as possible with the people—the mothers, fathers, children and students as well as with individual psychiatrists, psychologists, social workers, nurses, teachers, pediatricians, leaders of women's groups and government employees. I saw members of the national associations for mental health. I visited mental hospitals, regular hospitals, maternity clinics, social work schools, teacher training institutes, schools, child guidance clinics, child welfare centers, orphanages, homes for the mentally deficient, handicapped and disturbed children, where such institutions existed in a country.

Before sharing some of my observations regarding mental health in the Middle East and Asia, I think the general term "mental health" must be explained. The preamble of the UNESCO Constitution helps us when it says: "Since wars begin in the minds of men, it is in the minds of men that the defenses of peace must be constructed." Mental health begins with the minds and feelings of men. Mental health means more than trying to ward off mental illness. It is an effort to stimulate the growth of happier, healthier, more cooperative personalities creating healthier, happier more cooperative societies—our greatest defenses of peace. Mental health implies the interaction of individual and society, so it is a problem of human relations, of community living, of international relations in a constantly changing total environment. The mental health field is a new formulation of aspirations for a more fulfilling way of life. The focus is on how human beings can be helped to build more satisfying and loving relationships to live together harmoniously.

Some of the ways in which mental health aims are carried out in Western countries are through schools, through teacher training institutes where emotional factors in development are emphasized. Parent education programs, maternity centers, adult education, industrial programs of mental health, courses for professional and business people on human relations problems, and even special University Centers for Human Relations Studies are other evidences of mental health programs. There has been an increasing realization in the West that personality in disease and personality in the administration of public affairs is very important. In America and England, city, state, and national organizations devoted to mental health problems have been expanding and the boards guiding these associations are now composed of laymen and professionals. The whole concept and practice of volunteer work is an inherent part of our democratic system. This pattern is not used in the Middle East and Asia, for the democracy we know does not exist in those parts of the world. Our mental health programs are geared to highly-industrialized, large middle-class democracies. We cannot expect the mental health work of the Middle East and Asia to follow our examples. Our concept of the individual and his destiny is different, our philosophies and human values differ. We do have in common parental concern and protection of children. But respect for the dignity and worth of each human being is not a common belief the world over.

I found that in countries where there is a plethora of people and a shortage of food, one human being is not considered important. Under these conditions, consideration of one human being is almost a luxury. The prevailing caste systems in many of the countries we visited keep human relationships on a strict vertical level, everything being highly structured and in its place. The individual is not important under such conditions. It is a common pattern in the Middle East and Asia to risk your life for a member of your family who is in trouble because he is a member of your family. But if a friend of yours or most certainly a stranger, is dying right in front of you, you walk by because you feel this is not your concern, but his family's. This is not a calculated callousness but an expression of the way the society is organized. Part of this, I would guess, is due to the fact that until very recently all families lived under the joint-family system, where several generations lived together and were almost a community unto themselves as well as a social agency; within this orbit responsibility was taken, but no responsibility was assumed outside. The individual, as an individual, has not yet emerged in the Eastern, as he has in the Western, societies. A Turkish friend we met in Istanbul said he was most impressed with three things he saw in America in our newspapers. He listed them as follows: "one child; one woman; one dog." He went on to say, "the day when one child, one woman, one dog become important in my country, when the newspapers will devote headlines to such issues, I will rejoice for then we will be humanized." If we feel that the development of respect for the dignity and worth of one human being is essential to mental health, this concept must be interpreted in each country in terms of its present beliefs and aspirations and the way in which they may be redirected along these lines. Lawrence K. Frank has often said that the biggest job of mental health is "to help people reorient their own aspirations."

Despite the great nationalistic feelings in the Middle East and Asia, it was my impression that almost none of the people feel they are participants in their country's life. Part of this is the residue of occupation by foreign powers which made initiative punishable. Lack of participation also derives from feudalism which imposes so much from above, and the various types of caste systems which restrict the life of the individual, although these systems are breaking down slowly. The overwhelming poverty from which many millions suffer, the wide prevalence of disease, the enervating effect of the climate, have helped to create a feeling of resignation and hopelessness which does not encourage a feeling of participation in one's country 's life. Communication is limited in the countries we visited by the mechanical lack of radios and transportation. I never before realized what it means for a country to have 80 percent of its population illiterate as Egypt does, ninety-five percent illiteracy as in Pakistan, or to have ninety percent of India's 360,000,000 people illiterate. So very few must speak for so very many. The very means of communicating and sharing ideas is highly restricted by illiteracy and new ideas tend to be treated with even more suspicion. Illiteracy often invites exploitation. Most important, I believe illiteracy keeps people from knowing that they can achieve better worlds. So they react as the Egyptians often do, with a shrug of the shoulders and the word "malesh," which means that life is miserable, it always has been, it always will be, one life is just another, so why worry! Perhaps it follows that individual initiative and citizenship responsibility can be developed only as the way of living improves in a country, that social education therefore needs a sound economic base. Perhaps the assumption of individual responsibilities cannot come until the society assumes more responsibilities and encourages its population to do likewise.

The structure of the schools and colleges in the Middle East and Asia does not encourage responsibility. For the most part, the education system is devised and maintained to train clerks. It demands only the passing of examinations, and tends to discourage individual thought. The subjects are rarely related to the life of the area, and there is no practical education. Any kind of manual work is treated with disdain by those who have had education in the Middle East and Asia, to the degree that the chauffeur who has had a little education will employ a peasant to fix his flat tire because that job is beneath the dignity of an educated person. Life is highly compartmentalized as are human relationships. It is not surprising that the educated feel little responsibility to help the uneducated and few institutions encourage this responsibility. Cooperation in a stratified vertical society is quite another matter than cooperation in a vertically mobile society such as ours. At this time, a mental health society in the East finds it exceedingly difficult to work both with the villagers and the highly-educated upper classes.

One way, however, in which mental health ideas might reach the villagers, who compose usually eighty to ninety-two percent of the population in these countries, is through the local religious leaders and indigenous doctors. Those are the people who exercise the greatest influence over most of the population. Even among the most sophisticated families we met in Athens, Damascus, and in Lahore, the indigenous doctor was often consulted along with the Western-trained doctor. The local religious leaders and indigenous doctors are doing mental health work without knowing it, in their daily work with the villagers trying to help them fulfill emotional and social needs and iron out tensions within the community. Science must be prepared to accept what we call superstition while helping people to replace it. There is, for example, a Western-trained Sudanese psychiatrist presently living and working with the witch doctors in the Sudan. He has recognized the necessity for involving indigenous doctors in mental health programs and is teaching them modern medicine which they can apply in the fashion of their culture.

A problem of great concern to mental health workers is the position of women in the Middle East and Asia. The ancient Muslim pattern is gradually breaking down, and in some countries, as we have seen in Turkey, has been largely displaced. Despite our convictions on the subject, the inferior state of women in these countries was not a problem to them as long as no one knew there was anything better. But today the women of the Eastern countries are realizing that their status is not fixed and unchangeable. The impact of change is what constitutes the mental health problem!

The change in some of the countries, such as Pakistan, is very slow, so I was a bit shocked when I had to enter homes in Pakistan where I was permitted only to see the women, and when I saw screened-off ladies' sections in the movies. As we walked along the city streets we rarely saw a woman. When we did, she was usually clothed in the traditional all-enveloping white garment called "the burqa" (which resembles the Ku Klux Klan garb) with only a tiny perforated section in front of the eyes. Occasionally, we saw a high society lady, not veiled, step out of her chauffeured car into a shop, or a peasant woman walking several paces behind her husband covering her face with a scarf when a man passed by. A few times, we saw a bold girl student striding down the street. The veiled women we saw are in "Purdah," but so are some of those unveiled. The meaning of Purdah specifically is "curtain," but more fundamentally it means the separation of the sexes, and segregation. Purdah began as a privilege of the aristocracy during the Mogul Period (sixteenth-seventeenth centuries) on the Indian sub-continent. It is interesting and significant that ninety-nine and nine-tenths percent of the very small middle class observe strict Purdah. Only two or three percent of the small upper class observe strict Purdah. The upper class has been the vanguard in demanding women's rights, even though the wives of a number of Central Government Ministers, Provincial Ministers, and the wife of a former Prime Minister of Pakistan, maintain strict Purdah. The burqa is not worn by the lower classes for the women cannot afford them, and they would not be practical when working in the fields. But one often sees the village woman cowering along the lanes managing to cover her face with a scarf while balancing jars of water on her head. In the village joint-family homes, usually all the men sleep in one room, the women in another, and almost all activities are separated. There are still a number of little girls of ten who faces will not be seen again except by members of their families, their religious leader, and the husband who is chosen for them. It is still true in parts of the Middle East and the Sudan that the girls of seven are circumcised. It is still true that most Pakistani women would rather die than go to a male doctor, even though the medical facilities for women are scarce. It is still true that in Pakistan women are not allowed in the mosques on the principal day of worship and among very orthodox Jews and Moslems in other countries women and men are separated in houses of worship.

A study that has recently been completed in Lahore, Pakistan, regarding the social and economic position of women was quite revealing. Among five hundred male graduate students twenty-two to twenty-five years of age, asked about their attitude toward Purdah, ninety percent said they want their wives in Purdah and a fair number added: strict Purdah. Seventy-four percent of a larger group of women, the same age, said they did not want strict Purdah. They want mixing of the sexes "only when necessary," and want to maintain separate arrangements for women. They expressed the desire for more education to train them for careers dealing only with women. Thus it would appear, that the women themselves do not want unqualified freedom, but they do want to change their status. As the women rely less and less on tradition, so they must be helped to reorient their aspirations and goals, and helped to achieve them.

There are a number of women reformers throughout the Middle East and Asia. Many of them are not Moslem and thus exercise less influence. A number of women get carried away to extremes, such as the Moslem lady in India who said to me all housewives must be paid salaries by the Government so they would not be subservient to their husbands. Somewhat equivalent reactions have taken place in all countries as women slowly emerge from centuries-old subjugation. The very progressive wife of Pakistan's first Prime Minister, Begum Liaquat Ali Khan, head of the All Pakistan Women's Association, is now her country's first woman Ambassador (in Holland). Begum Liaquat, who reportedly is not Moslem, has spoken often of the need to teach school boys to respect women and the right women so they will grow up to be better husbands and fathers. She claims that too many children in the Orient, entirely women-raised, grow up in utter dread of their fathers, and that the whole area of male-female relations constitutes the core of mental health work. The Japanese women are clamoring for the same change of the education of their sons. The plight of women not only affects family life but national life. Economically, it holds back the development of the country, for the underprivileged woman who has lived according to an unchanged pattern of existence is not anxious to help others. The UN agencies have discovered that often women have fought innovations in medicine, agriculture, and such suggestions as cooperatives. The women say, in effect, that if they are not treated as partners at home, why should they be expected to participate as partners in technical change and development? Mental health programs in the countries we visited must reach the women and help them to help themselves. How to do this is an enormous problem. . . .

Underlining all that I have mentioned so far is the slow and sometimes violent social upheaval that is underway throughout the Middle East and Asia. Industrial revolution is commencing. The change is being made from agriculture to industry. The safe and narrow world of the joint-family system which provided the economic, social and cultural life of a community of family members is slowly breaking down with the shift toward the cities. The local religious leaders and indigenous doctors are not as accessible in the city as they were in the country. In the city, families are apt to be more isolated. There are many more physical dangers in the city. Housing is a problem in these overcrowded areas. The pace of living is more accelerated. For the first time, people are faced with problems of what to do with children since children need play space, and cities are not built for children, as we well know in the West! Many families are split, not only because of the shift to the city, but also because of the great refugee problem which affects many of the countries of the Middle East and Asia, where allegiances are split with one part of the family in the hostile neighboring country. The refugees who live in the city are living in terrible conditions, rootless, and without much hope of betterment. In Israel there is some exciting mental health work going on with the refugees in terms of research, treatment and prevention.

Under situations of stress and rapid change, in an aura of unsettledness, it is likely that mental ill health increases. But at the very same time, this enforced change offers the greatest teaching opportunity for the mental health field. In Zagreb, Yugoslavia, there is an unofficial mental health group headed by a public health doctor that has recognized that the small conjugal family, thrust in the midst of overcrowded cities where social welfare agencies are hardly developed, needs special attention and protection. This group has been reaching the parents through existing organizations, holding special seminars for teachers to help protect the child more in school, encouraging industrial human relations counselors, and has been helping individuals make reforms in existing institutions such as orphanages. The faith in what they are doing, the warm pride they take in their accomplishments and their recognition of the vast job ahead have created a spirit and zest such as I have rarely seen. In all of the countries we visited, there are immense resources to be developed and immense problems to be faced.

The work of mental health societies means different things in different countries and cannot follow any set patterns. I do not believe that mental health programs of the West can be adjusted to fit the Middle East and Asia. The layman in these countries, as is true in the West, is still frightened of the words "psychiatry," "mental illness," even "mental hygiene," but he is interested when he knows what it means in terms of his own life. The socially conscious laymen are willing to work for a movement that means a healthier society through better school and better teachers, through more loving and satisfying relationships between husband and wife and family, through more knowledge of daily problems, of general human relations between landlord and farmer, employee and boss in industry, government and people. Mental health is not a job for professionals alone. Certainly in the Middle East and Asia, where there is only a smattering of psychiatrists, mental health work must be an active responsibility of laymen guided by those professionals who have an understanding of the social and especially the cultural problems of their country.

I believe, the emphasis of mental health workers in the Middle East and Asia should be on facilitating harmonious change so as to encourage the greatest degree of social progress while at the same time respecting each country's values. Mental health workers must utilize the existing agencies and the existing patterns at the same time as they introduce new methods and concepts. As people can no longer rely on tradition, the greatest opportunity is available to mental health workers in the Middle East and Asia—to help their own people reorient their aspirations and goals toward a better way of life.

Ten — New York, Motherhood, and Geneva

In June 1954, Sally and Bob Smith returned to New York City and rented an

apartment in a new building at 2711 Henry Hudson Parkway in the Riverdale section of

the Bronx. Bob started assembling his nine months of interviews into his PhD

dissertation. As planned, Sally reported on her observations about mental health in the

Middle East and Asia at the Fifth International Congress of the World Federation for

Mental Health, held in Toronto, Canada, August 14 through 21. There she reunited with

her mentor Lawrence K. Frank.

As she explained in a letter to a *Mademoiselle* editor, "The World Federation for

Mental Health is the only voluntary international and inter-professional group concerned

specifically with securing better mental health. It has 86 members in 41 countries. Its

secretariat in London acts as a clearinghouse for information and research. It has

consultative status with the Economic and Social Council of the UN, the World Health

Organization, UNESCO, and the International Children's Emergency Fund, and it works

cooperatively on combined projects with these organizations. Until recently the World

Federation for Mental Health has been concerned primarily with the problems of the

West. In the last three years, it has been devoting increasing efforts towards helping the

Middle Eastern and Asian societies, partly by inviting representatives to special

seminars and meetings in Europe and partly through sending professional consultants

to the area."

In the ensuing academic year, Sally took five courses at NYU and conducted field

work in education toward her master's. In January 1955, *Mademoiselle* named Sally

one of its ten Young Women of Distinction, presenting her with its Award of Merit for her work in mental health. Her cohort of honorees included Eva Marie Saint, fresh from the

On the Waterfront role opposite Marlon Brando that earned her an Oscar for Best

Supporting Actress, and dancer Carol Haney, Gene Kelly's former assistant

choreographer, who won a Tony for her role dancing with Bob Fosse in the Broadway

production of *The Pajama Game*. Haney, who had danced with Fosse in the 1953 film

version of *Kiss Me, Kate*, is also remembered for injuring her ankle during the run of

The Pajama Game, providing an opportunity for her understudy, Shirley MacLaine, to

launch her career.[7]

In 1955 and 1956, Sally worked as an editor at the Mental Health Materials Center in

New York, preparing packets of mental health materials for educators to use with

guides. She received her master's in human relations from NYU on October 24, 1955.

In December Bob submitted his 426-page thesis to Harvard's Department of

Government. It was entitled *Cultural and Information Programs of Newly Independent*

Nations as Instruments of Foreign Policy: Case Studies of Egypt, Israel and Pakistan.

His preface read in part: "This dissertation is a study of cultural and information

programs as instruments of foreign policy of three newly independent nations, Egypt,

Israel and Pakistan. In undertaking this study, I conducted research in the Middle East

and Asia for a period of nine months, from October, 1953, to June, 1954. Most of my

information was obtained through interviews." On page iii of his preface, Smith noted,

"Only in India did I encounter some resistance to my research, and this came primarily

from members of the Ministry of Education. Special circumstances surrounding the

---

[7] Choreographers often quote Haney and Fosse's sexy moves in *The Pajama Game* song *Steam Heat*, performed in bowler hats, black vests over white T-shirts, capri-length black pants, and white socks. A recent *Glee* rendition of Britney Spears' *Toxic*, done in the attire described above, was punctuated by Jane Lynch, as the malevolent gym teacher, uttering, "This is a Britney Spears sex riot!" and pulling a fire alarm.

composition of this ministry, and the inopportune time at which I visited India, i.e.

immediately following the conclusion of the United States Military Aid Agreement with

Pakistan in the winter of 1954, contributed to my difficulties." In a footnote, Smith

elaborated that the Indian "Minister of Education is Maulana Abul Kalam Asad, a

Muslim, but a trusted friend and counselor to Prime Minister Nehru (see Chapter III,

Section E). His principal deputies are also Muslims. Since education plays such an

important part in the plans for Indian development, and since Pakistan, where the

majority of Indian Muslims pledged their allegiance after Partition, is still considered as

an unfriendly nation, there have been many suggestions of suspicion over the Muslim

domination of the education ministry. The representatives are therefore extremely

circumspect in their dealing with foreigners, particularly Americans. Other Americans in

New Delhi reported this same difficulty to me, and agreed it was more noticeable in the

education ministry than anywhere else in the government."

One of the givens of Smith's dissertation was the importance of influencing men's

minds in "comparatively recent times." (He defined "recent times" as the seventeenth

and eighteenth centuries in England, France, and America, when "the control of the

established rulers over their people began to be challenged by wide, popular

demonstration and popular force," citing Stalin, Hitler and Mussolini as having

understood the principle.)

Soon after Sally completed her master's degree and Bob submitted his thesis,

another life chapter began: Randall Alan Smith was born January 18, 1956, in New

York. He had blond hair and his father's blue eyes. On September 9, Bob was

appointed as acting secretary general for the World Federation of UN Associations in

Geneva. As Bob and Sally prepared to return to Europe, they visited Washington, DC, where they met an Englishman named Ray Goodman, who had just been hired by the World Bank, and his wife, Dorry (short for Dorothy). "Randy was an infant," Dorry Goodman recalled, "and our son Jeremy, who was born in December of 1956, had not arrived." Dorry had gone to Bryn Mawr and won a Fulbright Scholarship to England, where she earned her PhD in Russian and Balkan history from the University of London, and met Ray. When they moved to Washington with the World Bank, said Dorry, "We knew Sally and Bob immediately."

It is a remarkable coincidence that Dorry Goodman and Sally Smith would each successfully start an innovative school—the Washington International School in 1966 and the Lab School in 1967, respectively—and become an influential pioneer in education, Dorry as a founder of the International Baccalaureate program in North America and Sally with the Academic Club Methodology.

The Smith family moved and set up housekeeping at 8 Avenue de Miremont in Geneva. Sally served as the Geneva representative of the International Conference of Social Work at meetings of the United Nations' World Health Organization and other international agencies. She exchanged letters with Joan W. Blos in the Bronx, co-author of *A Year of Change: Six Months Before, Six Months After Childbirth.* "At present, representing the International Conference of Social Work at meetings of the WHO in Geneva," Sally wrote to Blos. "Mainly A MOTHER. HOUSEWIFE." Nicholas Lee Smith was born in Geneva on October 29, 1957, with dark hair and dark eyes.

Sally was an energetic, engaged young mother to Randy and Nick, while keeping up with her literary agent and Joan Blos, looking for opportunities to write. By late 1959, Sally was pregnant with a third child.

Gary Gordon Smith was born July 22, 1960. During a breech birth, the doctor did not do a Caesarean section, and Gary suffered loss of oxygen to the brain. On that day, Bob's and Sally's lives changed. The doctors were not sure Gary would make it, or be able to walk or talk. "The first thing everyone noticed about me as a baby was that I never cried," said Gary. "I had dyslexia, ADHD, hyperactivity, and many problems they didn't even have a name for at the time."

"From the beginning," wrote Sally in the Bennington *Quadrille*, "my husband, my two elder sons, and I looked carefully at each obstacle that the youngest child had to face. To encourage the infant to move more, we created all kinds of Rube Goldberg contraptions that made things spin or made loud noises at the slightest touch. When we saw how difficult it was for him to turn over from one side to another, we got down on the floor and analyzed the process of what turning over involved. We then worked on helping him achieve that readiness. Also, we turned him over so his body could feel what it was like, an organic kind of learning through demonstration hopefully setting a pattern."

That fall, John Kennedy defeated Richard Nixon in the presidential election. With Gary's continuing health challenges and potential opportunities for Bob in the new administration, it was a good time for him to seek a job with the foreign service in Washington and for the young family to return to the United States.

Eleven — Washington, Themed Parties, and *Nobody Said It's Easy*

Bob Smith joined the State Department soon after Kennedy was sworn in as

president. Bob started work in Washington early in 1961 and bought the house at 3216

Cleveland Avenue—in an idyllic neighborhood in the shadow of the National Cathedral,

which sits atop Mount Saint Alban, the highest point in Washington. Sally and the boys

joined Bob in late May, after Randy's nursery school let out in Geneva. Randy attended

summer camp at Beauvoir, the cathedral elementary school, before entering

kindergarten in the fall, when Nick started nursery school. Beauvoir was named for the

mansion it occupied, reflecting its panoramic view of the Washington Monument, the

Capitol, and the federal area of downtown Washington.

That November, Kennedy fashioned the US Agency for International Development

(USAID) out of previous State Department organizations with an eye to addressing swift

changes taking place as countries around the world gained their independence from

colonial powers. When Bob became AID's assistant administrator in charge of Africa, it

was a perfect opportunity. He had walked the streets of new nations. He knew the

complexities and the challenges. And Africa was very much on the mind of the Kennedy

State Department, which that year sent its first group of Peace Corps volunteers to

Ghana. Among the historical legacies of this period, newly independent nations like

Ghana, Kenya, and Gambia sent a wave of young Africans to American universities,

where they were to gain the education they would need to lead their new nations in a

modern world. One such Kenyan student at the University of Hawaii was Barack

Obama's father. Another, from Gambia, was Cheyassin O. (Pap) Secka, who went to

American University, lived with my family, and became, for all intents and purposes, a family member.[8] Like the senior Obama, Pap was the hope of a new Africa in an era of boundless idealism. In Bob Smith's role in the New Frontier, he forged new programs and new foreign policies for new nations in a new world.

Sally, meanwhile, became an active Beauvoir mom. She was pleased to see Nick show promise in his paintings, guided by the arts and crafts teacher, Alice Glass. Nick followed through with his artistic talent all the way to his career as an architect.

Among their fellow Beauvoir parents, Bob and Sally re-met their World Bank friends Ray and Dorry Goodman. Their son Jeremy and I were in Randy's grade, but a different class. Our "large" kindergarten class met in the Beauvoir gatehouse at the bottom of the hill on Woodley Road. The "small class"—code for advanced, or smart—convened in the mansion at the top of the hill. A recent phone conversation with Dorry Goodman served as a pleasant reminder of the durability of certain slights, as she recounted, some fifty-four years after the fact, a conversation that she and my mother had had with Mrs. Taylor, Beauvoir's principal, over our placement. "They told us that you and Jeremy, with your November birthday and his December birthday, were too young and shy and intimidated to keep up with the others up in the big school," she said. I had imagined that the sting of this underestimation of Jeremy might have been assuaged as he became the top scholar in our high school class at St. Albans, the cathedral boys' school. "There was Jeremy, and then there were the rest of us," says Jerry Howe, one of the handful perennially atop of our class rank. Or, I thought, this memory might have disappeared completely as Jeremy advanced to his bachelor's and master's degrees at

---

[8] A handsome, charismatic leader, Cheyassin O. (Pap) Secka was a leader in AU's student government, captained its soccer team, and led student protests in 1969, when the AU president would not allow Dick Gregory to speak. Secka went on to Oxford Law School, returned to Gambia, took part in a failed coup, and spent ten years in jail before returning to his law practice in Banjul. He died in 2015.

Harvard and his PhD at Princeton, where he has been an astrophysics professor for several decades. Nonetheless, despite these vindications, the episode of Jeremy being placed in the large class came up in my conversation with Dorry Goodman. This won't surprise educators and administrators who know the power of a determined parent. And, of course, this biography turns on the power and resilience of a determined Sally Smith. All that aside, to my shy and intimidated eyes, Randy, Jerry, and their "small class" mates, even as kindergarteners, were precocious, competitive, and one or two steps ahead in their academic development—a fact that, as we will see, may well have helped spark the Academic Club methodology.

Bob and Sally also came to know two other Beauvoir parents, Bob and Mary Lystad. He was a professor of African studies at the Johns Hopkins School of Advanced International Studies and an early advisor to the Peace Corps. She was a sociologist at the National Institute of Mental Health who wrote professional articles about families and children and eventually became a prolific author of children's books. Mary first met Sally when her daughter Lisa wanted to invite Randy to her Halloween party. Mary called Sally to see whether it was common practice at Beauvoir for boys to come to girls' parties. The answer was, "Why not?"

"The theme was to come as your favorite children's book character," said Mary. "Randy and Lisa were very inventive." Mary and Sally became immediate friends. Bob Lystad often gave seminars to young diplomats at the Airlee Foundation in Warrenton, Virginia. When he asked Bob Smith to give talks there, Sally and Mary went along. "We'd go off and talk," says Mary. "We had a lot to talk about. We had a very fun relationship. We talked child development all the time, because we had all these children." The Lystads had three girls—about the same age as Randy, Nick, and Gary—and two younger twin boys. "Gary and I had a particular affection for one another," Mary added. "He was the age of our third daughter."

Randy and John McTigue at the Civil War party

Another of Randy's precocious Beauvoir friends was John McTigue, a dark-eyed, dark-haired counterpoint to Randy's blond hair and blue eyes. "I spent quite a few days at Randy's house playing war games and more creative role-playing in those early days," John remembered. In January of 1962, Sally threw a sixth birthday party with a Civil War theme. Pictures in the scrapbook show us that John was Grant and Sarah

Sarah Peacock, Happy Sayre, Lisa Lystad, and Randy Smith play their roles in the Civil War birthday party.

Peacock was Florence Nightingale. Nick played a Union sergeant. Happy Sayre and Lisa Lystad, twirling a parasol, were southern belles. "We had just moved from New Orleans," explains Mary Lystad, "and Lisa really had a lot of that culture in her." Other boys played injured soldiers with bandages around their heads. Randy Smith, a Union officer, is shown blowing a toy trumpet, perhaps for a bugle call. John McTigue had the idea that the themed party might have grown out of Sally's observations of their history classes and role-playing in school. "Our teachers obviously

At right, Nick Smith plays a Union sergeant.

played off our natural competitiveness," he said. "Sally's parties for Randy fed off that in my recollection—fantasy role playing in which we adopted opposing roles. The fires were further flamed by Mrs. Dawson in second grade. Greek, Roman, British and American history. Anyway, I always suspected that Sally was watching the dynamics." It's also possible that it was the other way around—that the Beauvoir teachers took their cue from what they heard about Sally's parties. Either way, I remember watching a school play in which John played Grant, Jerry played Lincoln, calmly reciting the Gettysburg Address, and Randy not only played Robert E. Lee but then accompanied himself on the guitar as he sang the Civil War folk song *Two Brothers*.

The themed parties became a tradition. "They were awesome," said Randy, "and it's why to this day I love New Orleans, where at the drop of a hat people get into costume, and not just for Mardi Gras. I remember the Civil War, Pirates [1963], Round Table [1964], and Secret Agents [1965]. Sally decorated, designed, and organized all of them. They went on from about age six to ten for me. And the same for my brothers."

Our Beauvoir classmate Paul Shorb remembered, "I took my costume for the Knights of the Round Table party very seriously. I already had the Dad-made sword, shield, and helmet from a prior Christmas. Pretty awesome. My mom bought the metallic gold cloth to make the gown-like 'chain mail.' I sewed a dragon head onto the front for decoration. I guess that was the only part I did myself. But that was a nice stimulus to do something new—not sure I'd sewed anything before. And my mom said those little white dragon teeth were too small to stay on, but I was stubborn and it worked! Can you believe I still remember such a detail? It may support Sally's thesis that experiential learning is the best." (No surprise that as a 17-year-old, Paul was an

assistant teacher in the Lab School summer outdoor program on the island in the
Potomac.)

"My two brothers and I had many different kinds of parties over the years," said
Gary. "But the best for me was the one when all of us were dressed up as cavemen and
we had to grunt and make strange sounds to be understood. There was a lot of pointing
and make-believe sign language and fun was had by all."

For sure, Sally saw the power in what was happening. "As Gary grew older," she
wrote later,* "I discovered that birthday parties could be exciting learning opportunities.
One year we had an Indian party, all guests wearing appropriate costumes, and all
decorations conveying American Indian life. There were drum beats to accompany
Indian games such as 'follow the tracks,' table favors of homemade Indian drums,
feathered hats, etc., and the birthday cake was a recognizable teepee. We spent weeks
preparing and planning for this: reading about American Indians, listening to records,
visiting museums, looking at films, slides and photographs of Indian life. Our exploration
covered history, geography, government, science, art, music, dance, literature and
drama. Choices for the celebration had to be made constantly so decision-making was
an important part of the experience.

"Built on keen interests of the children, the parties were both fun and successful
experiences. Kids love to pretend and to do adult activities. They were totally immersed
in what they were doing. Some basic principles began to emerge: what children need to
know can be taught through what they like to do and want to do. Schools must tap the
ingenuity children use on the street and the play yard. Environments need to be created
with a few simple, inexpensive visual effects to help children believe in the dramatic

environment. They need 'to be' as well as to do, to see, to touch, hear, smell, taste, and discuss.

"The adult who guides the activity is also a learner, and doesn't need to know all the answers. The boys and I explored together. I learned easily what they knew, with what concepts they were struggling, which ones evoked questions."

Amid the creativity of the parties, Sally did what she could to address Gary's special needs as they arose. Demonstrating the power of a determined parent, she ignored the recommendations of doctors and experts. "My husband and I were told that our expectations for this child demonstrated our inability to come to grips with reality," she wrote. "'Keep yourself busy. Get involved in other things. Forget him. You have two sons who are in great shape. Two out of three is a fine average.' This was repeated by friends, doctors, and other professionals." As Gary became a toddler, it became apparent that his oxygen loss at birth had affected his motor skills. But Sally never wavered. "They said he wouldn't walk for years," Sally wrote. "He walked at fourteen months. They said speech would not come without specialized training. He talked at two years of age. One prediction after another went into the trash heap. The medical people were split when it came to predicting his learning abilities. The Medical Chief of Physical Rehabilitation insisted that this child had to be brilliant or be a genius to have physically accomplished so much. Prominent neurologists and psychologists took a dim view of the situation."

When Gary was two, he broke his leg playing with a wheelbarrow. "My foot got stuck in the handle and I fell," he said, "which meant I spent the next six months in a double leg cast being carried around everywhere. I slept in a bed in the playroom looking out to the backyard with my new friend Bird, a parrot. Being trapped like the

bird, I would let him out to fly around the house. Man, my parents really loved me when I

did that. The day my cast came off I let the bird free, and he soared away into the sky

never to be seen again."

Randy and Nick worked with Gary to address his challenges with motor skills. Amid it

all, Sally and Bob were noticing important facts about Gary's cognitive abilities. "At age

two," Sally wrote, "despite four operations, a broken thigh, and innumerable battles with

staphylococcus infections, he seemed to be amassing a great storehouse of information

and a large vocabulary. How was he learning it? Things we told him didn't stick in his

mind. Yet we found that he responded with alacrity to hearing highly dramatic stories

read aloud, stories (especially with pictures) that he could act out. Clearly, several

senses were being used at once."

As seeds of educational breakthroughs were sown, Sally and Bob were doing all

they could to deal with Gary's practical health problems. "I was very sick as a child for

many years of my young life," said Gary, "always getting colds, fevers, ear problems. It

got to the point that the doctor would have to make house calls, which was never done.

Mom used to have to take me into the bathroom and turn on all the hot water and steam

so my throat would clear up. As I got older, she would leave me in there alone for a few

hours until I got better. The one good thing about being sick was that Mom would treat

me like the king of the world, bringing me anything I wanted to eat or play with."

In August 1962, the Smiths were invited by a retired industrialist named Irving

Salomon to come out and relax at his ranch in Escondido, California. Salomon, an

original investor in Xerox, had been named as a member of the US delegation to the UN

General Assembly in 1958. At some point he had gotten to know Bob and adopted him as a protégé. "We called him Uncle Irving," said Randy. It was the first of five August trips to Rancho Lilac.

Gary remembered, "The first thing that happened to me was I was tossed into the pool by my father and told to swim, and I learned to swim before I learned how to walk again. I have been a fish ever since then, which means I love to swim." With a babysitter minding the boys as they swam in the pool, milked cows, and rode horses, Bob and Sally got some time together, playing tennis, reading, and writing.

Back in DC, Sally continued her work in the mental health field by organizing and chairing sixteen seminars in 1963 and 1964 for Asian and American women on subjects relating to social and technological change in Asia and America. She also began to map out her next book, which she envisioned as a guide for parents and children to help them understand their complicated feelings and relationships during the rocky teen years. It would develop and expand many of the ideas in *A Child's Guide* about parent-child relationships, and give practical advice for navigating the perilous teen years. The practical question for Sally was when could she possibly get to time and energy to write it. "She would try to write in the afternoons," says Randy. "But she was looking after Gary. It drove her crazy."

At the same time, Sally fulfilled the role of gracious entertainer to Bob's colleagues in the State Department and dignitaries, notably from African nations. "They had lots of nice dinner parties," says Randy. "We would get to greet guests and then wait upstairs to be brought our portions of the baked Alaska they usually had for dessert." In her role as the elegant, witty hostess, Sally was a valuable partner in supporting Bob's career.

She could charm the undersecretary of state as easily as the Senegalese ambassador.

The Smiths also began a tradition of hosting an annual Christmas party, always on

December 22 or 23. "They were beautifully done," remembered Ben Booz, who had

reconnected with Sally when she and Paul and their four boys moved to Washington

with the World Bank in 1962. "It was everybody she knew. They came in waves."

African and American diplomats. Young artists and teachers. Old friends like Ned Hall,

who in the late fifties had taught foreign cultures to Foreign Service officers in DC, then

in the early sixties continued his teaching and research at the Washington School of

Psychiatry, where his wife, Mildred, was chief administrative officer. "Most years it was

over 200 people," said Gary. "The food included roast beef, lamb, barbecued chicken, at

least two big hams, cakes, fruits of all kinds. Mom always had a great band that played

into the night." In her bright red lipstick and a zebra print dress, Sally greeted her guests

at the door, beaming and welcoming all comers. Attendees were energized by the red

wall of the dining room, the avant-garde paintings, kinetic animal sculptures, the

playroom with its zebra rug and African drums, and the wood chandelier crafted to look

like a lightning bolt. "They are always the best parties of the year," said my father.

"Everyone in Washington wants to be invited. The people are all so interesting."

Through most of 1963, including the August visit to Rancho Lilac, Sally completed

Nobody Says It's Easy: A Practical Guide to Feelings and Relationships for Young

People and Their Parents, which was published by MacMillan in 1965. On the cover,

above the title, was the question "Can the years between 13 and 19 be the best years of

your child's life?" The first paragraphs of her preface read, "This book was completed

before that agonizing date in American history, November 22, 1963. I feel I cannot leave unwritten a few words concerning President Kennedy's assassination, particularly in a book for young people exploring feelings and relationships.

Can the years between 13 and 19 be the best years of your child's life?

NOBODY SAID IT'S EASY
By Sally Liberman Smith

"President Kennedy was a leader of this age who ignited the fire of young people. He himself was young, courageous, modern. He symbolized trust in youth, a burning faith in the future." Her theme was that strong feelings can have untold bad effects, and everyone should use reason to understand the feelings inside and outside ourselves. The illustration at the start of the first chapter shows six pairs of moms and dads from cave days up through history alternately yelling at one another and lovey-dovey. The caption reads, "Our parents have more to do with the design of our lives than we like to admit." The line drawings look similar to Kiriki's in the first book. In fact, Sally had wanted Kiriki to do the dozen or so illustrations, but the editor at MacMillan told Sally it didn't work that way. Sally argued the point, but the publishing house picked the illustrator, Roy Doty. On her acknowledgements page, Sally wrote, "My appreciation is to Kiriki for all that she has gone through with me on this work." She also thanked Irving Salomon, "whose invitations to Rancho Lilac gave our family the relaxation that gave me the energy to write a book."

118

Sally also thanked, among others, Mary Lystad; her writer friend from the Bronx, Joan Blos; Mary and Lawrence K. Frank; Bennington professors "Smitty," Ned Hall, and Erich Fromm; and NYU professors Arnold Rose and Howard Lane.

The chapter headings are Relations, Feelings, Fear, Anger, Guilt and Guilty Feelings, Rivalry and Competition, Popularity and Conformity, Love, and Learning to Live with Ourselves. The discussion of parent-child relationships echoes many issues from *A Child's Guide*. Children don't want to be treated like babies, told what to do, preached at, criticized, or pressured: "Young people want the freedom to be themselves." The caption for the cartoon in the Feelings chapter reads, "We learn early in life to cover up how we really feel." In the Fear chapter, Sally writes, "When a family does not encourage a feeling of self-confidence in a child, the fear flourishes." Under the Anger drawing, the caption is "When no anger is expressed in a family, it gets bottled up and may explode later. In Popularity and Conformity, Sally tackles the esteem problems created by being out of work: "Today, close to a million out-of-school young people under twenty years of age have literally no employment opportunities. How do they feel? Many of them have dropped out of school, tried to enter the labor field, feeling inadequate and defeated because of difficult home situations and unsatisfying performance at school." In Learning to Live with Ourselves, she writes, "Many of us suffer from expecting too much or too little from ourselves. Why? It may be because we have not yet achieved the self-respect that families, that schooling, that extracurricular activities, that friends and others who influence our lives can help us develop." As the cartoon caption summarizes, "Like almost everything else in life, our aim is to attain a certain equilibrium." The words are practical, loving, and informative.

They remain as fresh and original as when they were written. And they give us a window into the empathy and awareness of the difficulties of growing up that helped Sally when it was time to develop her educational methodologies.

In the spring of 1964, Sally had the idea of hiring a teenage boy to work with Gary to develop his motor skills and improve his mobility. She asked her friend Joanne Macy, whose husband, Fran, worked with Bob at USAID, if she knew of a teenage boy who could help her.[9] Macy looked over the back fence of her Lowell Street home and saw a clergyman's family—mine—whose six children included several teenage boys. Macy broached this idea with my mother, Charlotte Clark, who thought of my older brother Stocky, a big brother by nature. "Stocky loves children," she said to Macy. Mom then asked Stocky, "How would you like to take care of young boy for July?"

On a recent Friday after Thanksgiving, on a family sun porch, holding a steno pad and pen in my hand, I sat with my ten-years-older brother and conducted a formal interview with him. A formal interview means, in this case, that the swirling, friendly members of our family were asked to leave us alone for close to two hours. This appeared to drive them insane, as they peered through closed French doors wondering what we could be talking about. Stocky is tall, about 6'4". But when he first met the Smiths, he was hovering around 5'9". He was a late bloomer, adding his inches in college, somewhere after he attended his first James Brown concert at the Apollo Theatre in Harlem and before he took up leathercraft and candle making as his creative reactions to the tensions of the Vietnam era. Sitting on the sun porch, I could tell that he

---

[9] Francis Underhill Macy served between 1964 and 1972 as deputy Peace Corps director in India, country director in Tunisia and Nigeria, and finally as director of all Peace Corps programs in Africa.

didn't think all this is formality was necessary—that he could rattle off the lessons of

Sally Smith anytime, anywhere. In fact, the process of revisiting these memories

brought us to some useful insights into his own development and how he was affected

by his lifelong mentor.

"I was reluctantly maturing as a sixteen-year-old kid," Stocky remembered. "I was a

kid without purpose, a kid without direction. I was not a particularly great student, and I

wasn't interested in fitting in with people's structures." He had moved in 1960 with our

family from Nashville, where he says he enjoyed a Tom Sawyer–like childhood among

unpretentious middle-class people. He had to repeat eighth grade as he entered St.

Albans, the cathedral boys' school. He always buckled at the preppy sarcasm of his

classmates and the English schoolboy strictness that the "venerable institution," as our

teachers called it, took such pride in. "I'm an experientialist," he says. "I'm an

experiential learner. Mom and Dad never told me we were leaving Nashville. They just

put me on a plane." Our father, the Reverend Bayard S. Clark, had been compelled to

leave his job as rector of an Episcopal church in Nashville because some influential

vestry members had objected to a *Tennessean* story by David Halberstam about a

prayer vigil of clergy from all denominations that Dad had led outside Mayor Ben West's

office window. The idea was to encourage the mayor to integrate the downtown lunch

counters. Dad had met with West and said, "If you integrate the lunch counters, we [the

clergy members] will support you." West replied, "I can't do that politically."[10] Dad found

---

[10] Halberstam covered the civil rights movement for the *Tennessean* in those tumultuous years, which he recounted in his 1999 book, *The Children.* Among the most consequential moments came two weeks after our father's prayer vigil, when young activists John Lewis and Diane Nash confronted Nashville Mayor Ben West on a street corner and had an historic exchange. Nash asked West to integrate the lunch counters. He said, "I can't do that politically." She said, "How about doing something because it's right?" West thought about it and said, "You're right. I'll do it." There is a plaque on the sidewalk on that street corner commemorating that moment.

a new job, as a canon at the National Cathedral and chaplain of the cathedral girls'

school. In the move, our parents had bought Stocky a blue blazer and put him on a

plane. He was met at National Airport by Craig "Rev" Eder, the kindly St. Albans

chaplain and a longtime family friend. Rev took Stocky up into the St. Albans boarding

area, where he was to stay until the rest of the family moved up from Nashville, and

introduced him to his roommate—another boy from Tennessee, whose father was a US

senator. Stocky and Al Gore played quite a bit of pickup basketball, and at some point

Stocky broke Gore's foot in a hoops game.

In the move from Nashville, our parents threw out Stocky's baseball cards, including

a Mickey Mantle rookie card. This misfortune—which seems to have befallen many

baby boomers as their church, military, and corporate families were uprooted on a

regular basis—serves as an emblem of resentments often harbored about saying good-

bye to friends and neighborhoods.

At Joanne Macy's suggestion, Sally and Nick visited our chaotic home on Woodley

Road, across from the Cathedral's College of Preachers. My older twin brothers, Rocky

and F. T., were probably practicing *Moon River* on their clarinet and trumpet,

respectively, in all their atonal glory. Our beagle, Yogi, was probably baying in the tiny

front yard. Sally liked to recall that I raced into the house in a Robin Hood costume—I

was obsessed with the TV show—and shouted, "Where is Maid Marian?" I showed Nick

my hamsters. I introduced them as the king and queen of Hamsterdam, which I viewed

as high verbal wit. My oldest sibling, Kathy, was off at college. The next oldest, Tucker,

was in prep school.

Sally probably saw a parallel to her own family growing up, with our four siblings at home, including an afterthought bringing up the rear. Like Ben Booz, my mother was a few years older than Sally. Like Ruthie Sussler, Mom was a graduate of a women's college (Smith) and a painter with New England roots (Mom's father taught English at Phillips Exeter Academy in New Hampshire). Along with her landscapes, Mom drew countless pastel portraits of children, for a fee of fifty dollars each, which later in the decade she put toward her MFA in painting at American University. She probably reminded Sally of Ruthie, although it was always Mom's dream to be a bohemian West Village artist like Kiriki. Sally, ever mindful of social justice, liked the civil rights story behind our family's move to DC and my father's continuing activism. (Dad was there for the "I Have a Dream" speech and later marched in Selma.) Mom and Sally became friends, and before too long Sally commissioned angelic pastel portraits of Randy, Nick, and Gary.

Stocky recalled his first introduction to the boys: "I met the Smiths on their front lawn. Gary was going to be four in July. Sally told me he had cerebral palsy and fluid on the brain and we didn't know what else. He didn't move well or easily. I more or less instantly realized he was suffered from something. There was fluid draining out of his eyes and, I think, draining out of his ears. I was told he had broken both his legs when he was a young kid and had more operations. I immediately took to him because he was the brightest bulb I'd ever seen. He was the most can-do, excited little boy. He'd been through so much. How could he have such spirit? His brothers were always attentive. They always tried to stimulate him. They were always in the backyard playing and fighting. Randy was perhaps more protective. My job was to just be with him. We spent all of our time playing games and playing with trips, learning interaction in a concentrated way. But there were opportunities to do more than teach him how to play Candyland. He was obviously very intelligent, but he had no fine motor skills. The act of moving pieces on the board and lifting cards became the therapy of the day. He rather quickly developed his fine motor skills, however awkward his overall locomotive skills were. His ability to walk was limited. He lacked balance. I think he even wore a helmet at some point.

"I realized at some point that Sally was extremely creative, as evidenced by Gary's caveman birthday party in July. She invited all these kids over and she created an environment of cave men doing art naturally with crayons, paper, and tempera paint and making things, and all the parents said, 'I haven't seen my son or daughter so happy.' She was always encouraging her kids to do things. They had a big playroom.

I was taken with her presence and her energy. That made my July wonderful. I loved the interactions and I loved her creativity and energy. One day she said, 'We'd like you to come out to Rancho Lilac.'"

Twelve — "My child needs a school now!" The Club Methodology is born.

At Rancho Lilac in August 1964, Gary remembered, "Stocky kept trying to tell me what a cow was. I called them Moo Moos. I knew they were cows, but I called them Moo Moos the entire summer just to mess with him. Then I said to one of the ranch hands, 'How are the cows doing?' Stocky heard me say that, and he said I was a little stinker." As the family settled in to a guest cottage, Bob Smith cooked hamburgers, played Risk! with the boys, and generally cavorted as a dad in a way that his work schedule rarely allowed.

"I looked up to Bob," Stocky remembered. "He was like one of the Kennedys. He was a star. He ran with the best and the brightest. He looked like a diplomat. He dressed like a diplomat, talked like a diplomat. He had the right facial expressions. Bob was going places and Sally was supporting him by raising these kids and throwing those dinner parties."

In early August, North Vietnamese torpedo boats engaged with a US destroyer in the Gulf of Tonkin. In the succession of events that followed, Bob was asked to speak at the University of California at Davis. "Those two spent so many hours working on his speech that you can't make it up," Stocky said. "What I noticed was that she was doing most of the talking—'But what I really think you might want to say is this.' I realized over time that she had been a ghost writer for him when they had lived in Paris. They were both very interested in his becoming a successful person in the State Department and rising through the ranks. She was helping manage his career." With women's roles in American society as they were in the early 1960s, Bob Smith's respect for his spouse's talents and judgment, notable in his PhD thesis, stand out. Her ambition and competence were a plus for his career. But for the most part, the emphasis was on *his* career. This was a simple fact in women's lives, even for driven, skilled graduates of Bennington, Wellesley, Bryn Mawr, Smith, etc., a fact easily lost on younger readers, since in this regard our world has changed so significantly.

One day at Rancho Mirage, Gary remembered, "Stocky took me riding on a horse with his legs dangling down and me in his lap. The horse got annoyed at the chafing and took off like a rocket. When he stopped, near the barn, the saddle had slid sideways so that we were hanging on for dear life with Stocky's hands able to touch the ground. I was laughing and thought it was fun. I am not sure if we ever told my parents." Stocky established some long-term bonds with Gary and the Smith family in these weeks. "The boys saw me as an older brother and Sally thought that was good," Stocky says. 'She saw a different side of me. She saw potential in me that others would not have seen. I was undergoing a transformation with the Smiths. From being a directionless and purposeless teenager, I changed big time, and I don't think my parents realized it.

"When I describe her as my mentor, I saw an idealized part of her character. I don't have to reach very far to say I saw an idealized parent – an inspirational figure who certainly had her flaws. I would label her as perspicacious because she had a level of mental acuity and an ability to deduce and synthesize that was startling. She was simply an unusual person. People were fascinated by her. I couldn't necessarily figure it out. I might have idolized her."

That fall Gary struggled socially in Beauvoir nursery school. "I got kicked out of sandbox play," he admitted. "I didn't know how to share. Everything was mine, mine, mine. When someone says, 'You were so bad you got kicked out of sandbox,' well, that was true."

In first grade, Gary was failing every subject. "I could talk about what happened in space but couldn't spell *cat* or figure out what two plus two was," he said. At one point he raised his hand to answer a question about Native American rain dances. As recounted in a *Reader's Digest* story, "Gary compared them with Greek myths and said, 'The Indians thought they could get what they wanted by doing a dance or telling a story . . .' His teacher grabbed him and said, 'If you know that, why can't you spell *cat*?' To the teacher, Gary's unexpected knowledge proved he could learn, that he had been doing poorly because he was lazy."

"One of the things I really remember was feeling really stupid," said Gary. "I remember I spent a lot of time in the bathroom. I couldn't read or write. So when there was anything with writing or reading, I'd raise my hand and say I had to go to the bathroom. After six months the teacher asked my mother whether I had a bladder problem. That's why my mother had me tested. We went down to the Kingsbury Center."

The Kingsbury Center, on Bancroft Place in the Kalorama Heights section near Connecticut Avenue, had been recognized since its founding in 1938 as a pioneer in the field of remedial education. It served as a diagnostic evaluation clinic for children having academic difficulties and as a training center with about seventy highly trained tutors backed up by advisors. The testers at Kingsbury revealed Gary's dyslexia. "He had been able to fake reading through using clues of pictures, inferences, or context clues," Sally wrote. "But when faced with the barren desert of letters placed together in a word he ran away." When successful dyslexic adults—Cher and Tom Cruise, for example— tell their stories, they often include the years of faking it. Often their intelligence and other talents enable them to persevere, pointing back to the above-average smarts that children like Gary neede just to get by.

Beauvoir, as enlightened as it was, could not accommodate a child who could not read, write, and do arithmetic. It didn't help that Beauvoir's assistant director was the Lincoln School alumna and principal's daughter Betsy Clark McIsaac, who was herself dyslexic and aware of her father's efforts on behalf of dyslexic Lincoln students like Nelson Rockefeller. Nor did it help that Beauvoir's reading teacher, Mary Gray Stoner, was the daughter of Darius Gray Ornston, a Philadelphia physician who was a close friend of Samuel Orton, the physician and researcher at the University of Iowa who first popularized the term *dyslexia*. Although Stoner, who had taught dyslexic high schoolers at Germantown Friends School,* was one of the very few educators in the area familiar with the condition and appropriate remediation, she told Sally with regret that she didn't believe that Beauvoir was able to meet Gary's needs. There is a difference between understanding a problem, and even having experience teaching students with the problem, and having the time, resources, and infrastructure to truly deal with that problem.

As Sally looked around, she realized that no other schools in the area could meet Gary's needs either. She pleaded with private schools to start a program for Gary and other learning-disabled children. "It would take at least a year," the educators said. "I don't have a year," Sally said. "My child needs a school now!"

She confronted the larger reality that, in 1966, schools for children with learning disabilities did not exist in the DC area. At the time, the number of children with specific learning disabilities was estimated to be as high as ten million.* The field of specific learning disabilities was in its infancy. A summary from the era read, "Learning disabilities is an umbrella term for dozens of different conditions, including minimal brain dysfunction and dyslexia, in which certain neural (nerve) pathways do not mature according to normal timetables, thus interfering with the processing of information from the senses. Symptoms often include distractibility, disorganization, little sense of time, an uneven memory, garbled eye-to-brain messages and the inability to plan a project from beginning to end. In addition, many of the children are immature, uncoordinated, accident-prone, or hyperactive. Rarely, however, is actual brain damage documented, and learning-disabled children frequently have average or above intelligence. But in many schools they grow accustomed to defeat and tend to give up, thinking themselves 'dumb' and beyond hope."*

At home, Sally experimented with ways to help Gary learn. She wrote, "Essentially, I was using a drumbeat . . . to corral his attention. We constructed big projects made of wood or heavy cardboard because his fingers and hands could not do coloring, cutting, gluing, and puzzles. Large projects were easier to tackle than small ones. We did eurythmics and jazz dancing. Drama was a basic tool I used to teach him vocabulary, content, and narrative techniques."* Friends and acquaintances who had attended the birthday parties started asking for help with their own children. Then friends of friends who heard about the success she was having with Gary began to drop off their own children, "claiming they had something wrong with them and asking that I please figure out what it was and fix it."

In the spring of 1966, Sally was asked to design an innovative summer program for 100 youngsters ages six to twelve from the inner-city Adams-Morgan community who were failing in school. "The Adams-Morgan Community Council had been given the opportunity, at no charge, to hold a summer program at the beautiful independent school called the Potomac School in McLean, Virginia," she wrote.* "They came to me because they were given a grant to pay for an innovative program, but they had no program.

"Mary-Averett Seelye, a friend of mine who was familiar with the activities I was employing with my son, was a member of the Adams-Morgan Community Council. She and I and a few other women had served on the D.C. Arts in Education Committee together, and she knew that I could handle the job."

Seelye, who had graduated from Bennington ten years before Sally, was a performance artist in the Washington area who had helped found a company, the Theater Lobby, which in 1958 had been the first in the DC area to stage Samuel Beckett's *Waiting for Godot*. In her own performances, Seelye combined poetry and movement. *Washington Post* dance critic Alan M. Kriegsman once praised her "courage, intelligence, charm and artistic integrity. She declaims the poetry clearly and artfully, and her tall, gangly figure has a natural, quirky expressivity in motion."*

Sally integrated the techniques she had used with Gary into a new program. It included graphic arts, woodwork, music, dance, and drama in the mornings; films at lunch, and fifteen "academic clubs" in the afternoon. "Because all the students had severe reading difficulties, I analyzed the skills that are needed for a child to be able to read, broke the skills down, and then asked each artist who was participating in the program to find ways to incorporate the in his or her art form without sacrificing the integrity of the art form. This meant that I had to develop my own form of training for artists and academic club teachers."

The clubs included the Secret Agents Club, the Smokey the Bear Club, the Storekeepers Club, the Pirates Club, the Civil War Club, the Caveman Club, and the Knights of the Middle Ages Club. "Each club had carefully structured academic objectives meshed into a dramatic framework that allowed each child to pretend to be a certain character. When assigned a character, a child took on another role and often had to do things he wouldn't attempt in a more formal learning situation."

Perhaps the most remarkable aspect about this moment in time is that Sally's strikingly original program and philosophy emerged pretty much as a functioning whole almost immediately. Over the years she refined it, expanded it, renamed it—we can call it the Integrated Arts and Academic Club Method or shorten it to the Lab School Approach—and of course she showed generations of teachers and parents how it can work. It's less surprising to see how she drew on so many aspects of her life experiences, including the revelations of the themed parties among other sources.

"I first used the Academic Club Method emanating from the birthday parties," she wrote in the Bennington alumnae magazine in 1971. "I designed fifteen of these clubs where carefully structured academic objectives are meshed into a dramatic framework that allows the child to pretend 'to be' certain characters. When he is assigned a character, the child can often dare to do things he wouldn't attempt in a more formal situation. The Clubs were designed to give reading readiness training as well as to build vocabulary and enlarge storehouses of information. They met daily for one hour, so they were an important part of the program. The children fought to in them. Three quarters wanted to be Secret Agents and the rest begged to be Storekeepers."

Each child had four forty-minute periods each morning, where through the arts he was taught academic skills. Math concepts as well as eye-hand coordination were emphasized in woodwork; listening skills and discrimination of sounds emphasized through music, body development through dance, and organization of thought and vocabulary emphasized in drama. Practicing artists, with high school students as aides, were hired to teach."

Stocky, back from his freshman year at Hobart College, was a counselor. "On the bus with the kids riding out to Potomac School, I'd play *Charlie of the MTA* on the guitar," he says.[11] "It was summer enrichment, merging Sally's love for the arts with her need to start a school." Sally signed up Bert Schmutzhart, a sculptor who taught at the Corcoran School of Art, to teach woodworking. As a fourteen-year-old in Austria, he had crafted a glider out of wood and had his friends snap him off a hilltop with huge rubber bands.* A lifelong flying addict, Schmutzhart had the adventurous spirit, creative mind, and technical expertise to translate the requirement of his craft into the visual-motor skills necessary for reading and writing, the planning and organization skills mandatory for academic success, and the basic concepts of math through woodwork.

---

[11] I hope the reader can understand my confusion, expressed earlier, in thinking that my brothers were the Kingston Trio.

Sally also tapped Turri Rhodes Herndon, a talented filmmaker who had been two

years behind her at Bennington, to develop a daily film program. Herndon's husband,

Gerald Olney Herndon, known to all as G. O., was an investigative reporter with the

Evening Star who broke the first stories linking smoking with cancer and started the

consumer advocate column "Action Line." He also mentored a young copy boy named

Carl Bernstein, who later credited Herndon with steering him toward becoming an

investigative reporter himself. In 1968, G. O. became public relations director for the

tragically short-lived Robert F. Kennedy presidential campaign.*

Turri Herndon showed films that the children "could relate to their own lives, such as

The Red Balloon, as well as short documentaries on interesting people, various

occupations, and animals. Animated films were also shown. My goal was to widen their

horizons, help develop their vocabularies, and increase their knowledge through film.

The emphasis was on the children's discussing the main point of each film and how it

applied to their own experiences in addition to comparing and contrasting films—a

different form of language arts training."*

"The children loved the program and asked for more," Sally wrote. "The guidance

counselor from the Morgan School, from which sixty of our students came, was thrilled

with the positive change of attitude and motivation to learn, explore and question when

the children returned in the fall. He was so excited by the results that he asked if he,

himself, could be employed in the next summer's program."

Sally tested some of her ideas in January of 1967, teaching creative writing with

experimental methods to fourth and fifth graders in demonstration classes at Stoddert

Elementary under District of Columbia Project 370. The classes were followed by discussion with groups of observing teachers.

That summer, wrote Sally,* "Sidwell Friends School, a private school in Washington, D.C., wanted to sponsor The Sidwell Friends Program and work closely with Morgan School faculty and with our artists. "By then I had explored in depth what it takes to read, and I was programming these reading readiness skills (often called perceptual skills) more systematically into the program. This time I designed the project so that each artist was assigned by a teacher. The rationale was that the artists could learn from the teachers about children's development and certain behavioral management techniques that could be woven into the art's or club's theme while the teacher could absorb some of the creative techniques from the artists. My techniques asked teachers to think, research, and plan activities differently from staff at traditional schools."

The Friends-Morgan Summer Project had 125 children with serious academic difficulties, mostly from inner-city schools, ages six to twelve. Sally wrote, "We offered physical education in addition to dance. Drawing and painting (stressing patterns) were offered as alternatives to woodwork. This time, there were many more Academic Clubs including the Seven Seas Club (emphasizing geography) and the American Revolutionaries Club (stressing history) as well as the Ecologist's Club, the Tarzan's Jungle Club, the Nature Detective's Club, and the Smokey the Bear Club."

The club format, wrote Sally, "enables each child to be an intimate and active part of the history of any topic being studied. I chose the word *club* to give a sense of belonging, ownership, membership, and privilege to children who tend to feel 'out' and

want to be 'in.' I developed passwords, routines, and rituals to help students pay
attention and focus, to make each student feel important, and to help the group be
tightly knit."

"In six weeks, although measurable changes in academic work showed up only with
our youngest students, the staff saw immense changes in attitudes toward learning. We
saw that exhilarating feeling of 'I can do it' that each child experienced. What the tests
didn't and couldn't measure was what these children carried away with them. Their
experiences were organic; they became part of their being. What they learned went
deep into their bones because they learned it through all their senses and understood
what they were doing. The child who made a stringed musical instrument out of wood
didn't just learn how to make a musical instrument. He studied pictures of similar
instruments and decided on shape and length and texture. He learned to plan what he
was doing and keep to his plan and make adjustments when necessary. He had to
measure the wood to achieve the proper dimensions and then sand and stain it. Then,
he had to feel the vibrations of the instrument on his neck and relate those vibrations to
the strings on the instrument, which had to be built in such a way that the frets the
student put the neck of the instruments achieved certain sounds. This child not only
went away with a tangible reward for his labors, but his mind had been opened to a way
to learn—a process that could be adapted to other situations. My staff and I were to
continue to be committed to the belief that we cannot just educate students for this year
and next year; we must teach them how to approach future unknowns.

"The Friends-Morgan Project was a great professional success for me, the children,
and the staff; but my youngest son failed first grade. How were we able to school him?

He was too capable verbally and too sophisticated in his comprehension and usage of ideas to be placed in a special education environment. And, even though he did not feel good about himself, he was not emotionally disturbed; therefore, it did not make sense to place him in an environment with children with mental illness. He was hyperactive, impulsive, and distractible with a very short attention span, and he had severe learning disabilities. Today, we recognize these characteristics as ADHD. His brain was damaged with a substrate of learning disabilities. He could not see the difference between a straight line and an angle, but there was nothing wrong with his eyes. He could not hear the difference between the word 'advertisement' and 'adbertizement.' He did not know the days of the week, could not count to 100, did not know his alphabet, and could not repeat other sequences. His thinking, problem-solving abilities, and vocabulary were ahead of his age group. Repeating a grade even twice would not do the job. He would still not receive the highly specialized help he needed. I tried to find schools, private or public, that would open a special program for children who were intelligent but had severe learning disabilities. Some of the schools were willing to talk about it and plan it over a period of years. My child needed a school in September."

Sally went to the Kingsbury Center and asked for help. It was impossible for the Kingsbury Center to run a school, Director Kenneth R. Oldman told her. She brought him to see the Friends-Morgan project, proposed a plan, and offered to help put the plan in action. He recognized that the need was great for numbers of children, but he did not have the money, the space, or the staff for a new program.

As Sally looked into different options for starting a school, she talked with Dorry Goodman, who was in the process of launching the Washington International School. "I just didn't think there were good enough schools in this area for the international

community," Goodman told me. "In fact, we contemplated doing our schools together.

We even looked at one of the big houses on Newark Street, number 2940 maybe. It has

twelve or thirteen bedrooms. We considered splitting it in half. But Sally's husband, Bob,

said, 'Look, that would never work. You are both very strong personalities, and these

projects are very different.' Both would have been compromised. I started with three

four-year-olds in my basement here on Macomb Street [in number 2946, where she still

lives today]. I had no idea that it would work."[12]

"By September 5, 1967," wrote Sally. "I was still desperately searching for a school

when I received a call from Oldman stating that he had just had been offered the town

house next door [1809 Phelps Place NW]. This was followed by the question, 'Can you

open a school in twenty days?' 'Certainly,' I answered, with a bravado that I laugh at

now."

---

[12] The Washington International School moved to the Tregaron estate several doors up from the Goodmans' home on Macomb Street, where is remains today. Ray Goodman died in 2016, just shy of his 100th birthday.

Thirteen — "I'm Not Stupid. Are You?" The Lab School Adventure Begins.

On the basement floor of a Washington townhouse, six elementary school boys crouched. Speaking only in grunts and holding flashlights, they got down on their hands and knees and crawled through a tunnel of blankets and into a closet, where they gathered in a circle. They were cavemen. Each picked a cave name. Gary Smith chose Slimbo Limbo. His friend Charles Perry was Mumbo Jumbo. "We didn't have language yet, so we had to grunt if we wanted something," Gary remembers. Ben Booz presided as the Cave Lady. "I tied the flashlights together and covered them with red transparent paper," she recalled in her conspiratorial British accent. "That was our fire. Someone's father had just bought a farm in New Jersey and sent some smelly big bones from a deceased cow, and we made weapons out of them. It was making something out of nothing. We experienced the early years of man. We invented the alphabet. We made cave drawings. The atmosphere remains with me." Accustomed to being derailed by the countless stimuli of a regular classroom, the children had a learning space of complete focus. "It was not planned," said Booz, "but there were no distractions." Instead, the boys acted their parts and were completely immersed.

"The first day of the Lab School was the happiest day of my life," said Gary. "There were six of us in our class. That first week, the thing I will never forget, was the first time I met my close friend for years, Charles Perry. He said, 'Hi. I'm not stupid. Are you?' I said, 'Well, I don't know yet.' It was more fun than I ever had before. We were all class clowns. One day we found the coal chute in the old house. We snuck out of class and went for a ride down the chute. We were head to toe in black coal dust."

Within six hours of Kenneth Oldman's phone call offering the townhouse next door to the Kingsbury Center as a school site, Sally had "a staff committed, a general plan for the curriculum, the schedules made for the three children we were to start with, and a long list of people to call to obtain financial backing."* Oldman had lined up one of his finest diagnostician-supervisors, Francoise Achilles, to do the testing and set up the reading program in the classrooms, and he had interested two Kingsbury tutors in being classroom teachers.

"The chairman of the board agreed to our plan and off we went," wrote Sally. "Private schools in the area gave us tables and chairs, friends brought in furniture, paintings, supplies, and junk yards in Washington welcomed us to their heaps. Our building was cleaned, and the staff, with friends, went to work painting, constructing equipment, and weeding the green outside. We opened at 9 a.m. on Sept. 25, 1967, twenty days after that telephone call I had received, with $7,000 that I had raised and with the belief on the part of the staff that I would find more money to meet the year's payroll."

So there was Sally Smith, red lipstick and a broad smile, on the sidewalk at Phelps Place welcoming each child to the new school, which she named the Lab School as a nod to educator John Dewey, "whose Lab School at the University of Chicago was known for pioneering work, innovating, trying new methods, centering all attention on children, and using all of their senses in active learning."*

The teachers in the early years of the Lab School occupy a special place in education history. In recounting their experiences, they tend to describe their experience as a whirlwind, or a carnival ride. They were drawn in by Sally and inspired to find new and creative ways to inspire their students. "She was simply brilliant in the classroom," said Diana Meltzer, a longtime faculty member and now the associate head of school. "There's no other way to say it. Hard work was really important to her. She had a great sense of humor, an optimistic point of view, and a commitment to problem-solving. She valued people. But there was nothing like watching Sally work to make you say, 'This is worth doing.'"

In assembling her staff of teachers, Sally made one of her first calls to Booz. Sally needed her to, as Booz put it, "lumber into the Cave Man Club and teach history, geography, civics and reading readiness to the seven-year-olds." Sally knew that an idealist who had met her husband wielding pickaxes in postwar Yugoslavia would jump at the challenge of becoming a Paleolithic woman in charge of six cavemen.

As Sally wrote, "Six and seven-year-olds who do not know their alphabet, cannot read, and usually have a difficult time associating a specific sound to the correct symbol, can enter the Cave Club, rise to a standing position and say, 'We slowly rise up like *Homo erectus*. We use our hands like *Homo habilis*. We speak and communicate like *Homo sapiens*. And we count one, two, three! Greetings, Wise Elder.' By chanting this daily, the children internalize the information and are comfortable with the terms *Homo erectus*, *Homo habilis*, and *Homo sapiens*."*

In casting her net for highly creative people, Sally often turned to Bennington graduates. "The quality of the human beings chosen to be the teachers was my foremost concern," Sally wrote in the Bennington alumnae magazine. "In ancient times the purpose of education was for children to be near the finest adults possible in order to absorb their learning and values. I realize now that in a way Bennington set that model for us, finding vibrant human beings actively engaged in their own intellectual and artistic pursuits, excited about learning and sharing it all with mostly eager students."

Sally thought of her avant-garde performance artist friend Mary-Averett Seelye and made the creative leap that she could help learning disabled children make sense out of the world of figures and numbers through dance. As recounted in *Reader's Digest*, an eight-year-old girl named Janet "spread her mathematics problems all over the page. Special dance routines taught her to organize her body movements. This 'motion planning' set up a pattern in her mind that eventually translated into an appropriate use of space on paper."*

Under the title of arts consultant, Seelye worked closely with Sally. "The program focus became clearly to strengthen basic learning skills in the children through the arts," Seelye wrote. "In Sally's method, 'programmed' and 'controlled' leads to creative learning. The words need no longer be equated with repression and rote. Furthermore, Sally's method of training her teachers turns out actually to be a series of experiences in which the participants find themselves plumbed for unexpected creative abilities. Everyone is generating teaching ideas for every else's need. By the end of the sessions every teacher's hopper of ideas to use in her classroom is replete for months to come, and she has found fresh skills in herself to apply to the classroom. Any teacher—open classroom or authoritative-type—is metamorphosed in three days! The very processes experienced by the teachers in these training sessions are what Sally envisions the teachers re-creating with their own students."

Sally signed up Bert Schmutzhart, the glider-building sculptor who had shown his teaching talents in the Friends-Morgan Project. "When he agreed to teach woodwork daily," wrote Sally, "I knew the Laboratory School of the Kingsbury Center was under way." Gary Smith remembered, "He was a short man with a very sharp way of talking when you acted out but was one of the smartest persons I ever knew when it came to explaining the right way to build something. None of the kids ever got hurt when working with his tools. He would not have allowed that. He had these big hands that didn't quite fit with the rest of him, but they could be very tender when you got upset about messing something up. Building a boat in the workshop took me nearly a year of very hard work and fun. I had to weigh myself and figure out how big it had to be to fit three people my size. This took out-of-the-box thinking and really using my brain, including math and all kinds of other academic thinking too. Then I had to build it on my own. Using cutting tools that were hard for my fingers to manage, but with my teacher showing me how to hold the tools right, I had to sand down the sharp parts and then paint the boat. In the end, making that boat was even harder than learning to read."

Turri Herndon agreed to develop a daily film program similar to the one she had run at the Friends-Morgan Project, but with more emphasis on studying the sequences that make up the totality of a given film. "All through the day," wrote Sally, "in the classroom as well as in the arts, I wanted the children immersed in patterns, sequences, sorting information constantly for reading-readiness training."

"For six months we ran our daily films without a projector of our own," Herndon wrote. "Thanks to the help of the kind people and an appreciation of Max Bennett-cum-Rube Goldberg situations, we didn't have to rent one. . . . The circumstance provided an invaluable teaching tool. Every projector works on the same principle but no one of them looks anything like another; so we learned something about isolating essentials (the basic feed pattern) from irrelevancies (dazzling arrangements of knobs). It's a simple exercise—but a way of learning how to sort out visual information, the skill with which these children have the least facility. . . . We used over a hundred short films and experimented with making our own sound tracks using tape recorders and records and the children's own narration. The latter revealed to us an astonishing secret—sound alters radically what is seen. . . . We learned that the skills required for the making of a film, or even for the viewing of a film, are those most necessary for these children to exercise: separate the part from the whole—focus and frame. (To read-write intelligently, there must be proper space between the words and/or letters. Words and letters are separate entities.) Put the action in sequence—cut and edit. (1-2-3 is very different from 3-2-1.) Determine what elements belong in the picture—background, foreground. . . . The arrangement of date or symbols on a page have special meanings. Plus and minus signs have a definite location in the space or they are meaningless. It seems so simple to look. To see is quite another experiment." At one point the films made by Lab School children under Herndon were shown at the White House conference on Children and Youth.

"Turri produced a sister-in-law to serve as our receptionist, administrative aide, and general coper," wrote Sally, who asked Marcia Ward Behr (Bennington '38) to develop a drama program "placing the emphasis on sorting information, organizing the role of parts to a whole, classification, categorization." Behr had studied under Martha Graham at Bennington and fondly recalled a dance class when Graham slapped her on her posterior and told her not to stick it out too much. Behr danced for a year with a vaudeville group, the Twinkle Toed Darlings, then acted with the Bulgakov Repertory

Company in New York City. Her proudest moment was when *New York Times* critic

Brooks Atkinson favorably reviewed her 1941 Broadway performance in *Kind*

Lady. During the Second World War, she served in the Red Cross in Australia and New

Guinea, an experience she recounted in her book *Coffee and Sympathy: World War II*

Letters from the Southwest Pacific (2002, Authorhouse). After the war, she met Edward

A. Behr, a journalist with *The Wall Street Journal*, on a blind date. They married, had

two sons, and moved to Washington, where she continued to work in theater, both

performing and teaching.* Like Booz, she was a person who didn't mind embarking on

an adventure.

Sally also cajoled Behr's Bennington classmate Sally Brownell Montanari into

teaching a club for older children. During World War II Montanari, another Sara who

went by Sally, cleaned spark plugs as an aviation mechanic at the old National Airport.

She taught English in the late 1950s and early 1960s in schools in Tehran, where her

husband, Valerio, was a Foreign Service officer.* She took her place on the list of

Sally's artistic friends who couldn't resist a challenge. "I had eight students in my

Renaissance Council," wrote Montanari, "a club designed to teach, among other things,

the Renaissance period of time to kids who had previously belonged to the Cave Man,

Egyptians and Greek Gods, and Medieval Knights Clubs. Run as a Council, we were

essentially a decision-making group, and I could relate to the District of Columbia

Council here in Washington, the Council for Human Relations, NAACP, etc. Sitting

around an old Persian rug, with corduroy hats squashed on our heads, and scraps of

brocade and velvet swathed around our necks, we looked like Italian Renaissance

paintings. We changed our names to Salliano, Davideh, Bobbino, etc. I would toss out a situation that had actually happened to the Medici family, for instance, and we would discuss what we would have done, and how we would have voted, if we had been members of the Florentine Council. I'd then read what actually happened: 'Lorenzo de Medici ignored the Council's advice, then regretted his personal decision, which left blood on his hands the rest of his life.' 'Ye-e-e-ek!' says Carlos. 'How come he couldn't wash it off?'"

"The basic philosophy was firm," wrote Sally about her new school. "We were committed to the belief that every child can learn; it is up to us, the adults, to seek out and discover the routes by which he does. In other words, we don't say that since we tried to teach him and he didn't learn, the child is either dumb or willful; we simply have to find other ways to teach him. We need to look at what he brings in with him, what he has going for him, his strengths, his interests. When we learn about how a child learns, we must teach him how he learns so that he can carry that armor through life. At every opportunity, no matter how far down we have to go, we must let the child taste success and succor the feeling of 'I can do it!' which so often breeds mastery of skills.

"It is a simple philosophy, though not one that is prevalent. Furthermore, the structure of the school and its curriculum contains another important facet of my philosophy. Only half of the child's school day is spent in the classroom; the other half is spent in clubs and in the arts. I believe that elementary schools demand the impossible of teachers and don't give them the time and freedom to do their job as well as they can. Artists have mastered the disciplines of their art, often in untraditional ways, and have had to indulge in non-compartmentalized thinking. Great ideas come in many fields and the artist avails himself of knowledge in the other arts, literature, science, often history. Part-time involvement in the schools by artists, creative scientists and other imaginative members of the community will perforce make a school come alive. Classroom teachers will be stimulated in new directions and will offer creative challenges to the part-time teachers. The adults will benefit enormously as human beings and as teachers, but most of all, the children will be wealthier in ideas and stimulation. It has been my understanding that elementary schools exist to excite children about learning and to give them the basic tools to pursue it further, but I feel that this point gets lost today.

"Another concept that rarely is discussed is that of children deriving pleasure from learning. Our Calvinist background seems to resist the idea that fun can be a part of learning, and when children do have fun, many teachers and parents worry that they are not learning at all. Every activity at the Lab School is the result of a highly systematic series of academic objectives, yet the children do have fun a good deal of the time. All learning is not fun, and hard work is definitely involved, but there are ways to incorporate pleasure as well as satisfaction into formal learning situations.

"For example, last year our son stunned his father when they went together to the National Gallery of Art and he said, as they were on their way out, that he had seen a 'Lippi.' 'You know, Daddy, the Renaissance painter, one of the first guys to use perspective. Mrs. Montanari had us line up on the street and look at street lamps. When you're fárther away, the lamp is tiny, and it's large when you're close to it, and that's 'perspective,' and we saw it in pictures. But we had a ball on that street!'

"I call that real learning. It's become a part of his being. Muscular activity has been related to ideas and ideas related to other ideas. Through the arts all kinds of learning can be internalized and thoroughly perceived. The arts are languages that people everywhere, at all times, have shared. Man's first communication was expressed through gesture, movement, dance, rhythm, painting, acting, acting and sounds. Then patterns of expression took on specific meaning, and communication became increasingly structured. It took man a long time to develop a spoken language that could be written and then read; is it any wonder that it takes children a number of years to decode the symbols in reading and then derive meaning from them? Reading follows a complex developmental sequence that begins at birth.

"After all, what constitutes a word? A word is a message that consists of graphic marks in space, a pattern of visual symbols written left to right that have no meaning unless you associate with them a series of appropriate sounds in the correct order. There is a prescribed order with definite sequences—a beginning, a middle, an end.

"Children with learning disorders suffer from difficulties in sorting information and putting it in order. Their brains take in all the sounds, all the sights without a proper screening and filtering out of the nonessentials. They very often concentrate on the details without seeing the whole, just as preschoolers have difficulty in breaking up the totality of a pattern or differentiating single parts. These children with learning disorders may require certain sequences, but cannot remember the correct order. They themselves lack the internal order. They usually have difficulty looking left to right, distinguishing varieties of forms and shapes. Their bodies, sometimes seemingly well-coordinated but more frequently clumsy and awkward, are not reliable instruments of measure; they are poor judges of space and their timing is off. Combined with a great deal of distractibility, short attention span, highly uneven strengths and weaknesses, it is difficult for them to integrate several processes at once. Since maturation is largely a process of integration and differentiation, it is not surprising that such children are said to be suffering from a maturity lag. The 'in' name for it is 'dyslexia.' 'Mild cerebral dysfunction,' 'neurologically handicapped,' 'neurological immaturity,' and the 'perceptually handicapped' describe the same child. Sometimes mild brain damage is found, but usually no evidence of brain injury is apparent. It is estimated that 15 percent of America's children of normal intelligence are not achieving their true potential due to learning troubles, and that about one third of those suffer the degree of difficulty that demands specialized training. Our students at the Lab School, who are of average to superior intelligence, are among the nation's five percent with severe learning disorders. Our job is to return them as soon as possible to the regular classroom."

In the middle of the first year, the Lab School had to rent a second town house next door to meet the demand. In those early years, Marcia Behr taught drama to four grade levels, ages six through twelve. "Since the sorting of information is one of the primary tasks of elementary school education," she wrote, "drama in our academic setting provides an excellent opportunity to do this. A child sorts as he acts out experiences involving categories, classification, sequences of action, similarities and differences. Another form of sorting is the development of judgment in social situations, learning the appropriate gesture, movement, action, and remarks in a given situation. This is dealing with the parts that make up the whole, and Lab School children have difficulty with the part-whole relationships. In order to tackle these objectives, I not only utilize exercises but involve the children in dramatic projects. *Aesop's Fables* has become the inspiration for a long session of improvisation, mask making, and a school production. The children are learning to sort differences and similarities in human characteristics, to determine

the appropriateness of each moral, and are practicing the coordination of the

appropriate movement of the body with the feeling and vocal expression." Behr's

methods worked so well that she published them in her book *Drama Integrates Basic

Skills: Lesson Plans for the Learning Disabled* (1970, Charles C Thomas Pub Ltd.).

In the fall of 1968, Sally got a Hattie M. Strong Foundation grant to train and

supervise teachers and parents at the Hardy Public School to set up seventeen

academic clubs for 250 students. The training took place on Friday afternoons from

January to June 1969.

That June, at the end of the Lab School's second school year, it received 194

requests for admission. "A fundamental decision had to be made," wrote Sally, "whether

to expand to 200 children or to remain, as we have, a small laboratory school, creating

and implementing new approaches and techniques and different styles of teaching and

learning, to be shared with other teachers."

As part of that sharing mission—and the start, it turned out, of Sally's career as an

advocate for her new methods—the Lab School made a series of 16-millimeter films in

1969 on the Club Methodology, using interviews from Friends-Morgan Project teachers.

"The US Office of Education Bureau of the Handicapped bought thirty-two copies of

each of the films, which were rented by people all over the country. All the Friends-

Morgan Project teachers who were interviewed for these films felt that they had grown

as teachers; they discovered that the adults who guide the activities are always learners

who, despite popular belief, do not need to know all the answers. They found that even in large groups it was possible to identify the strengths of each individual and to encourage each member to contribute the things that she liked and could do best." *

In 1969 Turri Herndon replaced her previous person at the Lab School front desk with another friend, Florence "T. D." King, whose neat and proper appearance masked a rapier wit. King recalled, "Turri told me, 'Sally needs a girl Friday at the desk.' It was supposed to be part-time, but nothing is part-time with Sally. I was there nine to three starting in September 1969. I occasionally took over a class. You were at her beck and call. That's how she got stuff done. I did it for a year, but it conflicted with my kids' schedule. If I had continued working there, I don't think we'd have been friends." In short order, Tidi King entered Sally's circle of long-term friends.

In 1971, the Lab School's fourth year, it had thirty-six students. Fifteen former students had returned to their regular classrooms. That year Sally produced a series of teaching films. "The Academic Club Approach is introduced via a 27-minute film," she wrote, "the first in a series, called 'Learning for a Lifetime' by Joel Jacobson. It features Allen Stevens (Bennington '65) teaching a Greek Gods Club, implanting the legacy of Greece right into the lives of Lab School children, exploring with them the difference between democracy and tyranny. Sally Montanari's Renaissance Councilors Club is on screen, vividly demonstrating how simple visual effects change room space, how club space is structured so that each child has his own prescribed Renaissance throne heralded by crests and banners, how discipline is worked into the dramatic framework."*

After Montanari's success with the Renaissance Council, she wrote, "This fall I visualized relaxing and doing a rerun of the Council with the upcoming class. 'Oh no,' says Sally Smith. 'I want you to go on with the later Renaissance and move into

American History.' That's when I thought I'd had it with the Lab School. How the hell can one jump in time from early Italian Renaissance to July 4, 1776? 'You figure that one out,' says Sally Smith. She's impossible to buck; besides, it was a challenge.

"So now I am running a Philosophical Society, based on Ben Franklin's. The room is decorated as a Colonial Tavern; we sit around a beat-up round picnic table with mugs for each and a pitcher of water (ginger ale on Fridays). To bridge the time gap: for the past semester the seven of us have been descendants of seven philosophers— Socrates (me), Galileo, Newton, Locke, Diderot, Rousseau and Voltaire—whose ideas influenced the thinking of our American philosophers Jefferson, Adams, Franklin, Madison and Hamilton. Each of the European philosophers has a block of time, his place on the map, ended by tacking on the wall a bit of that man's philosophy and having a 'birthday' party with food from the country of the particular philosopher. We ended with Voltaire. . . . I've never been interested in history before, and as for philosophers, I had to look the word up in a dictionary. My mind is exploding from constantly thinking creatively, and I shall surely resign come June. Then Sally Smith will say, 'Now next fall you will give this group American history through the year 2001.'"

Amid all the positive progress, one reality still remained in the social interactions of the students. "Even though the kids at the Lab School had more or less the same problems," Gary Smith remembered, "they still teased each other. They called me Mr. Potato Head. They'd say, 'You're a fat slob,' real loud in front of the class. I would say, 'Don't take it out on me because you're mad at my mother.' Or I'd say, 'Do you want to repeat that to the whole class?'"

Fourteen — Home Life in the Turbulent Late Sixties

Launching the Lab School consumed Sally. Bob Smith told Randy later that he thought the idea was for Sally to start the school, then turn it over to someone else to run. But Sally had discovered a calling. She had a unique vision, and it engaged her passion, dedication, and creativity. "By choice, she devoted that time and energy," says Randy.

For his work, Bob often traveled to Africa, Asia, and Europe, sometimes for weeks at a time. Unlike the heady days of their honeymoon, Sally did not accompany him on these trips. At first, it was the responsibilities of motherhood. She did not want to duplicate her childhood, when she was raised by nannies and she and her sisters were left at home when their parents went on vacation. "She wanted to be a hands-on mother," says Randy. "And she was. She was there to help us with our homework and talk about our days." In the later sixties, it was the responsibilities of the Lab School. "They never traveled or vacationed alone," says Randy. "This was the cost of living a life so devoted to her child and to the Lab School."

When Bob was at home, the nightly dinner was an important ritual. "We were supposed to eat at seven," says Randy. "Sometimes he'd be late. But when he got home we'd sit at the kitchen table, with that enormous map of the world on one wall, and talk over our days. Once the Lab School got going, the phone would ring at night with Lab School business, and it annoyed my dad."

In those years, Randy and Nick were in the St. Albans Lower School (grades four through eight), wearing a coat and tie, memorizing poems, playing sports, and acting in plays. For Randy, the regimen included doing his competitive best to "win the book"— that is, be named as the best student in each class section at the end of the year. "Mom pushed me to excel in school and in everything," says Randy. "Whenever I didn't get an A, she would ride me and say I hadn't tried hard enough." As the second child, just a year behind, Nick's pressure came mostly from being Randy's brother. Sally was tough in other ways. "If you were sick in our house," recalls Randy. "it was your problem." Although Sally rolled her eyes at much of St. Albans's uncreative rigidity, her approach to Randy and Nick's sniffles squared with the school's ethos of muscular Christianity. In a memorable February morning chapel service, Headmaster Charles Martin once praised us the red-nosed, coughing boys on hand for being present and chided our absent peers for giving in to a little discomfort.

The sixth-grade year at St. Albans revolved around the Europa project, a report on a European country. It was supposed to be twenty pages, but an arms race usually ensued, and the numbers of pages escalated. Randy wrote about Switzerland, naturally enough, since he had lived there in his early years. Our friend Paul Lee wrote about the USSR, in part to give a different viewpoint from the Cold War dogma that the Soviets, as our adversaries, were bad.

In early April of our sixth-grade year, the Rev. Martin Luther King Jr. gave a Sunday sermon at the National Cathedral. It was broadcast to the overflow crowd on loudspeakers mounted on the cathedral towers and echoed audibly in our neighborhoods. Later that week, after King was assassinated in Memphis, downtown

Washington erupted in flames. Even in our leafy area, we saw a few soldiers with bayonets and halftracks plying their way up Garfield Street. A 4:30 p.m. curfew was declared for all of Washington.

Senator Robert F. Kennedy had entered the presidential race, and at that moment he needed a campaign ad for the Indiana primary. Our next-door neighbor, K. Dun Gifford, was the legislative aide to Ted Kennedy (and later a cookie-selling partner in Cambridge, Massachusetts, with a young John Kerry). Gifford's wife, Pebble, called my mother and asked her to round up a bunch of children to be filmed with RFK. We were told to dress like farm children for an Indiana audience. Sally Smith got a similar call. We were asked to come up with questions to ask. "I was excited because I was pretty political," Randy remembers. "I decided to ask about the government's role in education." Nick was set to ask why the government didn't give more money to poor people. Paul Lee composed a list of questions that ran down an entire page. We all convened outside the St. Albans Lower School late on a Sunday afternoon. Sally stood with the parents, who were ecstatic about the opportunity but concerned about violating the curfew.

After an hour or so, Kennedy arrived in a red Chrysler Imperial convertible with a white interior, fresh from touring the riot zones. His face was bright red, presumably from the heat and the emotions of seeing the destruction. The film crew had set up lights and cameras in our one-room school library. Immediately Kennedy filled the room with his presence—the charisma, the reality of his being there. I can remember the sense of seeing someone from the big world come to life, someone intensely real. I remember his gentle eyes and the feeling he gave us when he talked. "Kennedy started by greeting us," Paul recalled, "letting us know he was pleased to spend this time with us." Paul's first impression was of a warm and caring man, his smile bracketed with wrinkles. "It was clear from the moment he sat down in front of me, however," Paul said, "that this was not to be a 'kids' time' spent on an informal chat. This was an appointment with the voters of America. I had never felt quite so adult. My palms began to sweat." Kennedy asked if we

Paul Lee sits across the school library table from RFK in a 1968 campaign ad.

knew any political speeches. Someone said, "Ask not what your country can do for you, but what you can do for your country." Then, says Paul, "he surprised us. Instead of diving further into politics, he said he loved poetry and asked if we had any favorite poems we could share with him. We were required to memorize a poem every week in school, so almost everyone raised his hand. He was playing to the whole room and wanted to draw everyone in." Kennedy shared some verse by Alfred, Lord Tennyson. One phrase stuck in Paul's mind: "my purpose holds to sail beyond the sunset, and the baths of all the Western stars, until I die." Paul recalls, "Kennedy talked about how beautiful the images were to him, and how they expressed a feeling for him about our lives—of being on a quest, reaching out in uncharted directions, with confidence in a better tomorrow."

Paul sat strategically at the library table directly across from Kennedy. "My first question came soon," Paul remembered. "I had done my Europa report on the fifteen republics of the Soviet Union, and I had developed a view that the people there were real, feeling people. I worried about the threat of nuclear confrontation. So I offered a leading question: 'If you are elected president of the United States, would you consider any unilateral steps to de-escalate tension with the Soviet Union?'" Paul was taken aback when Kennedy's expression turned stone cold. "His look seemed to pierce right through me. He answered bluntly, 'Absolutely not,' and didn't waver as he continued, 'My experience in the Cuban missile crisis taught me that the leaders of the Soviet Union cannot be trusted under any circumstance.' There were no follow-ups. The matter was closed." Later Paul asked what could be done about poverty in America. "Kennedy called for a partnership of government and private enterprise. One idea was to use tax incentives to stimulate investment in inner cities. Another was that people in these communities would have control over their own corporations, training programs, and schools. It wasn't a government benefits package, he explained; it would be a national effort to instill the benefits of an entrepreneurial economy." Paul's final question was about hunger in the world: What could America do? Said Paul, "I remember best how knowledgeable he was about all the programs that had been tried. He said the Agency for International Development, the Peace Corps, the United Nations programs, and the

Alliance for Progress all provided models. We would take what worked and apply it."

Randy recalled, "I remember feeling like I hadn't ever been talked to like that by an adult, talking to us on an equal level, as

Randy and Nick Smith in the RFK campaign ad

if he expected us to be at his level. It wasn't condescending." After the session, the students followed the senator outside. Kennedy talked to an aide who was animatedly reviewing the next item on his itinerary. Paul remembered, "Kennedy listened calmly, occasionally nodding or adding a comment to indicate that he was taking it all in. Yet he seemed to be somewhere else. While he waited for his car, I had a remarkable, tangible feeling that he somehow had an awareness that went beyond himself, that in his mind he was in touch with the hearts and aspirations of the American people."

"I remember him putting his hand on me, and feeling physically close to him," said Randy. "I remembered feeling that he cared."

The California primary in June was a must-win for Kennedy. "He'd become like a hero to me," said Randy. "The night of the California primary I was staying up. I could draw pictures of this, I remember it so well. My mom made me go to bed. 'You can find out in the morning.' When I woke up I asked, 'Did he win?' She said, 'Yeah, he won, but he was shot." I spent the whole day in the house. I sat by the radio in my parents' bedroom. I was completely depressed. I just felt like it was wrong." In the days that Kennedy was clinging to life, Nick and a friend went to the Children's Chapel in the cathedral. "We prayed for hours and hours that he would live."

I recently watched Emilio Estevez's remarkable 2006 movie *Bobby*, about the days leading up to Kennedy's assassination. I knew the campaign ad was in the movie, but when it flashed up, it still gave me an eerie feeling to see the camera zoom in on Paul's face as he nervously holds his black plastic glasses, and on Nick and Randy, looking like angels as Kennedy explains his concerns about the environment. "I was impressed at how pertinent Kennedy's comments were today," said Nick.

That summer of 1968 the Smith family took a trip to Tunisia, where they stayed for three weeks on the Mediterranean Sea. They also stopped off in Paris, London, and Rome. On all those trips," said Gary, "Randy would spend a couple of hours a day tutoring me, and we'd listen along to books on tape. At one point, Bob paid his respects to the governor general of Tangiers, who insisted that the family come for dinner, which started at nine. "He had multiple wives there," said Randy. "The feast went on and on. After each course, they would take up all the remainders in a tablecloth. Gary saw that there were eight tablecloths to go. "As the night went on I grew more and more tired and wanted to lie down. I started to slump down and Mom pointed at me and mouthed 'No.' I flipped her the bird and lay down anyway." Sally turned to two of the governor general's wives and waved her middle finger back at Gary, explaining that it was an American greeting. The wives, in turn, raised their middle fingers and happily copied the gesture.

In the fall of 1968, Bob took Randy and Nick to New Haven to see Yale's undefeated team, led by halfback Calvin Hill and quarterback Brian Dowling. In late November, Bob hosted Randy, Nick, and me at the Sheraton Park Hotel, where we watched a closed-circuit black-and-white TV broadcast of Yale's epic showdown with undefeated Harvard. With Yale ahead 29–13 with forty-two seconds to go, Harvard scored twice and got the two-point conversions in one of the most exciting finishes in Ivy League history. The Harvard *Crimson* headline read, "Harvard Beats Yale 29–29." Dowling's lasting fame was as "B. D." in his Yale classmate Garry Trudeau's comic strip *Doonesbury*. Hill, after his storied NFL career with the Dallas Cowboys, had another round of athletic note as the father of the Duke and NBA star Grant Hill, and then, in a political footnote, as the husband of Hillary Clinton's close friend at Wellesley, Janet Hill.

For the Thanksgiving holidays, the Smith family would always fly to New York to see the grandparents and cousins. They would stay with Bob's mother, then spend the day at the Libermans' apartment. "We always had to look our best during these trips, with coat and tie on at all times," said Gary. "While dinner was going on, anytime that Gram wanted anything she would ring a little bell and the cook would come in. Their cook always treated me like I was the king and always had special treats hidden away for me. Then came watching different football games for the rest of the day, which was boring to me, but I knew better than to misbehave at those times. The last part of the day Gram would give all the boys a twenty-dollar bill and say, 'Don't tell Popa.' Popa would give us one hundred dollars as we left the apartment."

Cousin Jonathan Low remembered, "the Liberman holiday dinners were festive affairs, with lots of relatives we barely knew and everyone seated around a huge dining room table groaning with fruit, breads, pastries, centerpieces, silver, and crystal. The walls were hung with expensive old brocades and tapestries. Dinner was served by servants in formal uniforms overseen by Karl, the Swedish chauffeur-butler. Their apartment at 875 Fifth Avenue overlooked Central Park and the view, high above the treetops, was always beautiful. Afterwards the women would play gin or canasta and gossip while the men and boys would retire to another room to watch TV—usually after an obligatory one-on-one conversation with Pop, who encouraged us to be industrious, though I'm not sure any of us knew what that meant. Gram was famous in my mind for demanding that we have another piece of cake or serving of ice cream as she always said we looked so thin. I also remember Pop slipping us twenty-dollar bills when we left to go home."

"I never saw my grandfather when he didn't give me a hundred-dollar bill," said Randy. "We were the sons he never had."

After Christmas mornings at home, the Smiths would fly to visit the Libermans' in Palm Beach, staying at a hotel around the corner from their apartment. "I always thought of this trip as another time we had to get dressed up in coat and tie," says Gary. "The hotel was filled with old people, and we were the youngest people there. The thing I remember the most is taking walks with him near his apartment. He was in his eighties and walked three miles every day. The path seemed so long, and I was the one who always got tired."

That January Randy, Nick, and I watched the third Super Bowl in Bob and Sally's bedroom. I think I realized even then that it was a showdown between the new and old, the upstart AFL and the stolid NFL. Randy identified with the flamboyant New York Jets quarterback Broadway Joe Namath, while I was rooting for the old-school Earl Morrall and Johnny Unitas. When someone said of Sally later on that she never saw a rule she didn't want to break, it helped me understand this aspect of Randy's character better. History was on Randy's side, as the Jets won 16–7.

In the Lower School, the weekly winter sports schedule included respective days of soccer, basketball, swimming, and wrestling. Nick was drawn to swimming; Randy to wrestling. "My brothers and I would have wrestling matches in the living room right after dinner," says Gary. "We always had to wrestle." Later on, Bob Smith converted a basement dog pen into a padded wrestling cage.

Nick did his Europa paper on the Netherlands. Around the neighborhood, we played war games in the alleys. In the Smiths' backyard we played Wiffle ball, often ending in an argument over who was safe or out. Inside, we played board games, notably Risk!, in which each of us strove to conquer the world. Sometimes it was the more sophisticated Diplomacy, about the complex alliances leading up to the First World War.

"There was another game Randy liked to play that I always hated," said Gary. "He would put me on trial for all kinds of things. I was always found guilty in the end." In the winter of Randy's eighth-grade year, he won his weight class and the Best Wrestler award in an intramural wrestling tournament. The Upper School wrestling coach recruited Randy and saw to it that wrestling became Randy's sport through high school.

At some point in these years, Bob Smith was offered an ambassadorship to an African country. Sally said she wouldn't go, because of Gary's needs and her commitment to the Lab School. Bob turned the opportunity down. Later he had an offer to become the president of the State University of New York. "It would have required us to move to Albany, which my mom nixed," says Randy.

April 22, 1970, was the first Earth Day. While some 3,000 people, including folk singer Pete Seeger, gathered at the Washington Monument, our eighth-grade class boarded a school bus for a tour of the eco-friendly planned community of Columbia, Maryland. As a follow-up, our class camped on the sand of Assateague Island, Virginia, planted pine seedlings, and learned about the fragility of brackish marshes and the role of beach grass in preventing dune erosion. A group of students then formed the Assateague Action Committee to fight the planned commercial development of the island.

That summer the Smiths again spent three weeks at a Mediterranean resort, this time in Morocco. They loved the Moroccan culture, played with Moroccan children, and named their second dog Salah, Arabic for prayer.

On October 15, anti-Vietnam groups staged moratorium protests in various US cities. Our school headmaster said, "Many of you will choose to take part. Just remember that when you are out in public you represent this school." Escorted by my mother, Randy and I walked in front of the White House holding candles, then saw Peter, Paul, and Mary performing at the Washington Monument. "I remember the SDS students with armbands," said Randy. A month later, another moratorium protest focused on Washington. My older twin brothers—both facing the draft after their graduation from college that spring— drove down from their respective campuses with a few friends. My father donned the hiking boots he'd worn in Selma, and our family drove together in our white Comet station wagon to join the 400,000 people or so on the Mall and around the Washington Monument.

During the 1971 baseball season, Bob Short, a Minnesota trucking magnate and the owner of the Washington Senators, announced that he was moving the team to Arlington, Texas. The Senators were perennial losers, but they were *our* losers. When 6'7" slugger Frank Howard hit a homer, the ball leapt off his bat on a line drive, angled only slightly upward in an elegant parabola that peaked deep in the outfield, then descended only slightly in its flight path out of the park. We were faithful to our team in a way that only Cubs fans and other disciples of futility can truly understand, and the theft of the team was a betrayal.

On a Thursday evening, September 30, a school night, my mother loaded several of my neighborhood friends, Randy, Hank Staples, and Evan Bayh, into the station wagon and drove us to RFK Stadium for the last game, against the Yankees. Effigies of Bob Short were festooned from the upper decks, along with banners reading "We were Short-changed" and "Senators to Texas/Short to Hell."

In the sixth inning, with the Yankees up 5–1, Howard came to the plate in what was likely to be his last at-bat in Washington. He took a fastball and drilled it in a majestic line drive. It was the last of his 237 homers as a Senator. The ovation lasted a full ten minutes. Fans dropped torn-up copies of Manager Ted Williams' autobiography *My Turn at Bat,* which had been given away at the gates to clean out the team's promotional gift closet, from the upper decks as confetti. Somewhere between second and third base, Howard tipped his cap. When he emerged from the dugout for his second curtain call, he broke out in tears. "It was utopia," he said after the game, "something I'll take to my grave."

As the game went on, there was a smoke bomb or two, and fans started leaping onto the field to run the bases or shake hands with the players. At one point a long banner was unfurled from the center field upper deck reading "Short Stinks." An ominous chant of "We want Short" ensued for several minutes.

With one out to play in the ninth inning and the Senators ahead 7–5, fans swarmed onto the field and began to make mayhem. We all made our way to the field-box level, where we saw bases being pulled up and the scoreboard dismantled. The last out was never played. How appropriate, I've always thought, that in those years even baseball was a source of cynicism and upheaval.

In the spring of 1972, Randy was in his sophomore year in high school, feeling good about the world. He had his driver's license and a red-haired girlfriend. The wrestling team had won the conference. He was president of the class. Nick was a freshman, doing well in painting and establishing himself as a backstroker on the swim team. They were both looking forward to their summer lifeguarding at the Beauvoir pool.

The dinner hour had festered as a point of contention. At least once, when Bob was later than usual, Sally fed the boys and sent them off to do their homework. "My father didn't like the fact that she would feed us before he got home," said Gary. "She said, 'I'm willing to eat with you. What's wrong with that?' It was continuous fighting—verbal, that is." One day in April, Randy saw his mother crying. "It was only the second time I'd ever seen her cry," said Randy. "The first was when she picked us up from school after John Kennedy had been killed. She said, 'Your dad and I are having problems.'"

One weekday in May, Bob told Randy that the family would be having a meeting on Friday evening. Randy had planned to go out with our friend Evan that night. Randy told Evan that he would be delayed, that they were having a family meeting. "That doesn't sound good," said Evan.

"Early that night I was fighting about something dumb," said Gary. "Randy told me we were going to have a family meeting and that I needed to cool it. We were all in the living room. My father was sitting next to the tree lamp in a rocking chair. Nick was sitting on the red couch with Mom and me. Randy was sitting in the big red chair across from Dad."

Randy recalled their father saying, "We both love you kids and we want this to be amicable," and Sally saying, "It can't be." Gary remembers his father saying there was no more love left in the house and he was moving out for good. "Mom started to cry," said Gary, "which as I remember was one of the first times I'd ever seen her bawl like that, and it really scared me. Both Nick and I started to hug her, and Dad said, 'That's good boys. Your mom is going to really need you now.' After the meeting Dad and I played chess and I won for the first time," said Gary. "Then went into the bathroom and really started crying. I felt like I was in a movie about something that had gone wrong, and that it was not really happening."

Afterward, said Randy, "The weirdest thing was watching my dad packing." Afterward Randy went out with Evan, drank a little, and spent the night at the Bayhs' house without calling home. "Under the circumstances nothing was ever said about it," says Randy.

"I didn't know anything about divorce," said Gary. "For a long time, I wondered whether it my fault that he left. One of the reasons that they divorced was that she started the school. For years I blamed myself. I don't anymore, because I finally realized it was his decision. I would not have wanted them to be back together because they were both happier not being married."

For some time, though, Sally stayed angry at Bob. "In the two years after their divorce," says Gary, "she would say, 'It's your f---ing father on the phone.'" After Bob remarried, Sally told her friends that if they went to a dinner party and the new couple was there, Sally expected her friends to get up and walk out.

That summer Sally took the boys on an Italian cruise ship, the *Rafaelo*, which stopped in Cannes and other Mediterranean ports. The summer after that they returned to Tunisia.

In the Lab School, said Gary, "Every day there were new things to try and learn. In drama class I got to act in plays and pretend to dance as one of the Jets in *West Side Story* too. The only problem I had with that show was that I could not snap my fingers, so I had to fake it. At school I was studying with a tutor every day, learning the tricks of the trade—sound it out and it will usually make sense. My thirteenth year I was slowly getting it that the words went together.

"One day I was given a group of tests by my tutor. She showed me the answers after, and I had jumped three grades in my reading levels since the last test, six months before. We went to my mom's office to tell her the good news. She was on the phone with someone. She covered the mouthpiece and asked, 'What's he done?' The tutor told my mom and she screamed, 'Holy shit! You know how to read!' Mom hung up the phone and hugged me so hard it hurt, but in a great way."

Randy went off to Amherst College, and Nick, in his senior year, served as editor-in chief of *The St. Albans News* and got into Yale. But the divorce still hung over the family. "It took me years to realize it wasn't my fault," said Gary. "Dad and I discussed it the week before he died. We talked about his life in general. I went over because I knew he was sick. All she cared about was that he didn't hurt any of us. Once it was over with, it was so much better for her. After she finished being angry with him, she became a better person because of it.

"I didn't show her how I felt, because I bottled it up. I'd get mad at other things. At eleven and a half, you're looking for a father figure, and your father walks out. He said, 'I'm not leaving you boys. I'm just leaving your mother.'" Bob went on to remarry. He got an ambassadorship to the Ivory Coast from 1974 to 1976, retired in 1979, and died in 2013.

"He was brilliant in his way," said Gary. "But my mom was a shooting star."

Fifteen — American University and *No Easy Answers*

On the first day of class in Education 545: The Arts in Special Education, forty students take their seats. The professor, in red heels, a geometric print skirt, a bright purple blouse, and an orange scarf, strides up and down the aisles, leaving a hint of Giorgio perfume as she goes. Her earrings, concentric gold ovals, sway back and forth as she speaks. Like an actor filling up a stage, she fills up the classroom with her personality, making eye contact with her new students, rattling her bracelets with the occasional shake of her arm. They notice that her lips are painted a cardinal red and her nails in a multicolor pattern, like mini Picassos. All the students have heard of the professor and the innovative teaching methods she invented. They also know about her demanding reading list, which includes her own book, *No Easy Answers: Teaching the Learning Disabled Child*. But mostly the students know that, with this prof, you better be on your toes and ready to think of creative answers on the spot. No dozing or daydreaming.

Loud music blares from a boom box. A teaching assistant flicks the lights on and off. The professor says, "This is a test." On either side of the room, two other TAs talk loudly as the professor announces, "Sarah will show you vocabulary words that you need to remember." Amid the cacophony, a TA walks up and down the aisles flashing cards with words on them and saying them aloud but at low volume and not clearly articulated. After this ends, the professor says, "Now write down all the words you remember." As the students put down the words they can recall, the professor says, "This is what the classroom can feel like for a child with learning disabilities.' On the board she'd write

"This si wkat a learming bisadleb qerson frepuently hasto conteub eith wheu attemqting ot nead a dook."*

"The reason it really stuck with me is my husband suffers from ADHD," remembered Elizabeth Elizardi, a former American University student who now runs the Green Trees Early Childhood Village preschool program at Isadore Newman School in New Orleans. "What she really impressed on us was, 'No matter what a child presents to you, you can always find something that child does well.' She was all about being inclusive and said it was our responsibility to advocate for them. It was a hard class to get into. She was a campus icon. People were clamoring to get into the class."

In 1975, Sally had been asked by the American University School of Education to teach its fifty-nine master's and PhD students in their classes on learning disabilities. The course started in three days. "I had never taught at a university before," Sally wrote. In fact, she had plenty of experience bringing along her young teachers at the Lab School as they developed their methods for instructing LD children. She had also gained practical experience when she designed and directed the Urban League–Lab School Summer Session for forty-two failing readers under a Title I ESEA grant in 1970 and organized and directed workshops on learning disabilities for thirty-five District of Columbia junior high school teachers in 1974.

At AU, she introduced her students to the Integrated Arts and Academic Club Method and gave many of them opportunities to test their own abilities at the Lab School. She also introduced her colleagues to her flamboyant fashion style. During one large staff meeting of the AU Education Department, one professor suggested that it was not proper for an august professor to sport exotically painted fingernails, as Sally did, sometimes in a crossword puzzle pattern, often in a colored pattern, carried out by an artistic nail cosmetician at the Four Seasons in Georgetown. In response, Sally gave a joyous laugh.

After a successful school year, Sally was named acting chairman of the special education department and an associate professor in charge of the master's degree program in special education: learning disabilities. She redesigned AU's program to make sure students had the necessary theoretical constructs and practical experience. Each year, around a dozen graduate students from AU, along with several from George Washington University and Howard, served their practicum experiences under master teachers at the Lab School. Thus began an interchange between teachers at the Lab School instructing AU students and AU students learning their craft at the Lab School. This symbiotic exchange has sparked the careers of hundreds of the brightest teachers in the LD field and continues to the present day.

In that 1976–77 school year, the Lab School had fifty-four students—forty-eight boys and six girls. They were in five groups— 6–9, 9–10, 10–11, 11–12, and junior high, 13–15. On the tenth anniversary, May 23, 1977, the Lab School Parents Association gathered some 250 parents, teachers, and other prominent people in education, foundations, and the arts for a reception at Georgetown Day School to honor Sally. The Lab School's numbers were impressive: In its first ten years, it had successfully moved eighty-five children on to other schools. "It is our estimate that ninety percent of them are now succeeding in regular public and private schools. Six are known to be in college and a good number who are now in the 10th, 11th and 12th grade are definitely college bound." *

NBC aired a one-hour special on the Lab School and Sally's teacher-training methods in the fall of 1976. That year Sally also served on the US Task Force on the Definition of Developmental Disabilities and as a consultant and field reader on learning disabilities for the Bureau of the Handicapped under the Office of Education in the US Department of Health, Education, and Welfare.

With all he'd been hearing about the Lab School and Sally Smith, Bertram Brown, the director of the National Institute of Mental Health, decided to give the Lab School a look. "At first I was skeptical," he said. "But I found that in coping with her own problems, she rose heroically to help others with theirs. In that is the glory of this woman and the power of her school." * As a result, Brown awarded Sally an NIMH contract (also under the aegis of HEW) to write a book on learning disabilities for laypeople, for which he eventually contributed a foreword.

So, while running the Lab School, teaching at AU and running a department and a master's program, Sally had a book to write. She turned to her old friend and former Cave Lady Ben Booz. After a three-year posting in Indonesia and the death of Paul in 1971, Booz had taken a job teaching history at the Sandy Springs, Maryland, Friends School. "It was a very patchy beginning," Booz said of the creation of *No Easy Answers*, "coming out by fits and starts. Sally had an article here, a lecture there, at least a couple of exposés in the important educational magazines."

In March 1977, Sally spoke to the National Association for Children with Learning Disabilities Conference in Washington. Her topic, presented jointly with the clinical psychologist Edna Small, was "Support and Supervision of the Learning Disabilities Teacher." In September, *Developmental Disabilities Digest* ran a story, "Mother Designs

Own School for Child's Learning Disorder," that read in part, "Today, the Lab School of the Kingsbury Center enrolls 56 children with similar disorders. . . . 'Every part of our curriculum is geared to helping students organize themselves, their bodies, their minds, their work,' she said. The slogan on the bulletin board in the front office: 'Nobody here is a nobody.'" In its fall 1977 issue, *Washington Review* ran a Q&A, "Learning Based on the Arts: An Interview with Sally L. Smith." In November Sally addressed the University Leadership Training Conference of the National Committee on Arts for the Handicapped in New Haven about special education and art education.

Sally wrote "What Kind of Conference Is This?" for the May 1978 *Arise*, the magazine of the American Research Institute in Special Education. On May 11 she spoke to the Rhode Island Hospital School and State Department of Education in Providence, Rhode Island, on teaching basic academic skills in alternative ways.

In a family moment, Sally, Nick, and Gary— along with Bob Smith and his new wife, Didi—convened on May 26 in Amherst, Massachusetts, to watch Randy graduate Phi Beta Kappa from Amherst College with his degree in history and a respectable minor in fraternity life.

In October Sally gave speeches to three DC groups: the Potomac Art Therapy Association of the DC Metropolitan Area, "The Arts and Educating the Learning Disabled Child"; the Area A Community Mental Health Center learning disabilities workshop, "What Is a Learning Disability?"; and the Sidwell Friends School faculty, "Educational Strategies for the Learning Disabled Child." In June 1978 she chaired a panel at a conference at the Sheraton Park Hotel on the arts in education, and she wrote an article, "When Learning Is a Problem," for the November 1978 *American Educator*, the magazine of the Office of Education.

Building on this considerable body of material, Sally worked with Booz to craft a book that answered practical problems but also addressed tougher emotional and developmental problems. They worked together in a house at Rehoboth Beach, Delaware, in late May 1978, then August 20–23 in Bermuda, then back to Rehoboth for August 25–31. Published in 1978 by the US Government Printing Office, the first version of *No Easy Answers: The Learning Disabled Child* ran 131 pages, with very much the no frills, no color look—on the outside, anyway—of an official handout. Sally wrote in her acknowledgments, "Elisabeth Benson Booz played a vital role in the development of this manuscript and provided creative criticism and substantial help in every facet of its creation."

In the distinctive style of *A Child's Mind*, Sally lists the questions in *No Easy Answers* that she knew were eating at troubled parents, because she had lived them. As in,

- "Why does he read SAW for WAS?"
- "Can't he see the difference between b and d?"
- "How come she could read all of these words yesterday, and she can't get a single one today?"
- "Will he ever learn the days of the week?"

- "If he can talk about life on Mars, why can't he add 2 + 2?"

- "Can't he stop talking for 5 minutes?"

In the next section, she lists adjectives: "Exasperated . . . Puzzled . . . Desperate . . . Uncertain . . . Frantic . . . Exhausted . . . Helpless . . . Hopeful." She starts the next paragraph, "These are the feelings of the mother or father of a learning disabled child." The twelve chapters are titled Disordered, Immature, Inflexible, Lost in Time and Space, Clumsy, Free Spirit, Defeated at School, Why?, Parents, Teachers, Adolescence, Order. Its six appendices include one headed "Some Typical Academic Problems of Learning Disabled Children." In all the sections, brilliant insights, lively, conversational prose and practical, how-to approaches jump off the pages.

No Easy Answers became one of NIMH's best-selling titles,* issued in many editions over the years, and, in its various incarnations, established itself as the go-to text of the learning disability field. Sally and Ben quickly realized they had struck a chord and enhanced the book as *No Easy Answers: The Learning Disabled Child at Home and School* for a commercial publisher, Winthrop, which issued the book in June of 1979. The chapter titles were more direct, and they added a Chapter 10, "Teaching Through the Arts and Academic Clubs."

Sally dedicated it "To my son Gary, who has been my finest teacher and my hardest taskmaster. He, who did not read until he was thirteen years old, because of his severe learning disabilities, once said, "*Now* I understand how people can read to themselves. They have to share it with their brains!"

Ben Departs to Teach in China

On February 7, 1979, Sally hosted a farewell to Ben, who, ever the international adventurer, had jumped at an opportunity to relocate with her third son, Paddy, to teach English in China. "Paddy was graduating from the University of Wisconsin in Asian studies and Chinese language," wrote Booz,* sounding more than ever like a Kipling character, "and he thought we might make a good pair. The authorities in Beijing must have agreed because they appointed us to Yunnan University in Kunming, in the far southwest corner of China. Before we departed, the editor of *National Geographic* magazine told us we would be the first Americans to enter remote Yunnan Province since the Communist revolution of 1949. Out of curiosity he lent Paddy a Leica camera and lots of film, asking him to snap photographs of anything he saw in Yunnan and send back his undeveloped rolls of film to the *National Geographic.*

"We arrived in Kunming at the Chinese New Year 1979. Yunnan University was somewhat in ruins after the ravages of the twelve-year Cultural Revolution, but restoration was beginning. There were no books in English later than 1936 and no copying machine in the whole province. We shot off letters howling for help. Friends and relatives in Europe and America responded by emptying their bookshelves and a 'book-lift' of second-hand books continued to arrive through the whole three years I remained in Yunnan. The National Geographic sent us atlases and reference books and we were able to establish a workable English language library. We taught English to doctors, professors, leaders of institutions, and others who could read English but not speak it. We tried unsuccessfully to teach former 'foreign language teachers' who knew only Russian.

"Our students in the Foreign Languages Department were brilliant. In 1977 they had outstripped thousands of competitors in the first university entrance exams in twelve years despite little regular schooling. As Red Guards burning libraries, some had managed to steal books, but even the lucky ones were only haphazardly educated. They begged us to teach them 'knowledge.' A new dean joined our department and he agreed. For starters he asked us to teach 'The History and Culture of the English-Speaking World.' That course lasted a year but we did it. When communist officials came to see if we were corrupting the students, our dean explained we were only teaching the vocabulary of economics, law and history, and they appeared satisfied. I invented many other courses and published two text books. Paddy and I worked nonstop, using every bit of experience, imagination, and knowledge we had ever acquired. Paddy stayed for two years but I remained for three, to see our first class through to their graduation. Whenever he had time, Paddy snapped pictures and sent them, unseen, to the *National Geographic*.

"During our second year, a staff photographer came through Kunming and some months later I got an urgent telegram from Washington, asking me to send a 5,000-word story on our life in China as soon as possible! How could I? I had minimal free time in any day and there was so much to tell! Somehow I wrote a story at high speed during ten sleepless nights, but I made no effort to construct a balanced account. I told truthfully about the multitude of positive things that were happening at Yunnan University, but did not discuss the setbacks, difficulties, or the anxieties of living with no foreign support in a communist country.

"The story appeared almost unchanged in the *National Geographic* of June 1981 with four of the photographs by Paddy. It had one fortunate outcome for me in China. Leaders in Beijing liked my optimistic story about Yunnan and I got permission to visit Tibet four years before it was officially open to foreigners." This led Ben to write a guidebook to Tibet in 1984, then a guidebook to New Zealand in 1985. No surprise, either, that Ben got her job with NatGeo's Books Division in Washington, where she worked for twenty years.

Sixteen — Sally the National Advocate; Buying the Castle

In 1979, Sally continued her role in the national and sometimes international conversation about educating the learning disabled. She filled the entire June issue of the NIMH-HEW pamphlet *Plain Talk* with "About Children with Learning Disabilities," which was reprinted two years later in the journal of the National Education Association, *Today's Education.* * The UN Secretariat for the International Year of the Child commissioned "The Learning Disabled Children: Who Are They and How Do We Teach Them?" It was published in English, French, and Spanish and sent to 192 countries.

Sally wrote a chapter, "Teaching Academic Skills Through Drama to Learning Disabled Students," in *Drama, Theatre, and the Handicapped*, edited by Ann M. Shaw and C. J. Stevens and published by the American Theatre Association, and the foreword to Marcia Behr and her co-authors' *Drama Integrated Basic Skills: Lessons Plans for the Learning Disabled.* *

Over the course of 1979 Sally gave nine major speeches, including three of particular significance: In July she gave a talk titled "Drama, Theatre and the Handicapped" at the American Theatre Association Conference O'Neill Theatre in Waterford, Connecticut. In October she returned to New York to deliver the keynote address at the 92nd Street Y, describing the Lab School program and showing slides of her innovative teaching methods at a conference on the arts, recreation, and religion for children with learning disabilities. On that trip, she visited her parents and saw Tom Stoppard's *Night and Day* at the Eisenhower Theatre. In November, her address to the Woodrow Wilson International Center for Scholars at the Smithsonian Institution Castle was titled "The Theoretical Framework for Employing the Arts as Part of the Program for Learning Disabled Children."

A glance at Sally's calendars from these years is a varied symphony of unending energy and variation. While carrying out her roles at the Lab School and at AU, attending conferences, visiting universities around the country for smaller talks (e.g., July 18, 1979, at Bradley University's Sleni School of Music in Peoria, Illinois), and touching base with Gary in his residence house in Orlando, Sally kept up her dinners and social gatherings with family and friends old and new, played tennis, spent time with her boyfriend, Norman, and decompressed on occasional weekends on the beach in North Carolina or Rehoboth. And yes, she hosted her Christmas parties.

In February and March of 1980, Sally prepared yet another edition of *No Easy Answers*, this one for Bantam, which came out the following January. Her calendar allots a chapter for each of twelve days of February, with "revisions due" penned in on the thirtieth. On March 1, after "Irene 60th" is BANTAM Book. Same on March 2 and March 3 "Book deadline." March 4 reads "SEND TO BANTAM—Collapse".

The 1981 Bantam edition of *No Easy Answers* firmly established Sally as a national authority and her book as an indispensable resource, reprinted many times over the years and issued in a revised edition in 1995.

Days after her post–Bantam deadline "collapse," Sally spoke to the Connecticut Association for Children with Learning Disabilities and then, on March 13, to the University of Michigan Institute for the Study of Mental Retardation and Related Disorders, with the Washtenaw Intermediate School System, on the topic "Children and Adolescents with Learning Disabilities: Strategies for Learning and Living."

In May she returned to Bennington to speak on the arts and the educative process, a theme she reprised in July in her talk "The Arts: Central to Learning" at the Institute for Cultural Progress in Washington. Later that month, Sally and the Lab School attained a measure of celebrity when the Q&A "In Her Own Words" appeared in the July 28 issue of *People* magazine. The interview was done by Garry Clifford, *People*'s Washington bureau chief, who had been a Lab School parent since 1973. In a story like that of many Lab School parents, Clifford had discovered that her youngest son, Eamon, was "very dyslexic" after his kindergarten year at Chevy Chase Elementary School. His teacher suggested that Eamon might have to repeat the year, and also suggested that Clifford have Eamon tested. When the results came in, Clifford says, "I spent the summer educating myself" on coping strategies for dyslexia. Eamon had a late birthday, so Clifford had hopes that his development would catch up in first grade. Three weeks after school started in the fall, Eamon's teacher asked Clifford during the afternoon pickup, "What is he doing here?" Clifford called the Kingsbury Center, ostensibly to get a tutor. "I threw myself into my car and went down there," she says, remembering the panic of almost every parent of an LD child looking for an answer. She was shown the Lab School next door, where a child had recently left the youngest group "I met Sally," she said, and heard about the tuition, which in 1973 was $3,800 a year. "I took Eamon down the next day, and when I picked him up the kids were screaming goodbye to him, and he was rushing down the stairs with a smile that went from cheek to cheek. He stayed there until graduation from eighth grade."

Clifford's husband, George, was a former newspaperman then working on political campaigns. With three boys at home, Garry had not been working. She had been a reporter at *The Ottawa Journal* in Canada. Through a connection at a *Washington Daily News* party, she got a job working half-time for five dollars an hour as a researcher at an NBC-TV weekend show. It enabled her to finish work at 3:00 p.m., then pick up Eamon at 3:30 at the Lab School. Early on in Eamon's time there, the children were playing at Mitchell Park, across the street from the school, when a ball hit Eamon on the head. "Sally carried him all the way back to the school," Clifford remembers. "They called me, and I picked him up." The other teachers told Clifford what Sally had done, and it impressed her. This head of the school was most certainly hands on—and definitely cared about her students.

Clifford and Sally became friends, and Sally started inviting the Cliffords to the epic Christmas parties. Garry Clifford's career took a turn when Betty Ford went to NIH for a mastectomy and a new magazine in the Time-Life family, *People,* hired her to report on the operation and the First Lady's refreshing openness about breast cancer. As *People* took off, Clifford was hired by the Washington bureau and became its chief in 1979. Her July 1980 Q&A with Sally put the Lab School and dyslexia in front of some 40 million readers. It also planted the seeds for a relationship between the Lab School and celebrities that—fertilized by some innovative thinking by Sally and Clifford—bore fruit a few years later and continues to the present day.

Among Sally's dozen speaking engagements in 1980 and 1981, two were to the Washington School of Psychiatry—"Precursors to Learning" in November 1980 and a "The Relationship of Learning Disabilities to Emotional and Social Problems" a year later. With her Bennington background under Erich Fromm and his friend Ned Hall, a School of Psychiatry faculty member in the 60s, these topics very much inhabited

Sally's wheelhouse. She was hired as an adjunct faculty member in the psychiatry school's Child and Adolescent Therapy Training Program.

As of December 1981, the Lab School had nine full-time teachers plus many artists working part-time, eighty students ages six to sixteen, and a long waiting list. It was housed in three adjacent townhouses. In seven out of ten cases, the tuition—$6,700 yearly in the elementary school, $6,900 in the junior high—was paid by the local school districts, which were mandated by federal law PL 94-142 to "provide free and appropriate education" for handicapped students. That month the school's national profile hit another high-water mark with "The School That Sally Built," Earl and Miriam Selby's story* in the December *Reader's Digest*, reaching a worldwide circulation of thirty million. The story introduced many readers not only to the Lab School and the Academic Club methodology but also to the very concept of learning disabilities, and the fact that they affected an estimated ten million children. The school was flooded with calls, some from parents wanting to start a Lab School in their area, others from educators wanting their schools or systems to adopt the Lab School methods. There were so many calls, in fact, that board member Susan Hager of the K Street PR firm Hager, Sharp & Abramson deployed her employee Karen Lubieniecki to provide the Lab School staff with advice on handling them. The result was a five-page letter. The Lab School was national news.

In 1982, American University elevated Sally to the status of professor with tenure, and the Lab School took the enormous leap of becoming independent of the Kingsbury Center. This made sense, since the offspring had grown up and begun to overshadow the nurturing parent. More than that, the Lab School, like a teenager bristling under the constraints of living at home, had developed various gripes, even down to the mail being delivered to the Kingsbury Center then passed along to the building next door, sometimes promptly, sometimes less so. When Sally discussed the options with her friend Tidi King, King asked her, "Do you want them reading your mail forever?"

In August, Sally officially became executive director of the Lab School of Washington, a new tax-exempt nonprofit institution. Its proposed budget for 1982–83 called for income of $649,900 in tuition (forty-five lower school students paying $7,300 each and forty high school students at $7,500) and expenses of $655,066, including $425,595 in salaries. "Independence allowed the school to expand from 80 students to 250 students spanning kindergarten through twelfth grade with an after-school arts and sports program," wrote Sally.*

In October and November, Sally's speaking engagements included three keynotes at state associations for children with learning disabilities—in Atlanta for 400 participants and leaders of workshops at the Georgia association; at Michigan State University for 1,010 participants and workshop leaders at the Michigan association's annual conference; and in San Juan, Puerto Rico, to 400 participants at the Puerto Rico association. In San Juan she also ran two workshops, one for parents and one for teachers. In February 1983, Sally addressed the National Association for Children with Learning Disabilities. A month later she was appointed to the NACL's sixteen-member Professional Advisory Board. If she hadn't been before, Sally was now a national figure in the field of learning disabilities.

Then came the Lab School's biggest leap yet. In the spring of 1983, the former Florence Crittenden Home for unwed mothers, a 3.6-acre property at 4759 Reservoir

Road NW, came on the market. It included a brownstone mansion and two other buildings nestled on a hill facing the Georgetown Reservoir. "I told her not to do it," remembers Stocky. "I told her, 'Don't tie yourself down with a major asset like that. You'll spend every waking hour doing what you hate to do, raising money.'" Still, it was perfect for an expanding school. The Lab School bought the property in May for $2.4 million. "We were able to buy it because we have raised $450,000 in cash this year through donations," said Sally, then a vibrant 54. The rest of the money came from bank loans. Tuition was listed as ranging from $7,800 to $8,000 and the annual budget, with its new mortgage payments, at about $1 million.

In August of 1983 the Lab School of Washington moved to its larger permanent headquarters, which permitted an expansion of the student body from ninety to 124 students, with a potential future expansion to 250. The school also added a diagnostic clinic with testing and tutoring services for the community, a training course for tutors, a kindergarten program, and plans for a night school for learning disabled adults.

The night school opened its doors in January 1984 to some seventy-five to ninety LD adults. It was one of the first such night schools in the country, if not the first. "Precise teaching methods are geared to the needs of each individual," wrote Sally. "At this school, adult students working with master teachers find out how they can learn most effectively. And they continually teach their teachers more about learning disabilities." The first batch of students included an engraver, a foundation executive, a salesman, a furniture mover, a telephone-company worker, a secretary for the FBI, a nursery school assistant teacher, a restaurant owner, and an athletic coach. As other classes followed, it became clear that most night school students had not been previously diagnosed as learning disabled.

In May, among her dozen other speeches and workshops in the 1984–85 school year, Sally was the luncheon speaker at the Hay Adams Hotel in Washington for government and corporate officials. As part of that appearance, she introduced Mrs. James Totten, the daughter of General George S. Patton and the grandmother of a Lab School student, who discussed her father's learning disabilities and gave Sally several pages of Patton's fifth-grade schoolwork, both writing and math, which now reside among Sally's papers at AU.

In the summer of 1985, the Lab School hosted a summer school for 120 children, thirty-five adults, three graduate interns on their practicum experiences, and three AU students. In September, Lab opened with 160 learning disabled students, fifty youngsters in an after-school program, and fifty-five adults in the night school. The school also provided diagnostic services to about a hundred clients a year, tutoring to some eighty to ninety students a year.

Ever since the early seventies, Sally had been a regular figure in radio and TV interviews, short and long, for stations near and farther away. As the Lab School moved and expanded, her appearances had increased. In Washington, these included an hour-long interview with call-ins on Dr. Joseph Novello's "House Calls" on WMAL Radio in October 1981, an hour-long interview with New Republic editor Morton Kondracke on WRC radio in January 1982, and two hour-and-a-half interviews and call-ins on WRC Radio, The Joel Spivak Show in May 1983 and the Rudy Maxa Show in November 1983. In August 1985, Sally taped an hour-long interview with John Merrow of New

Hampshire Public Radio as part of a series of the New Hampshire Committee for Citizens in Education.

As part of its new status as an independent nonprofit, the Lab School started holding luncheons for the community at large at which celebrities spoke about learning disabilities. The purpose was to raise public awareness, but they quickly grew into daylong celebrations. With the Lab School ensconced in its castle with many new bills to pay, Sally tapped into her twenty-year history of putting on rollicking parties that no one in Washington wanted to miss.

Seventeen — The Dawn of the Galas

Sally Smith, glowing in a white V-neck blouse, white and brown beads, and white pleated skirt, looks out over the crowd of a thousand, dapper in black tie and formal gowns. She welcomes them to the first Outstanding Learning Disabled Achievers Awards. She smiles and thanks Hecht's Department Store executive Henry Hemsing for adopting the Lab School as the store's official charity, hosting the gala, and donating the Waterford crystal awards. She compliments Hecht's expansive, just-completed Metro Center store, scheduled for its official grand opening the next day. Built on G Street Northwest, between Twelfth and Thirteenth Streets, it will be the flagship of Hecht's 142 stores in forty-two states, a jewel of off-white honed granite and white marble in a revitalizing downtown.

For the event, the Lab School staff and gala committee have pushed away the dress racks on the third floor and made room for a hundred tables, Gene Donato's swing band, and a dance floor. During the cocktail hour, the decibel level of the conversation reaches those of Sally's Christmas parties. When the most interesting people in Washington get together, they can't stop talking—and no one wants them to. Sally circulates from person to person, touching arms, bearing her trademark red-lipstick smile, the aura of her Giorgio perfume perceptible even on the department store floor.

The first lady had agreed to lend her name to the gala, so the invitations read

"Under the gracious patronage of Mrs. Ronald Reagan,

an Award ceremony honoring Outstanding Learning Disabled Achievers"

When Sally and her high-powered gala committee members promise a party, Sally's friends, cabinet members, congressmen, and Lab School parents don't mind ponying up for the tickets, which range from $150 to $5,000 for benefactors.

Tonight, says Sally, you will meet six amazing individuals who have contended their whole lives with learning disabilities and successfully beaten the odds. They are investment banker G. Chris Anderson, the incomparable Cher, actor Tom Cruise, Olympic decathlon champion Bruce [now Caitlyn] Jenner, modern artist Robert Rauschenberg, and Dallas real estate developer Richard C. Strauss.

Like the children at the Lab School, she says, these award winners have experienced the slights and humiliations of life as a dyslexic. To one, she says, 'You were called stupid, someone who'd never amount to anything." To another, "You were held back in third grade because you couldn't read." To another, "You felt ashamed of what you'd received on a test and hid the paper, but one teacher took you aside and said, 'Let me help.'"

How had Sally and her benefit committee, co-chaired by publicist Joe Canzeri and Carol Laxalt, wife of Senator Paul Laxalt of Nevada, assembled such a list of achievers? "We got lucky," Sally told the papers. Actually, she had the help of Garry Clifford, who noted the celebrities who talked about their dyslexia in news stories and used her *People* connections to reach out. "I suggested that we invite all these people and see if they'll come," said Clifford. For Tom Cruise, Clifford asked *People*'s Los Angeles bureau chief to contact Cruise's agent and made the invitation. Strauss, son of political insider and US Ambassador to the Soviet Union Bob Strauss, had written a piece in *Dyslexia Today* that Sally had spotted.

Majestic white-haired Speaker of the House Thomas "Tip" O'Neill, the living legend who said "All politics is local" and lived it, hands a Waterford crystal goblet to the winners, each of whom makes heartfelt remarks. "I was told at one school I was word-blind," says Anderson. "Another school, they blamed it on the previous school. It wasn't until a few years ago I discovered this was a problem that could have been diagnosed."

"It's exciting to get an award for being a dummy," says Cher, wearing a spiky black wig reminiscent of costumes from *Cats*, a black sequined sweatshirt under a black tail coat, over shiny black Wonder Woman tights and black satin over-knee boots. She tells the audience she can't dial a long-distance number. She dropped out of high school, bored and discouraged by her classroom failures. She speaks of her visit to the Lab School earlier in the day. "I found children that were having the absolute best chance at an education and I really felt jealous and happy for them." Cher had told the benefit committee that she always thought she was just plain stupid and began to think differently when her and Sonny Bono's teenaged child Chastity [now Chaz] started showing signs of dyslexia in high school. Cher says she finally decided to accept the award to help Chastity.

Cruise describes feeling "really embarrassed" about his reading problems, and how his frustration in the classroom had led him to acting. Likewise, Jenner, looking like someone straight off a Wheaties box, tells the crowd about turning to athletics to escape his defeats in the classroom: "It was very, very difficult. For some reason the [reading] process didn't work. It just didn't want to come off the paper like for everybody else. The biggest fear I ever had in my life was reading in front of my classmates. I was absolutely terrified." Jenner ends by encouraging other dyslexics to persevere: "If he wins, he knows the thrill of great achievement. If he loses, he loses while daring greatly, so his place in life will never be with those cold and timid souls who know neither victory nor defeat." *

Rauschenberg says he didn't discover his dyslexia until he was about seventeen. "No one cared or knew anything about learning disabilities," he says. "You just feel terrible about it, like you're the dumbest person around. But thank god for my learning disability. Otherwise I'd be an accountant where I grew up in Port Arthur, Texas, instead of pursuing the only thing I was good at."

Strauss admits he can barely write. "Like many dyslexics," he says, "I became the class clown to get attention and win social acceptance. Unable to compete academically, I drove a go-kart through my school hallways and sold pencils I'd stolen from other pupils' desks."

The crowd stands and cheers. The dancing lasts into the night. Cher and Tom Cruise bond, talking for much of the night in their hotel. The gala raises $386,000.

That morning, October 30, 1985, Randy Smith, then a lawyer at a New Orleans

law firm, had picked up Cher at the Hotel Bristol and taken her to the White House, where they walked to the Rose Garden to meet with Nancy Reagan and the five other winners. Cruise had brought his mother and two

Sally Smith at the first Gala with Tom Cruise, Bruce Jenner, Richard Strauss, Robert Rauschenberg, and Cher.

sisters.

For the occasion, Cher was draped in black and gray gabardine with what Desson Howe of *The Washington Post* described as a sculpted "haute punk goddess" hairstyle. After posing for a picture with the first lady (below), the group visited the Lab School, where they talked with the students. One asked Cher, "How do you approach reading a

script?" Cher replied, "First of all, I don't approach anything. I just fall in or fall out! I'm a terrible reader. I see words and jumble them together. But my

brain has a way of compensating. I read my scripts very, very slowly, but I memorize them almost immediately." *

"I'm a terrible reader," she said in an interview. "I don't write letters. Numbers and I have absolutely no relationship. I can dial a phone OK, as long as it's not long distance. I write the first letter of the word, and my mind races to the last letter. I see words and jumble them together. I see great billboards, billboards no one has ever invented. But my brain has a way of compensating. I read my script very, very slowly, but I memorize them almost immediately. Now, my problem is annoying more than anything else." *

"Going to the school was pretty terrific," said Cruise, who was described in the *Post* as wearing a "1920s-chic gangster suit, hair glopped in grease."

Clifford remembers Rauschenberg's Harris tweed jacket. "He was so cute," she says. "It was all browns and golds and greens. I think of it as an artist's jacket. "It [dyslexia] can make your life absolutely miserable when you can't keep up with the other people in your school," Rauschenberg said. "Your whole social life is based upon it, and, you know, it took me years to realize that I wasn't stupid. If anyone with learning disabilities can learn that when they are still young, they can be saved from an awful lot of pain and disturbing memories."

The galas threw the Lab School into the arena of celebrities and glamour, further reinforcing Sally's growing reputation as a national advocate. In March 1986, Gannett filmed a fifty-five-minute documentary titled *I'm Not Stupid* at the Lab School, featuring day and night students. That month Sally was on stage four times at the ACLD National Conference. On day one she presented "What LD Adults Can Teach Parents and

Teachers." On Day Two she moderated two panels, "I Am an LD Adult Who . . ." and "I Am a Parent of an LD Child Who . . . ." On day three she presented "Masks That LD Adults Often Wear." That autumn the Lab School honored *Night Court* comedian and actor Harry Anderson, Artic explorer Ann Bancroft, Head of the US Fish and Wildlife Service Frank H. Dunkle, Olympic diving champion Greg Louganis, and the Fonz himself, actor and producer Henry Winkler. The following February Sally presented "Systems that Work for the Learning Disabled" at the National Association for Learning Disabilities Conference in San Antonio, then reprised her panel moderations on "I Am an LD Adult Who . . ." and "I Am a Parent of an LD Child Who . . . ."

In a perhaps predictable reaction, some voices in the congregation dissented from Sally's highly developed view of learning disabilities and her practical methods for addressing them. In early 1988 Gerald Coles, an associate professor of clinical psychology at the Robert Wood Johnson Foundation and a fellow at Rutgers, published *The Learning Mystique: A Critical Look at LD*. Among many points, Coles downplayed the notion of specific learning disabilities and "minimal brain damage" and challenged the educational practices that addressed them. As *New York Times* reviewer Vivian Gussin Paley noted, "Mr. Coles puts the matter into broader perspective. 'Learning difficulties, and any neurological dysfunctions associated with them, develop not from within the individual but from the individual's interaction within social relationships. Brain functioning is both a product of and a contributor to the individual's interactions, it is not a predetermined condition.' "

Sally rebutted Coles's positions in interviews and speeches. In her notes, she mapped out a letter to Coles: "You criticize all research in the field of LD but your research refers to a series of laboratory experiments with rats—not LD children—refers to a set of studies on psychological dwarfism where physiological causes were found to be child abuse . . . and five adults with reading problems in the specialized-instruction program you direct. . . . You state that the field of LD was created for Middle Class kids who had 'unexplainable' failure and tend to want to blame the dysfunction on an affluent society, but later on you talk about the preponderance of these problems among minority groups. The book is destructive—Have you been the parent of an LD child? You blame parents . . . and they blame themselves too much already. They need practical help. The same with teachers. We don't need whipping boys."

In April 1988, the CBS television show *West 57th* featured the Lab School in a fourteen-minute segment. "The telephones of the Lab School rang off the walls for ten days," wrote Sally. "Parents, teachers, and administrators were brought in to answer more than 700 telephone calls from every state in the nation. All of them requested written material and asked us to start a school in their locale. Alas, as a nonprofit institution we had no funds for expansion and barely the funds to meet the costs of the mailings we sent out. The very same passion that I had felt for the unmet needs of my own son twenty years before was the same passion we heard from all corners of the country. Parents were saying, 'I know my child can learn in this way.' Teachers were saying, 'I could do this in my classroom.' "

Spreading the Lab School methodology to the far corners of the nation was a dream that had to wait, but in DC, the galas took on a life of their own. "Over the years they kept getting better and bigger," says Clifford. Susan Hager, who later chaired the Lab School board from 1995 to 2004, took over the galas, delivering award winners

194

over the years that included *Washington Post* columnist Richard Cohen and scholar, author, and professor Roger Wilkins (1987); American Express Vice President Malcolm Goodridge III, NBA great Magic Johnson, and then-governor of New Jersey Thomas Kean (1988); singer Harry Belafonte, Washington Redskins defensive end Dexter Manley, and Kinko's CEO Paul Orfalea (1989); *The Heidi Chronicles* playwright Wendy Wasserstein (1991); photographer Richard Avedon and comedian Fannie Flagg (1994); and actor James Earl Jones and Olympic decathlon champion Dan O'Brien (1996).

In 1997, Pulitzer Prize-winning *Wall Street Journal* writer Ron Suskind and his wife, Cornelia Kennedy, were searching for ways to meet the challenges of their autistic son, Owen. As Suskind writes in *Life, Animated: A Story of Sidekicks, Heroes, and Autism*, Owen could communicate through Disney characters. With the Lab School's emphasis on drama, it was a natural choice. "Sally had pulled Cornelia and me onto the gala committee in our first days at the school. As journalists, we were good at getting phone numbers and breaking through the protective webs around the powerful and celebrated. With Cornelia's plate full, this was more my job. Smith and I bonded. We had many meetings each year about the gala, which became a passion—some might say, an obsession—for Sally." Suskind helped land Vince Vaughn in 1998, was part of the team that got longtime San Diego Chargers coach Don Coryell in 1999, and helped bring *Witness* star Kelly McGillis and politico James Carville in 2000.

Nonetheless, said Clifford, "It was getting harder and harder to find people." In the early 2000s, Sally Quinn, wife of legendary *Washington Post* editor Ben Bradlee, took over the gala. Their son, Quinn Bradlee, had gone to the Lab School in the eighties and wrote a memoir, *A Different Life: Growing Up Learning Disabled and Other Adventures*. Sally Quinn opened up a whole new avenue of connections for finding honorees.

The gala still reigns as a premier event of Washington's philanthropic season. Throughout the years the awardees, like Tom Cruise and Cher, have counted their visit to the Lab School, taking questions from the children and seeing the way they are learning, as the highlight of the occasion. "Most people found it rewarding to talk to the children and to offer their own experiences as a way to say yes, you can succeed if you work hard enough."

Eighteen — Writing More Books with Ben

In a pink stucco house in the medieval fishing village of Yvoire, France, Ben Booz sits in a large-backed wicker chair with her feet on a big footstool, looking out across Lake Geneva and scribbling on a legal pad as Sally Smith lies on a bed throwing out ideas in an energized staccato. "We start with the Lab School, which led to the night school," she says. "In those Tuesday-night seminars with the adults at the night school, I've learned what it's like to have grown up with the pervasive feeling of not being OK. Again and again I've been overcome with how rotten these adults feel about themselves. This book comes from those adults, from former Lab School day students, from AU students with learning disabilities, from letters, and from the celebrity winners of our Outstanding LD Achiever Awards who have shared their secret pain and strategies for success in their visits with Lab School students."

Throughout the nineties, the last half of June or first half July was Sally's creative time, between end of the Lab School year and her summer session at AU. Sally would join Ben at her house in Yvoire, and they would set to work—throwing out ideas for books, getting down the key chapters, or shaping existing manuscripts. Sometimes Ben packed picnics and they drove in her car to settings like Venice, Lucerne, and Giverny, where they could draw inspiration from Monet's gardens.

In Yvoire in 1990, the project was *Succeeding Against the Odds: Strategies and Insights from the Learning Disabled*. Taking the ideas laid out in June, Sally, sometimes with help from "Bozo," as she sometimes wrote Booz's name in her monthly calendars, worked on the manuscript in three-hour blocks of time in January and February 1991, with final revisions and edits done in time for her to speak at the LD conference in

Chicago from February 26 to March 1. All the while Sally was keeping her regular schedule of teaching at AU from 2:00 to 7:00 p.m. on Wednesdays and from 5:30 to 8:00 p.m. on Thursdays, along with the night school on Tuesday evenings at 6:30—not to mention grading papers, playing tennis, and enjoying social occasions with her wide circle of friends.

Succeeding Against the Odds was published in 1992 by Jeremy P. Tarcher Inc. of Los Angeles, dedicated "To my three sons, Randy, Nick, and Gary, each an only child. You have been my backbone and my pride! Thank you." The acknowledgments begin with "Elizabeth Benson Booz, one of my dearest friends in the world. I thank you profoundly for your enthusiasm, for all your sage advice, and for your professional talent as an editor. You provided a beautiful and uncluttered existence

for me in Yvoire, France, to write this book, and I am forever grateful."

Succeeding Against the Odds grew out of the many stories gathered from winners of the Outstanding Learning Disabled Achievers Awards over the years. (The acknowledgements also include thanks to Joy Galance, who gave Sally tapes of all the galas.)

The first chapter, "The Hidden Handicap," outlines the enigma of talented students who fail, pointing out examples like Nelson Rockefeller and George Patton. She touches on the strides that were made in the 1960s and 1970s toward understanding and recognizing learning disabilities, and its definition in Public Law 94-142, the Education for All Handicapped Children Act. The chapter revisits in bullet form the many ways that LDs show themselves and how they occur. It includes a checklist headed "Should I be tested to see if I am learning disabled?"

Chapter two, "Feeling Stupid, Acting Smart," touches on the stories of night school students and the gala awardees, including their recollections about how they discovered their LDs.

Chapter three, "Masking Secret Shame," offers many more anecdotes collected from the gala award ceremonies, such as Harry Belafonte's recollection, "In the West Indies, as a student, I was constantly being physically abused, because the whipping of students was permitted, and in America, the degrading way in which I was ostracized and punished for my dysfunction made my childhood a very unhappy experience."

Chapter four, "Talent," starts with a quote from Robert Rauschenberg—"If I hadn't been able to escape to the art studio and paint, I think I'd have died!"—and includes many others from award winners. The remaining chapters are "Drive," "The Need for Order," "Learning by Doing," "Responsibility: Preparing for Adulthood," "The Emotional Toll, "Family Tensions," "Socializations," "What Parents Can Do," "What Teachers Can Do," "What the Learning Disabled Can Do for Themselves," and "Strategies for Success." Many of the tips in the last chapter are just as handy for young people without learning disabilities as they are for those with LDs. Everyone can use tips on job interviews or with college admissions officers.

On July 12, 1991, Sally flew on KLM airlines to the Netherlands for three days. From there she went to Paris and Giverny, then camped for eleven days in Yvoire, where she and Ben discussed a booklet to help children understand disabilities.

When *Succeeding* was published in January of 1992, Sally did book signings in Los Angeles and Dallas, and read at a book party at the Politics and Prose Book Shop on Connecticut Avenue in Washington. That summer she left on July 10 for four days in London, two days in Giverny, and four days in Yvoire. From there she went on to Portofino for four days, then back to Yvoire and home on July 25. Back in the United States, she worked on the book on August 8 and 16.

In February 1993, the Learning Disabilities Association of America presented Sally with its highest honor, the LDA Award, in recognition and appreciation of outstanding leadership in the field of learning disabilities. On June 26 Sally left for Yvoire, spending four days in Lucerne, three in Yvoire, four more in Lucerne, three more in Yvoire, three days in Venice, including Booz's sixty-eighth birthday on July 5, then back to Paris and back to Dulles Airport on July 10.

Different is Not Bad, Different is the World: A Book About Disabilities, which Ben illustrated, was published in 1994 by Sopris West of Longmont, Colorado. It was widely used in elementary school classrooms and stands up today as a primer on tolerance and open-mindedness—and perhaps as Sally's

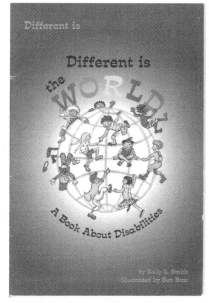

most concise, eloquent, and persuasive statement of her philosophy of education and the world.

The dedication, "For Randy, my lawyer, my friend, my firstborn son with love," is high praise. The words and scenarios in these thirty-six pages come directly from Sally's heart, echoing the concerns about children she expressed as far back as *A Child's Guide to a Parent's Mind*. An introduction sets out the purpose of the book: "To help young children (grades 2–6) realize that being different is O.K.; in fact, it makes people more interesting and the world a better place. This book is intended to help children with disabilities feel better about themselves. Plus, children without disabilities will see that people who are different have different ways of accomplishing everyday tasks, but people can do almost anything in their own way. The message is: Respect and prize diversity!" A note headed "For Teachers, Parents, and Other Adults" concludes, "You will need to read this book to the children several times and help them to look at all the pictures very carefully." On the next spread, a grid of thirty squares is headed with the instruction "Color your own quilt of CAN Dos and CAN'T Dos. The bottom of the page reads "Each DIFFERENT. Each of VALUE." The illustrations start with comparing the cultures of different countries around the world—their holidays, homes, climates, methods of transport, clothes, faces, bodies—always echoing "VERY DIFFERENT. ALL GOOD. Each of VALUE." This segues on page 12 to "Sometimes differences in our bodies mean that we must DO THINGS DIFFERENTLY." Ben's drawings depict children who are blind, deaf, and in a wheelchair, which leads to children with learning disabilities, notably a thematic spread on pages 18 and 19. "Remember: Different is NOT BAD. Different is NOT LAZY . . . NOT WEIRD. NOT

DUMB. Different is NOT STUPID . . . NOT UGLY . . . NOT DORKY. Difference is NOT NERDY. Different can be a NUISANCE when you can't READ, can't concentrate, don't know up from down or RIGHT from LEFT, can't SPEAK CLEARLY, or can't understand NUMBERS." Page 20 shows how those "The NUISANCES can make you feel . . . depressed, angry, guilty, NO GOOD, like wanting to HIDE from shame, like PICKING on others, OR nuisances can make you feel MORE DETERMINED THAN EVER to succeed." The facing page shows a happy boy lying beneath a patchwork quilt: "DIFFERENT often makes you feel like a patchwork quilt of abilities and nuisances, of CAN DOs and CAN'T DOs. Everybody has a different-looking quilt. THEY ARE ALL GOOD." The next spread shows children with learning disabilities in school. The one after that shows great figures of history, from Thomas Edison, Auguste Rodin, Nelson Rockefeller, Leonardo da Vinci, and General George Patton, who are thought to have been learning disabled, along with Ludwig von Beethoven, who composed some of his great music while deaf, Franklin D. Roosevelt, who was physically disabled, and Helen Keller, who earned a master's degree and became a writer while deaf and blind. The final page reads "Different is NOT BAD. In fact, different is GOOD, to be PRIZED, DIFFFERENT is the WORLD. How boring it would be if we were all the same!"

From June 26 through July 10, 1994, in France and Italy, Sally celebrated Ben's sixty-ninth birthday and revised *No Easy Answers: The Learning Disabled Child at Home and*

School, which came out as revised edition in January 1995 and a Bantam Paperback in March.

In the fall of 1994, Robert Rauschenberg began a tradition of sponsoring the Arts and Disabilities Workshop at the Lab School for thirty art teachers from all over the United States. Picked from hundreds of applicants, the teachers would come to Washington for a reception on a Thursday evening, then an early breakfast meeting at the Lab School for a workshop led by Sally on the characteristics of children with LD, ADHD, and language impairments. "We discuss how specific art forms can help students who have particular learning problems, and we do some role-playing activities." Rauschenberg would arrive at lunchtime to meet with all the winners. The Lab School students would then put on a multimedia presentation, Rauschenberg style, after which Rauschenberg would discuss his work, techniques, and methods. As Sally recounted, "When an artist asked Rauschenberg, 'What is the most important thing an art teacher can do for a student?' he quickly responded that it is vital to foster curiosity." The evening was capped with a dinner reception at the National Gallery of Art, where Rauschenberg handed each winner a hand-painted certificate he had created specifically for the day, as well as a present of $500 to $1,000 worth of art supplies for each teacher's school.

In 2003, the tenth year of the awards, Rauschenberg was ill and unable to attend. In her remarks to the thirty winners and other attendees, Sally gave a passionate summation of learning disabilities and the arts' importance in addressing them. "We have discussed today how confusing it is to teach children of average to above-average intelligence who look typical but don't learn typically. They have a disorder of the central nervous system that short-circuits information coming in to the switchboard of the brain, often scrambles information, and interferes with the way it comes out. This impairs the orderly acquisition of knowledge and contributes to the devastating failure at school of intelligent, often gifted students.

"Parents don't cause learning disabilities. Teachers don't cause learning disabilities. They can make the problem better or worse, but the problems are intrinsic to each individual. It's often called the 'hidden handicap.' Children and adults who are trying hearts out are frequently called lazy and told they are not trying hard enough. Often they are called stupid. Many of them are not comfortable in the world of words. They are visual thinkers. They see shapes, forms, contours, colors, textures, movement. When they see a chameleon, a lizard that changes color, they don't say to themselves, 'That is a chameleon,' as many of us do. They study the shapes, forms, contours, colors, textures, movement, and want to touch it, feel it, play with it. As our artists here know, most children with learning disabilities have to learn through the visual, concrete teaching, through touching and doing. When imparting knowledge, we need to paint pictures in their minds through involving them thoroughly in in experiences, hands-on-project learning and active learning. We see astonishing successes when we honor their different styles of learning.

"Art teachers, for years you have provided the refuge for the different, solace for the wounded, nonjudgmental listening for the troubled. You provide a training ground for the talented artists but also a comfort zone for the students who feel alienated from schooling. You tend to accent the positive, build on strengths, value uniqueness. As writer Marcel Proust remarked, 'The real act of discovery is not in discovering new lands, but seeing with new eyes.'

"The Lab Schools of Washington and Baltimore believe, as you do, in the power of the arts, particularly with the children who have special needs. The arts demand involvement. They counteract passivity. The arts ignite the whole learning process. The arts help organize knowledge. Our experience is that the arts hold children's attention and deal constantly with sequence and order—areas that cause the learning disabled so much trouble. The arts provide connections, linkages, and often clarify relationships.

"You art teachers know that all the art forms help our students to build large storehouses of information. The arts are scholarly pursuits. When a student experiences an art form, usually it leads him or her into legends, myths, great literature, poetry, history, geography, anthropology, psychology—a whole host of academic subjects. Paintings from the Lascaux caves, Indian rain dances, jazz music introduce us to the history and spirit of the times. Shakespeare tutors us on the ways of human beings. The arts must be treated as rigorous academic subjects because they require reflection, high-level thinking, critical thinking, and intense problem solving. . . . Children who feel bad about themselves can earn approval, applause, accolades through what they do in the arts.

"Art teachers, we honor you today. We celebrate your giving. Too often you are the hidden treasures in our schools. . . . Robert Rauschenberg said in this room a few years ago, 'The possibility always exists to nourish an important new genius in learning disabled children, if their spirit is not broken and creative dreams are allowed to develop."

In June 1995, Sally won the American University Faculty Award for Outstanding Scholarship, Research, and Other Professional Contributions. At the time she was shopping for an assistant professor. Sarah Irvine Belson—then Sarah Irvine—had just received her PhD from Arizona State University and was entertaining offers from Oregon, among other universities. She flew in to Washington for two days of interviews and was taken by surprise. "I saw myself as a traditional academic," said Belson. "Sally offered this opportunity to do research and teach and be at the Lab School two days a week. My background in special education was in using technology and game design, so the Lab School provided an opportunity to test out these approaches with the kids." In July of 1995 she settled in at AU. "We wired the Lab School for internet. That was a big deal at the time."

Belson had been born at Fort Sill, an Army base in Oklahoma. Her father, Randy Irvine, had been in the Army during the Vietnam years and returned to his native Arizona to work in graphic design. As a teenager in Arizona, Belson remembers hearing Sally speak. "My brother Zack had significant learning disabilities. My mom went to a lecture and my sister Bonnie and I were dragged along." Afterward, as Belson and her sister looked on, Deirdre Irvine talked with Sally about her struggles in getting Zack the attention he needed. "At one point my mom was sitting outside the door of a principal literally for 24 hours. She did not go home. She said, "This is a mess that needs to be fixed."

As an undergraduate student at Northern Arizona University, Belson had started off as a computer science major but grew bored with the programming. "I felt like I wanted to make a difference," she said. At AU and at the Lab School she had that opportunity.

"Working with children every day is awesome. Supervising the interns is rewarding, as you see them discover that there's this face in front of you that wants to learn. I got addicted to being happy."

One day she started talking with Stephen Belson, who was the assistant to the head of the high school, Dick Meltzer. Belson had gone to Lab from fourth through eighth grades, then on to Gonzaga High School and West Virginia Wesleyan. Both Dick and Diana Meltzer had tutored him through high school, and after college Dick gave him a job in Lab's high school. On his way to his career at the World Bank, Steve Belson was helping out at the desk on the second floor. He had a real talent for breaking his computer, and eventually invited Sarah to a football game. To this day they don't agree on who won—the Arizona Cardinals or the Washington Redskins. They were married in 1997. In 2002 Sarah was promoted to associate professor and wrote a textbook on technological innovation in special education. In 2003, she was named dean of the AU School of Education, Teaching, and Health, a position she held until 2015, when she became executive director for AU's Institute for Innovation in Education. They have two children, Deirdre and Griffin, and Griffin is tutored by none other than Dick Meltzer.

In 1995, around the time that Sarah Irvine was joining the AU School of Education, the US Department of Education identified the Lab School as a National Diffusion Network (NDN) Model Education Program. "A panel of experts called a Program Effectiveness Panel (PEP) validated the Integrated Arts and Academic Club Method of the Lab School and acknowledged its effectiveness," wrote Sally. "The PEP encouraged the Lab School of Washington to disseminate the Integrated Arts and Academic Club Method and materials to public and private schools around the country."

This led to Lab partnering with Martin Luther King Jr. Elementary School in Anacostia, an inner-city school, to implement the Integrated Arts and Academic Club Method. "The relationship we formed with the administration of the school blossomed, and by 1997 we had a second partnership with the Brent School on Capitol Hill. In 1999, both schools asked the Lab School to do staff development for them—ten workshops on their campus and a number on our own." By 1999, Stuart Hobson Middle School from Capitol Hill Northeast joined the partnership.

It was around her seventieth birthday, on May 7, 1999, that Sally spent the weekend at Birmingham Southern College bonding with her fellow Woman of Distinction honorees, including Wendy Lee Gramm and Olivia de Havilland. To truly mark her seventieth, though, Sally decided to gather her fondest friends for a special adventure.

Nineteen — A 70th Birthday Aegean Cruise and *The Power of the Arts*

On her second day aboard the 108-foot *Aegean Princess*, Kitty Klaidman was suffering from a bad cold, jet lag, and seasickness. She made her way on deck as the *Princess* was anchoring off the Greek island of Kea. She mentioned to her host that she was a little under the weather. "Get over it and jump into the water," said Sally.

"After that I felt great," said Klaidman, in her gentle Slovakian accent. "For Sally it was always 'Get over it.' That was her mantra throughout her life. There was nothing that could stand in her way if she needed to do something important."

Klaidman and her husband, Stephen, were among the group of twenty-six that Sally had invited to celebrate her seventieth birthday with a two-week cruise to nine Greek islands in June and July of 1999. In some cases, Sally had to encourage her friends. The Klaidmans, who were then living in California for a year, had just returned from Europe. Kitty wondered if an Aegean cruise might be too much for her. "Get your behind here immediately," said Sally.

The celebrants included Randy, Nick, and Gary, several of their friends, and Sally's closest friends, including **Ben Booz; Stocky Clark and his wife, Judy; Garry Clifford; Tidi King; longtime Lab School board member and chair Pauline Schneider; and the Klaidmans. As a child Kitty Klaidman, a painter,** had hidden with her family in a Slovakian rural attic during the war years. Some of her most memorable paintings depicted the dark hiding places where she was confined with her parents and brother. "Somehow, it seems to take about forty years for survivors to come to terms with their personal Holocaust experiences," she said during one of her shows. "I have been working out my feelings about this part of my past through images on canvas and

paper." Stephen Klaidman had started out as a copy boy with *The New York Times*,
become an editor and reporter with the *Times* and *The Washington Post*, written books,
and become a senior research associate at the Institute for Health Policy Analysis at
Georgetown.

"Most of that trip was spent talking about life as the sun set," said Gary, "or
swimming off the boat in the sea, or going to different places to shop and wandering
around looking at all the wonderful sites of history." At Santorini, they had ridden the
donkeys up the steep paths to the city above and lavished in the beauty of the white
buildings and their cobalt blue roofs. In a museum they had seen murals excavated
from before the eruption, perhaps from an ancient bordello, depicting playful monkeys
swinging on vines and an alluring Minoan woman, all rendered in a strikingly modern
style. Kitty was amazed by the excavations on Santorini, showing the world that ended
with one of the largest eruptions in recorded history around 1650 BC.

Stocky was taken with the reconstruction of history, how the volcano and tsunamis
that hit Crete wiped out the Minoan civilization, but not immediately. "Several of us
thought up the notion that the tsunami born from the eruption of Santorini completely
wiped out many of the crops, livestock, houses, boats, and people on the island of
Crete. The devastation was so great that the remaining people gradually died out and
simply couldn't sustain themselves without their boats for trade. They were easy prey to
invaders, which ushered in the Mycenaean civilization from Greece. There is actually
some theory to support this theory. We presented this to our merry band of travelers on
the boat after dinner." Throughout the voyage from Flisvos to Kea, Mykonos, Delos,
Paros, Naxos, Santorini, Sifnos, Andros, and back to Flizvos, Ben Booz drew sketches

with colored pencils, which she made into a book and presented to Sally afterward. "We ate too much and had the time of our lives," said my sister-in-law Judy Clark.

Later in July, Sally and Ben sojourned to Elounda Beach on the island of Crete to work on what became Sally's ultimate summary of her methodology and its practical applications, *The Power of the Arts: Creative Strategies for Teaching Exceptional Learners*. "After that she never went anywhere but Crete," said Booz. "We had a cottage with our own swimming pool. She would wear a T-shirt and her underwear and sit in the pool, and we would work through the book."

Brookes Publishing Company released *The Power of the Arts* in 2001. In her acknowledgments, Sally wrote, "First and foremost, I thank one of my dearest friends in the world, Elizabeth Benson Booz, for all your wise counsel and enthusiasm regarding this book. . . . It was you who made me focus and get the job well started, and it was you who took out your editing pen and gave of your professional talent. I am

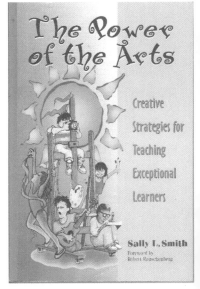

deeply appreciative that you took time out of your busy schedule to read, critique, and improve this book. Thank you."

Sally dedicated the book "To Nicholas Lee Smith/who has the artist's eye and/who sparked so much of my creativity. Thank you my friend and my son."

She thanked many others involved with the Lab School and AU, as well as Robert Rauschenberg, who contributed a foreword that says, in part, "The hope of a fuller world lies in the recognition of many more ways to teach and learn, rather than exposure to predigested memory that insists on the flat projection of repetition.

"Like the arts, play helps children understand relationships: they think, compare, analyze, generalize, and solve problems. During play, a child makes things happen. Often, he is surprised by the results and filled with the wonder and awe of it all. According to Plato, 'You can discover more about a person in an hour of play than in a year of conversation.'"

The preface includes a pithy summary of the Integrated Arts and Academic Club Method: "It is a format that enables each child to be an intimate and active part of the history of any topic being studied. I chose the word *club* to give a sense of belonging, ownership, membership, and privilege to children who tend to fall 'out' and want to be 'in.' I developed passwords, routines, and rituals to help students pay attention and focus, to make each student feel important, and to help the group be tightly knit. I called it *academic* because, done right, highly academic material is presented through visual, hands-on means. I chose the arts because every art demands active participation, concentration, and discipline. I also chose the arts to capture the ingenuity and imaginations of children who tend to be written off."

The preface continues with a chronology of the Lab School and its methods. The chapters stand as an irresistible summary of Sally's insights, philosophies, and commitment to reaching every child. Chapter one, "The Power of the Arts with Exceptional Learners," is a manifesto and an argument, with support from scholars. "All art has symbolic meaning: It can be understood without words. Therefore, the arts can and should play a central role in academic learning. All the art forms can help ignite the entire learning process. They are motivators. They demand student involvement. Every child can succeed in at least one art form, whether it is photography, modern dance, puppetry, sculpture, music, or computer art." Chapter five discusses the Lab School "educative process" and chapter Six describes its curriculum. Most powerful of all, chapters seven and eight present the words of Lab School visual and performing arts teachers. From Dieter Zander on woodworking to Sean Rozsics on secondary music, these interviews offer insight into the creative process along with practicalities of the classroom. In answer to the question *What is the classroom routine?,* for example, Zander writes: "Students form a line and are asked to be silent for a few seconds before entering or leaving the workshop. This enables the students to disengage themselves from any previous activity and helps them to 'change gears.' At the same time, it permits the instructor to look for signs of possible difficulties with focusing and listening to directions."

Kelly McVearry, the plaster art and painting teacher, is among those quoted. "Art offers inherent problem-solving activities in an exciting form and makes a bridge to other academic areas," she writes in *The Power of the Arts*. "Projects expose children to different modes of organization, as each project requires a different organizational strategy. Art helps to cultivate longer attention spans. Engagement in an intriguing project keeps a student focused. Art instills a respect for quality. The process of creation, of being fully engaged, is more important than any specific product, but the visible accomplishment can also be a source of pride."

Twenty — The Baltimore Lab School and *Live It, Learn It*

As national interest in the Lab School spread, Sally entertained the idea of franchising. She had established the framework in her works, articles, and books on the Academic Club Methodology. But an unavoidable conundrum of selling school franchises was that, as Sally knew better than anyone, startup schools have no money to spend on franchise fees, and even successful schools never have a spare dime after paying for buildings, teachers, school supplies, and operating expenses. Defining the reality of nonprofits, schools never make a profit.

Beyond the annoying impediment of money, a built-in problem with establishing Lab Schools in faraway places was that, when it came to actually operating a vibrant, innovative Lab School, the essential product was Sally herself. She possessed that inexplicable ability to pick out creative adventurers who could succeed as Lab teachers. She had the educational framework at AU to provide the formal training the teachers needed. And in the trenches she knew how to direct and motivate them. Moreover, a built-in contradiction to the idea of creating an exportable book of Lab School lesson plans was that Sally pointedly *avoided* imposing set lessons plans on the artistic adventurers she hired. Rather, she gave them the freedom to invent those lessons themselves.

Amy Aden Dunn, who taught at Lab starting in 1998, remembered Sally saying, "Amy, come in here for a minute. I want you to teach a club this summer. The theme is mysteries. What are your strengths? What are your passions?" Dunn had never read mysteries, but she suggested Agatha Christie as a unifying idea. "Fine," said Sally. "Write me up a description and bring it to me tomorrow." Dunn wrote up her ideas and created the Library Mystery Club. "Now," she said, "I have a lifelong appreciation of Agatha Christie. Sally could make you feel like you could do anything, but it was pressure to do a club for Sally, because she was watching you. She gave you all the time and space and energy and enthusiasm that you needed to succeed. We did great and creative and fun things, and the kids were always engaged. It was so hard to do the same thing in other schools I taught in since then, without Sally's enthusiasm and energy and support."

All this made nearby Baltimore the best option for expanding the Lab School franchise. Being only a forty-five-minute drive away, the Baltimore campus could be established as "the first authentic duplicate of our Washington program,"* administered by Lab School people in the Lab School way. The Lab School board voted in April 2000 to go ahead with a Baltimore school. In a remarkably short time, on September 13, the Lab School of Washington Baltimore Campus opened in the Port Discovery Children's Museum, starting out with nineteen children ages to eleven. "It was a typically Sally kind of move to open that quickly," said Diana Meltzer, now associate head of school at Lab but then Sally's special assistant. Typically, every other week Sally and Meltzer would drive up to spend the day in Baltimore, for which her title was founder and director, as it was in DC. The school prospered, outgrowing its first location in two years, and its second location two years later, ending up at Goucher Hall. "They kept to the mission," said Meltzer. "They used the club methodology and kept the curriculum art focused."

With this expansion in place, Sally continued to strategize ways to spread the Lab School message. *The Power of the Arts* had gone a long way to laying out the Academic Club methodology. Its subtitle, *Creative Strategies for Exceptional Learners,* was general enough to appeal to anyone seeking new pedagogical ideas. But Sally

knew she could refine her messages in a more focused, persuasive way. So it was that,

when Sally and Ben Booz next retreated to Bungalow 18 at Elounda Beach in Crete, the

opus that Sally presented was to become *Live It, Learn It: The Academic Club*

Methodology for Students with Learning Disabilities and ADHD. It was a specific,

focused, and refined restatement of the club methodology. Illustrating the idea that

teachers can always learn best from other teachers, the book includes conversations

with club leaders Amanda Wolfe, Carrie Hillegas, Gina Van Weddingen, Ursula

Marcum, Donald A. Vicks, Noel Bicknell, Kelly McVearry, Graham Houghton, Sarah

Lowenberg, and Betsy Babbington.

Live It, Learn It, in some ways Sally's *Abbey Road*, bears this dedication: "To Gary

Smith, who forced me to think differently / *Thank You My Friend* / to Nick Smith, who

tutored me with his artistic eye / *Thank You My Friend* / To Randy Smith, who

contributed brilliant ideas for birthday parties and Academic Clubs / *Thank You My*

Friend / To all of The Lab School of Washington and Baltimore Lab Club Leaders, who

bring magic, excitement, and profound knowledge into schooling /*Thank You."*

Starting with chapter 1, "What Is the Academic Club Methodology?" *Live It, Learn It* lays out Sally's playbook. Chapter 2 is "Why the Academic Club Methodology Works for Students with Learning Diabilities and ADHD." Chapter 3 is "How to Keep Students

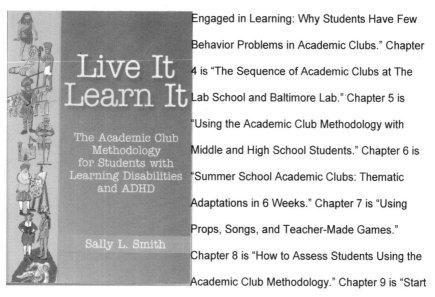

Engaged in Learning: Why Students Have Few Behavior Problems in Academic Clubs." Chapter 4 is "The Sequence of Academic Clubs at The Lab School and Baltimore Lab." Chapter 5 is "Using the Academic Club Methodology with Middle and High School Students." Chapter 6 is "Summer School Academic Clubs: Thematic Adaptations in 6 Weeks." Chapter 7 is "Using Props, Songs, and Teacher-Made Games." Chapter 8 is "How to Assess Students Using the Academic Club Methodology." Chapter 9 is "Start Your Own Academic Club: Here's How!" Chapter 10 is "Conversations with Club Leaders" and chapter 11 is "Academic Clubs Can Transform Schools: Dare We Do it?" Paul H. Brookes Publishing Co., of Baltimore, London, and Sydney released *Live It, Learn It* in 2005.

At that time, the Lab School had about 310 students in grades K–12. More than 80 percent of the students were funded by the District of Columbia, Maryland, and Virginia based on PL 94-142, requiring free and appropriate education for disabled children. Also around that time, a group in Philadelphia was preparing to incorporate the next line extension of the Lab School model, in Manayunk, Pennsylvania.

Patricia Morgan Roberts and Nancy Blair had been working for the Institute for

Educational Excellence and Entrepreneurship (3E Institute) at West Chester University.

"It was time to nominate and entrepreneurial educator to receive the President's

Educator 500 Award in the spring of 2004," they wrote in their 2010 history of the

Academy In Manayunk.* "We could think of no better nominee than Sally L. Smith.

"There was no missing her in the crowded 30th Street Station as she emerged from

the Amtrak tracks below. Sally was covered in colorful scarves and had a large set of

dice dangling from her ears. It was hard to comprehend this vision, but one thing was

clear . . . this was going to be fun!

"[Over time] we realized her colorful persona was truly by design. It was a signal to

the students that this school is different from all the rest, and that teachers, and, yes,

the head of school, were there to engage every child in the process of active learning

through doing. Well, we have never painted our nails with polka dots, but we do think of

Sally as we reach out to children at the Academy in Manayunk every day and make

those *fun* connections."

"Sally's acceptance speech at the Union League in 2004 before an audience of 400

educators and business leaders brought awareness about her program and a unique

understanding of the challenge of children with learning disabilities in a real and

personal way." Morgan and Blair took professional development courses at Lab and

were inspired by the faculty. They raised $750,000 in the first six months.

At the November 2005 gala Sally announced that a Lab School would be launched

in Philadelphia. It did so in September 2006 as the Academy in Manayunk (AIM) in

Conshohocken, Pennsylvania, with Roberts as executive director and Blair as associate director and director of admissions. At AIM, the partners included the Wilson Reading Method Partner School and partnerships with local universities, including an online master's program in special education at St. Joseph's University that included twelve graduate credits for a clinical residency at AIM. To supervise the master's students, Sally dispatched Jackie Ford Gilbally, who had gone through the AU program and taught at the Lab School of Washington.

After the Lab School, Gilbally's first job was at a traditional school. In "Bringing Sally Smith's Vision to Manayunk," she writes of applying *Live It, Learn It* to a social studies class: "I employed weekly passwords to facilitate vocabulary development, and our opening and closing ritual reviewed the big ideas of the age of exploration. . . . Our activities varied from fur trading to dramatic representations of explorer's conquests. By the end of the year, my students were well versed in the motivation, discoveries, and ramifications of the age of exploration. But more importantly, the members of my class discovered something invaluable about themselves and their classmates. The desire to learn and the value of their own abilities were re-ignited. . . . Quickly, I began to find the success that Sally had found. My students were begging (yes, begging!) to have more time to learn about their explorers. I was delighted to see once-reluctant readers going home and reading printed pages all about their characters so they could challenge me on trivia they had independently learned." Sally then called Ford about a new school in Philadelphia following the Lab School Methodology, and she became a part of the launch, teaching her own club class and mentoring the master's students from local university programs when they came for their internships.

"And so it goes," wrote Roberts and Blair. "It is these university partnerships that hold the key for developing future best practices and the professionals who will implement them."

Twenty-One — A Wedding, a Birth, and a Goodbye

As you enter the lobby of the Hotel Monteleone in New Orleans, the ornate continental grandeur fills the senses. As Karen and I checked in on a January afternoon, Sally was there to greet us. The next evening her son Randy was to marry Diane Sinclair. The magic of New Orleans is that the spirit of the French Quarter never takes long to inhabit visitors from straight-laced suburbs and button-down businesses and inspire us all to relax. On the Monteleone's top floor, Randy and Diane were toasted and roasted in a rowdy rehearsal dinner. Sally noted that New Orleans is a perfect adopted home for Randy, because he has always been a bon vivant. True enough. Stocky gave an earnest toast about his longstanding, cherished role as a big brother. Randy's Yale Law School friends, former Whiffenpoofs, sang a bawdy a cappella medley. Amid the adult-oriented tone of the discourse, I put my G-rated childhood memory of watching Super Bowl III on TV—about Randy identifying with Broadway Joe Namath and joy at the flamboyant new era of pro football he was ushering in—in my pocket.

The next morning Diane's mother, Charlene Sinclair, gave the out-of-town guests her tour of Saint Louis Cemetery No. 1, including the grave of Plessy (he of *Plessy vs. Ferguson*) and a detailed description of the above-ground disposal of bodies in a city with a water table too close to the surface for in-ground burial. Under the deep blue January sky, Sally, with boas and scarves framing her beaming smile, led us from the gate of the graveyard into hansom carriages. To melodious clip-clops, she rode in the lead carriage, hands gesturing along with the top-hatted drivers pointed out the "rising sun" grillwork of an iconic bordello, Truman Capote's elementary school, and a pirate-era Bourbon Street bar. In front of the pink walls of Brennan's, we disembarked and headed up the red-carpeted stairs for a luncheon punctuated by a chef relating the history of the restaurant's gift to the culinary world, Bananas Foster, while he created it before our eyes. The next evening Randy and Diane were married amid the deep mahogany woodwork of the Round Table Club, an Uptown District mansion. In black tie amid the iconic hallways, Randy's school friends looked like cast members of *The Great Gatsby*. Michael Dolan, hearing Stocky recall his late-sixties hobby of making leather belts and wallets, recalled that he had bought a Stocky-made belt from me in eighth grade. "It was the best belt I ever had," said Mike, with new respect for Stocky. "I don't know what ever happened to it. I'd like to get another one just like it."

If Sally Smith was ecstatic at the wedding, she was over the moon eleven months later, on December 10, 2004, when Diane and Randy were blessed by the arrival of Maggie Smith. Ben Booz painted a tribute card for the occasion.

Like her grandmother, Maggie has blond locks and angelic features. From Maggie's earliest days, she has embodied Sally's spirit, energy, and creativity. When friends comment on it, Maggie accepts the compliments gracefully. She is pleased to be compared to her grandmother. In fifth grade, she played Tiny Tim in *A Christmas Carol*. In fourth grade, playing Michael in *Mary Poppins*, she sang and moved like a dancer. Watching a performance, Randy was late to a hearing. When the judge was told that Randy was attending his daughter's play,

Maggie Smith

he happily moved the hearing to a later time slot. The judge had met Maggie many times and liked her. Such is life in New Orleans.

Around 2005, Sally was slowing down. Over the course of the next two years, her condition worsened. She had trouble walking, and by the fall of 2007, she was in a wheelchair and unable to climb the stairs at home. "They put in electric chairs and ramps," remembered Diane, but still no one knew what was wrong. Near the end of October, she went to see a rheumatologist at Johns Hopkins Hospital, who thought she might have amyloidosis, a rare disease that causes the abnormal protein amyloid, usually produced in the bone marrow, to build up in the organs and tissues. Although there is treatment, there is no cure. She was admitted to Johns Hopkins to have tests and get a definitive diagnosis. "This was right before the gala that year," said Diane. "They did tests and determined that she had multiple myeloma. Her type of multiple myeloma produced amyloid as a by-product. Sally found out all this Thanksgiving week. She went home the Wednesday before Thanksgiving thinking she would start treatment for her cancer, but before any treatment started she threw a pulmonary embolism. She went back to Johns Hopkins. Gary spent the next weeks virtually living in that hospital room. As she began to slip away, Gary called Randy and Nick. "Pounding, pounding, pounding," Randy wrote later. "Her clenched fist onto my hand. Over and over again, for what seemed liked forever. Time standing still, at her deathbed. Surrounded by family and very close friends, unable to speak, unable to feel the pain, but knowing it was close to the end. I take her hand to squeeze it lovingly and say goodbye to my mom. She, not content with that, starts pounding my open hand with her fist and intently staring into my eyes. For years, I have been haunted by that pounding. What was she trying to say? And why to me?" Sally died on December 1, 2007.

American University hosted a celebration of Sally's life in its Bender Arena. Sarah Belson helped make the arrangements. "At first the folks at AU said, 'We can't have a funeral in the arena. It's way too big.' Well, Bender Arena was full. She was simply adored on campus."

I arrived with my older brother F. T. and sat with old friends, including Jerry Howe, Fred Vinson, Mike Dolan, and Evan Bayh.

AU President Neil Kerwin led off with gracious remarks on how special a presence Sally was on the campus a how much she had contributed to the university:

"Professor Sally L. Smith's many successes underscore the idea that teacher training in universities and in 'real-world' schools are strengthened greatly through interaction with one another and through their shared commitment to improve the lives of learners of all ages. Without Smith, the nationally recognized Lab School of Washington would not exist; without her, AU's master's degree in special education focusing on learning disabilities would be only a desired but not realized goal of the university. Under Smith's direction, however, both the Lab School and AU have created a model of innovation and educational achievement that is respected, admired, and even envied by other institutions.

"The higher education community recognizes her groundbreaking curriculum design, which integrates theory and practice not in separate courses or during separate semesters but every day in every activity. Students working with Smith reap the benefit of her experience in designing programs of study. All collaborate with her to design their own programs, which build on what they already know and challenge them to stretch in new directions. Few master's programs like this exist, where students are guided so closely both in their academic work and in their practice."

Ben Booz talked about her role as Sally's editor, as she referred to herself. She told of Sally's creative genius and their creative process in conceiving and developing Sally's books. "I spoke extemporaneously," said Ben later. "I didn't realize how large a gathering it was going to be. And how do you summarize a lifelong friendship and a dynamic person like Sally who accomplished so much?"

Kim Palombo, Sally's graduate assistant at the time, read from Sally's collection of sayings that she saved, starting with the proverb "In the land of the blind, the one-eyed man is king" and Gandhi's "Live as if you were to die tomorrow. Learn as if you were to live forever."

Lawyer Pauline Schneider, a longtime Lab School board member and chair from 1987 to 1992, remembered how close a call it had been in the tough times to keep the Lab School going and moving from one stage to the next.

Shaun Miskell, then and now the head of performing arts at the Lab School, added some more of Sally's favorite quotes, such as Erik Eriksson's "Caring is the virtue that is born from the struggle to take responsibility" and Paul Gaugin's "Color is the language of the listening eye."

Stocky Clark eulogized Sally as the mentor of his life and that of many people in the arena. As a younger brother, I was proud of Stocky's eulogy and especially proud for my old friends to hear it. Here are few selections:

Like you, I am not ready to let Sally go. I imagine her pulling up to her house in her bright red Mercedes and throwing open the front door to her house. As usual, her fingernails are painted like the top of a ladybug; her scarves are some bright combination of colors, mostly purple, her smile is broad. Here are some things to keep in mind when dwelling in the Land of Sally:

1. **You are special and don't forget it.** The smaller you are the more important you are. One of Sally's favorite quotes is by Georgia O'Keefe: "Nobody sees a flower—really. It is so small—we haven't time—and to see takes time like to have a friend takes time."

2. **Celebrate life. Laugh, play, be creative . . . and don't forget to use bright colors.** They make everything more exciting. Another of her favorite quotes is: "If you do what you like, you never really work. Your work is your play" (Hans Selye).

3. **Bring out the best in people.** If you give a little bit of yourself, you get a lot more back.

4. **When you get knocked down, get over it.** Start making lemonade.

5. **Don't believe the National Weather Service when they tell you in early December that the hurricane season is over.** Sally made her own weather and made you believe you could do the same.

Part of creating worlds was her challenge of rules. "I never saw a rule I didn't like— to break!" would be a quote I would ascribe to Sally. This is the woman who signed her will with a purple pen, whose dining room is orange, whose bathroom is lime green, and whose house is a gallery of creative art. Her creativity gave her the amazing agility to handle almost any situation.

One of the quotes you have heard, by William Arthur Ward, is "The mediocre teacher tells. The good teacher explains. The superior teacher demonstrates. The great teacher inspires." Sally was a GREAT teacher, as all the great teachers from Lab School must feel. Sally has always been a ball of fire. The flames from her fire have instilled passion, innovation, and creativity in everything she has touched. How many of us have lit our torch from the fire of Sally Smith?

One of Sally's favorite quotes has been up on my office wall for as long as I can remember. "Are you in earnest? Seize this very minute. Whatever you can do or dream, begin it. Boldness has genius, power and magic in it" (Wolfgang Van Goethe).

So build your world as Sally would have each of us all do: Believe in yourself and others. Imagine the possibilities. Act on your passions. Strive for more than you think you can achieve. Laugh whenever you get the chance. Wear color, especially purple. Celebrate life often. Be strong. And…. do good.

After the memorial service, AU hosted a reception in its art department. Afterward, many friends adjourned to 3216 Cleveland Avenue for an after-party. Everyone chatted, visited, and gave solace to Randy, Nick, and Gary. Then the spirit of Sally—which, as Stocky said, inhabited every corner of the house—took over. It did not seem fitting to leave our friends alone in their old home on such an evening. Fittingly, the arts provided an answer. Our classmate Fred Vinson darted off to his home and returned with guitars and harmonicas. With Mike Dolan blowing on his blues harp and Fred on guitar, we played blues, the Allman Brothers' "Stormy Monday," the Beatles, the Stones, "The House of the Rising Sun," and on and on. At 1:45 a.m., it was time to leave. "That was the best night," Randy has said more than once. "It was totally impromptu, and it was magic."

Twenty-Two — Gary's Journey

On a gray November day on upper Connecticut Avenue, I walk into the bustling lobby of an apartment building in which Gary Smith and his cats share a pleasant apartment. He is waiting for me in an armchair. We walk down the block to the Parthenon restaurant, sit down, order, and begin talking.

Gary Smith at the Parthenon Restaurant.

I have so many memories of the young Gary—playing Risk! or wrestling in the living room; setting up Wiffle ball diamonds in the Smiths' back yard; bartending at Sally's parties, when Gary loved to flirt with the ladies. All these clear pictures make it especially interesting to sit down with the fifty-something Gary and hear his insights into his own life.

Gary has settled into an appealing, generous figure, reminiscent of his second cousin Marcie, who presided over the Albion Hotel in Miami Beach and the barbershop across the street much as Gary holds court in his apartment building lobby and the Parthenon. After Sally's death, Gary lived in an apartment in McLean Gardens off Wisconsin Avenue for a few years. After nearly dying from leukemia in 2009, he is in remission.

For many years he worked at a playground near the Smiths' home. These days, he teaches computer skills to youngsters and works as a research assistant with Sarah Belson, now the executive director of AU's Institute for Innovation in Education.

He has been writing his own reflections on his life. "Sometimes when I'm bummed out and I'm missing her, writing helps," he says. "At one point, when I was really sick and almost died, the day that I woke up, the *reason* I woke up was that I smelled her perfume. This was two years after she died. Even now, I know she's here."

Gary talks every night with Nick, who lives in a small town in Maryland. "Sometimes he says I preach at him," says Gary. "Nick sells stuff on eBay, looking the stuff up, where the book came from. He's just like me, to be honest. He doesn't like being told what to do by a boss. He'd rather do it his own way."

Gary reflects on the arrival of a daughter in Randy's life: "Maggie's the one that's mellowed him. She's got him wrapped around her little finger."

We have been to a Lab School gala the Friday before. To Gary, it wasn't the same without his mother. It was just another fundraiser, lacking Sally's special élan, focused too much just on the money. "She often said, 'The one thing I never wanted to do was beg people for money, and what do I do every day? Beg people for money.'"

Gary reflects on the oft-recounted fact that the story of his young years is the story of the Lab School. This has always made him a little self-conscious and proud at the same time. Even at Sally's memorial celebration, he felt an occasional twinge of embarrassment when the speakers—including Stocky Clark, who remains a friend and mentor—recounted anecdotes of Gary's early years. For his own part, Gary is bemused as he recounts the timeline of his schools and jobs, describing his younger self with remarkable distance. "I stayed an extra year at the Lab School, until I was thirteen, then went up to Landmark School, in Beverly, Massachusetts, a boarding school, pretty new at the time, for teenagers with learning disabilities. I stayed there one year and six months. I got into a little bit of trouble. I disturbed—quote, unquote—kids. Then I went to the Grove School in Madison, Connecticut. I had a temper. I threw soup on the director. I was an evil little rug rat. In the end I went to a residence house in Orlando, Florida. I lived there for almost two years. I was going on eighteen. That's when I really grew up. I was told by the director that I had to go out and get a job. I spent two summers working with autistic kids. I kept that job for six months, then I told my mother I wanted to come home. I got homesick."

When he returned to the house on Cleveland Avenue, Gary realized that his mother had a romantic life, which brought some surprises, along with other realities of adult life. "I started job hunting. I worked at a hospital for sick children in Southeast and quit after about a year. I walked up to John Eaton [Elementary School]. I had a volunteer job doing before- and after-school care. They hired someone else to help the teacher, and I was standing there and the kindergarten teacher asked, 'Would you like to work with me?' I helped the kindergarten teacher and got paid by the teacher. At the end of the year the parents were so happy. At some point in May they gave me Gary Smith Day. I got a plastic key to the school. They sang songs for me. Randy came and my mother came. She said, 'From now on I'm going to shut up and let you do what you want to do.'

"For nine years I would go over to the playground. The director of the rec center, she hired me the first summer to work with the little kids. Then she hired me full time as assistant director. I worked for a year and a half at another rec center.

"I had gone to culinary school and bartending school. One day I was sitting on the computer playing a game and it dawned on me, 'Why not?' I love computers. I went to computer school, and I've been teaching computer ever since. I've been working at the University of the District of Columbia on the weekends and in the summers teaching computer and computer science to kids from kindergarten through eighth or ninth grade.

"My way of teaching computer skills is I would write down questions on the board— *When did the first star appear? How would you build a farm on Mars?* I'd have the students look it up and write me a paper. It was good practice for learning about the way of learning information. I'd have them list each site they went on. I teach the elderly in my building and I do computer research at AU, working with Sarah [Belson]. Four or five doors down from where I work is my mother's old office. I work typing different books for Sarah. I do all the grunt work for her and for those in Learning Disabilities. What I like about working on the computer is that I use my mind more than my body.

"I still have bouts of anger. It's taken me a long time to calm down. But life's too short. I don't tolerate idiots very well. People who ask dumb questions. That's what I'm still working on, blowing up for no reason. I've gotten a lot better at it. I love working with kids, because I understand the kids, where they're coming from. I can take them aside and explain step by step."

Gary still looks back on that moment when he was thirteen and a half, when the tutor told Sally that he had jumped up three reading levels. "Holy shit!" said Sally. "You know how to read!" Gary says, "I've been making up for lost time ever since. I read twenty books this past summer. I read every day for three or four hours."

I note the word of salty language in Gary's life-changing moment, and Gary smiles. New Yorker that she was, Sally could in private moments deploy a lively lexicon from time to time. "My mom could cuss like a drunken sailor on shore leave," he says, deploying his own mischievous grin. On phone calls at home on some evenings, as Sally hashed out some work problems, Gary relates that she might tap her colorful vocabulary. After she hung up, she'd say to Gary, "You didn't hear that."

"One thing I always think about is not being able to talk with my mom," Gary says. "Even though I talk with her in my head. She was my sounding board. If I did something stupid and wondered, 'How do I get out of this?' She'd say, 'Admit what you did and go on from there.' My mom and I were wrapped up in each other's lives. We were more friends than mother and son."

Sally is buried in Oak Hill Cemetery down in Georgetown. "Randy found one of the board members who helped us get that," says Gary. "There was a view that looks down a hill, so she can keep an eye on everybody. It just fit with her. It's bittersweet when I go to the Lab School. They always expect me to say something. They don't get it that there are times when all I want to do is enjoy. The first year that she was gone, they wanted me over there all the time. Now I just show up. I was the cause of the Lab School but my mother was the one that did it, and then she did so much more. As I liked to say to her, 'I gave you a career.'"

Twenty-three — Measuring Sally's Impact

As Sally's chief protégé at AU, Sarah Belson has a unique perspective on her long-term contributions to the Lab School, the AU program, and the larger education world. "This woman had two jobs," said Belson. "She was running the school. She was not a slacker at AU. She always taught the Arts and Special Ed class and Introduction to Special Ed. Everybody loved that class—there were always thirty or forty people in it. Her classes were demanding. She really was a force on campus. She said what she wanted to say and she meant it. She asked a lot of her faculty: She expected everybody to put out a book every year."

The cooperative use of AU master's students as Lab School interns continues to the present day. Belson spends two days a week at Lab and works with the AU students who serve as interns in the elementary and intermediate programs. Not long ago one intern was working on a problem in the classroom, and Belson wondered if the challenge might be too much for her. "She said, 'No, it is my life's ambition to be at the Lab School. I want to figure this out.' When we look at what makes the AU program unique and special, it's the Lab School. It's always been the Lab School approach that no challenge is insurmountable," Belson said.

When it comes to Sally's broader impacts on the education community as a whole, Belson started with arts integration. "She had her finger on that well before it happened in elsewhere. The idea of teachers creating theater, doing improvisations as they teach, understanding that children always did role-playing. Sally was also way ahead in understanding why woodworking is important to kids."

Sally opened up important and ongoing discussions about neuropsychology. "She was really on to the fact that LD students need to have an opportunity to develop their cognitive skills," said Belson. "They need to understand spatial relations, their own processing speed. The student needs to be fully involved in the way they learn—not just in a hands-on way but in a body-on way. That's an essential component of the Lab School philosophy."

The spring/summer 2010 edition of *Learning Disabilities: A Multidisciplinary Journal* was a 118-page special issue dedicated to Sally L. Smith and the Lab School Methodology. As noted in chapter one, it was guest edited by Luanne Adams, the Lab School's longtime head of psychological services. In her editor's note, she wrote that Sally's books "tell us a lot about her methodology for making magic. . . . There is much to be told, however, that cannot be found in her books. Those who studied and worked with Sally know things about her methodology that Sally did not know—things they have learned from years of applying her methodology." The special issue collected seventeen articles, arranged in five sections: The Sally L. Smith Methodology, Art and Education, The Academic Club Methodology, The Related Services Integrated Model, and Replication of the Lab School Approach.

Mark Jarvis, a Lab School art teacher since the late nineties, leads off the first section with his article, "What Sally Knew and How I Found Out." He describes the experience of being drawn in to Sally's "special brand of passion and enthusiasm. . . . We were allowed a great amount of freedom but woe to anyone who was uninteresting or uninspired. . . . Sally taught us that every aspect of our school, from the color of the walls, to the outdoor sculpture, to the joy in the classroom, should telegraph to the prospective student that this was going to be a new beginning."

In his third year, Jarvis faced the challenge of creating a high school math curriculum that would make the subject less threatening and use art to make it more compelling. He thought of the models created by the architecture students at the University of Maryland. "It occurred to me that our kids might find that building a model of their dream house would be enticing. For centuries people have been enchanted by miniaturization. Doll houses and model trains have filled many an imagination. These projects have allowed us to help the students with basic math, life skills, measurement, simple civil engineering, and design. This curriculum has enabled students to visualize in three dimensions the geometry concepts that previously eluded them. For some it provides an opportunity to experience something less rigorous but similar to a freshman college course in architectural design. They developed a new vocabulary, learned to defend their work in critique, and most importantly, began the ongoing process of rehabilitating self esteem and awareness of the nature of their learning styles."

Some of Jarvis's words on Sally's emphasis on self-esteem for children with learning disabilities are quoted in the chapter. He writes that he understood this intellectually but truly internalized it when he was humiliated in a swing dancing class. This lesson, as self-evident as it might be, is among Sally's most important legacies.

In "Sally Smith's Arts-based and Integrated Curricular Approach to Educating Students with Learning Disabilities," Jennifer Durham, a Sally protégé, recounts, with scholarly citations, the history of the Lab School and Sally's arts and club methodologies. "And 50 years after the fact," writes Durham, "educational research has begun to catch up with what Sally has known all along. The arts are being proven to be powerful partners in learning, especially for the population of students who need it the most."

In "Sally L. Smith: A Genius at Seeing the Potential in People," Mary Allen Edgerton, then the Lab School curriculum coordinator, began with her first encounter with Sally: "I met her for ten minutes or so while she scribbled out in her signature purple pen the next two years of my life on the back of a used envelope—what classes I would take at American University in the master's program in special education that she directed as well as what my jobs would be at the Lab School. At that moment, I had some sense that I had lost control of my life and Sally had taken charge of its course. And what a course it has been!" She writes that Sally "saw more potential in a person—young or old—than anybody or even they themselves, frankly, had ever even considered possible." Edgerton goes on to break down the moving parts of the oft-described magic of Sally's approach to teaching. "She used to say, *If the child isn't learning, it's because we aren't teaching.* For students in Sally's graduate courses the words task analysis, diagnostic-prescriptive, hands-on and manipulative-based, as well as engaging the senses, and including an auditory, visual, and a tactile piece to every lesson became the lens through which everything else was considered. One could not understand how to teach a child with learning disabilities unless he or she could break a task down to its smallest components and discern at exactly what step, no matter how miniscule, a child might be encountering difficulty." At the same time, Edgerton notes, "the best lesson Sally taught her students was to love and value teaching through games. . . . Learning could be, and, most importantly, *should* be fun and engaging."

Lab School parent Kim Tilley, who also went through the AU master's program, wrote "Understanding the Parent's Perspective." She tells an all-too-familiar story of her older son having trouble in the classroom. "Events finally reached a breaking point when one afternoon our son threw his pencil down and began hitting himself on the forehead saying repeatedly, 'I'm stupid! Stupid! Stupid!'" She tells another familiar story: "Little in our experience prepared us for the flamboyance of Sally. From her brightly colored scarves to her polka-dotted fingernails to her deep-throated laugh booming out in response to our son's negative answer when she asked if he wanted to go to Lab and he said, 'Not really.'" When she read one of Sally's articles that came in the school packet, Tilley writes, "I began to cry—not quietly. I put down the article, unable to continue. The next day I picked it up and once again tried to read it. Same reaction, but this time I finally accepted the tears needed to come. Sally had put into words all the pain we had been going through. She knew. As a parent of a child with learning disabilities herself, she knew our struggle, she knew our pain, and she knew we hadn't failed as parents—she knew."

In "Revisiting *No Easy Answers*: Application of Sally Smith's Methods in the Lab School of Washington High School Program," Meredith Reynolds, the school's longtime high school curriculum coordinator, outlines the ways that the Academic Club Methodology is used in Lab's high school, which didn't exist until 1986. "The first edition of *No Easy Answers* (Smith, 1995) was published in 1979, thirty years ago," writes Reynolds. "That seminal work is as relevant today as it was when the book first appeared." Reynolds stresses that "High school students with learning disabilities must learn the process of learning," and that organization is essential. She quotes from *No*

Easy Answers, "Teaching the learning disabled child, the approach to a task is as important as, if not more than, teaching the task itself." Lab high school teachers must have complete mastery of their subjects, because the students bring considerable expertise and enthusiasm to many topics, exemplified "by the student who has conducted paleontological research and is joining a six-member team to look for fossils this summer," and another who "can recite game statistics for all Washington sports teams, past and present."

In Sally's tradition, "Teachers are given much liberty in the LSW high school to design their curricula and determine how they will teach." At the same time, they are held to Sally's credos that "a failing student really means the teacher has failed to teach" and that her teachers have a passion for their subject. "No matter how obscure the topic of interest, she held fast to the idea that if you love what you are doing, the enthusiasm is contagious." For high school students, as with younger ones, the Lab School emphasizes teachers knowing and teaching their students in a holistic way: "In order to teach the *whole student*," writes Reynolds, "the teacher must be aware of a student's composite parts: what the person's strengths, weaknesses, interests, pitfalls, maturity are, as well as which strategies are effective, along with his social emotional state, his health, coordination, cognitive ability, and communication skills."

Reynolds's article outlines the priority that Lab's high school places on organizing students, problem solving, encouraging students' self-advocacy, and assisting their continuing work of learning how to learn.

Art and Education

This section leads off with M. Sean Rozsics, the Lab School's music maestro since 1987. In "Sally Smith's Art Methods Applied: Music Education for Adolescents with Learning Disabilities & ADHD," Rozsics writes, "Sally was brilliant, hip, funny and a voracious reader. She exhibited a quiet confidence and exuded a calm, sage wisdom, but she did not suffer fools well and her bluntness could intimidate. Yet, she was genuine, sincere and endearing, and when she truly expressed her confidence and belief in your abilities, it meant everything. While many of my less fortunate colleagues around the country struggle to obtain mere support and recognition, Sally Smith continually provided all of her arts teachers with inspiration and encouragement as well as a reasonable budget."

Rozsics notes that "every member of Sally's arts staff is a functioning artist in their own right, accomplished in their craft and active in the local arts community." But later on, he hits on a nugget of gold: "Sally did encourage all teachers to develop the capacity to break down any action or activity to its most basic and primary components. She called this task analysis and in written form one could easily consume twenty pages. This arduous and exacting deconstruction of a task allows the instructor to become aware of each aspect of the task so that he/she can then better identify and correct any flaw or problem that the learner is having with the task."

Rozsics eloquently describes a philosophy of teaching music that includes his frustration with those who can play the notes on a page but not improvise a 12-bar blues progression by ear. Rozsics designed a curriculum around the organization of notes, which enables students to develop a *tonal vocabulary* that enables them to identify, by sound, most intervals, chords and chord progressions.

In "Discovering Science Through Art-based Activities," Rebecca Alberts describes Lab School strategies for connecting art to science, such as tying the works of Leonardo da Vinci and Rube Goldberg to their scientific basis or investigating the physics of Calder mobiles. In the Periodic Table of Elements project, students are assigned an element, gather images based on their research, and create a collage. To understand the different parts of a cell, students can use candy, Jello, or 3-D plaster relief models to recreate them.

In "Embracing the D," Lisa Holley, a 2005 graduate of Sally's master's program, writes of learning and teaching differently and of making scientific topics fun and approachable. Having studied fine arts as an undergraduate, she was at first dismayed when Sally hired her as a science teacher. "Photosynthesis in and of itself is not a very thrilling to subject to 9-year-olds," writes Holley, now at a DC charter school. But Holley found a way. "When I asked the class who wanted to audition to be the new *sales rep* for my Photosynthesis Machine 3000 on the Lab School Shopping Network, however, every hand in the room went up enthusiastically." Using a cardboard box, she created the machine, complete with a leaf, water, and sun lamp. "As I was embarking on my fourth year teaching science, I had the opportunity to teach art again. I promptly turned it down. I enjoy teaching science. Who knew? Sally did."

The Academic Club Methodology

In "The Academic Clubs: Theory to Practice," Noel Bicknell, who has led the Lab School's academic clubs since 1999, lays out the framework for Sally's most original, brilliant, and enduring breakthroughs. In the process he eloquently expresses some of her most important educational philosophies.

"The academic club model is designed to deliver to our students the social studies content they would otherwise miss due to their reading and language deficits," writes Bicknell. "Our use of academic clubs enables a child to feel like an intimate part of a time and a place and to become a vital part of the topic studied. It demands total involvement and gives each child a voice."

- Cave Club studies human evolution and the origins of language, shelter, agriculture, and culture.
- Gods Club makes kids gods and goddesses in ancient Egypt, Greece, and Rome.
- Knights and Ladies Club is all about medieval Europe.
- Renaissance Club, set in Florence, sets students to work as guild artists.
- Museum Club studies world history through the eyes of museum curators preparing exhibits.
- Industrialists Club studies American history through the eyes of industrialists and their adversaries.

One of Bicknell's subheadings reads "Beware of the Quick Fix—*There Are No Easy Answers*." He writes, "Wary of educational dogma and those who claimed to cure students of learning disabilities, Sally reminded her teachers that there was no single way to help all students and that the learning problems these students struggled against would likely follow them for a lifetime. Instead of chasing the easy fix, it was our responsibility as special educators to find out how each child best learned and to help these students understand their needs as learners. She designed the academic clubs as a venue, a laboratory, where teachers and students explore these individual learning strengths and seek a path to their full potential."

In a section on dramatic framework, Bicknell writes, "No matter what subject is to be taught, Sally believed that the dramatic framework is at the core of every successful academic club. By creating a compelling landscape that captured the child's imagination, the teacher can hook the child's full attention and natural curiosity."

In his section on total involvement, he writes, "Sally understood the challenge of the passive learner. Whether the result of distractability, learned helplessness, or years of painful classroom experiences, the need to engage passive learners is clear."

And under "Depth Is More Important Than Breadth," Bicknell notes that the Academic Club Model lends itself to deeper investigation of a content subject. Lab School students do poorly with connecting rote facts to a meaningful context. "For example," he writes, "the muddy single paragraph on Renaissance science found in a typical world history textbook is not the place from which to build a storehouse of knowledge. Instead, we look for a bedrock moment on which to build, such as when in 1609 Galileo lifts a spyglass skyward and becomes the first person to study the magnified night sky. That moment leads to so many great questions: Where did he learn about telescopes? How did he make his telescope better? How did he make the lenses? How was glass made back then? What did people know about the night sky?"

Under "Make It Visual, Make It Big," he writes, "Sally never lost the ability to see the world through the eyes of children. Her mantra was always, *make it visual, make it big*. By this she meant to start with the concrete and build to the abstract and start with the whole and move to the part."

Lab parent and reading teacher Susan Wolk lays out an outgrowth of clubs in a piece titled "An Actor's Role-reading Approach to Reading Fluency with Junior High Students," describing how students' immersion in their reading—making gestures and facial expressions—can help them improve their reading.

Longtime Lab School democracy teacher Nancy Rowland writes, "Sally sat me down in her office and explained to me what her plans were for me—*You will use your drama background to teach democracy*. I was as stunned as a deer in headlights, because in my mind I never was a *history person* and, therefore, never imagined teaching it." Rowland's article is titled "Becoming a *History Person* or, If Sally Says It's Possible, It Must Be."

The Related Services Integrated Model

In "Speech/Language Pathologists Reflect on Sally Smith and The Lab School of Washington," members of the Lab School's speech and language department recall Sally's vision of not only integrating language therapists into the school but also indoctrinating them into her commitment to creatively and collaboratively find a way to teach students who had not succeeded elsewhere. "We understood the need to summon up the best of our education and training in order to help find a way to get the kids to learn and to make it stick. Although the Cs that follow our degree stand for

Clinical Certificate of Competency, here at the Lab School those Cs have taken on a new meaning that reflects Sally's philosophy: follow Sally's lead in teaching and do it Collaboratively, Creatively, and Constantly."

Occupational therapist Christine Chang writes in "Memories Are Made of This" of Sally's ability to find innovative solutions to problems. When the school needed to replace a wetlands area that had been lost to the gym and pool construction, it became a lesson in wetlands and the waterfowl that nested in them. And building bridges over "our swamp" became another learning experience in sequencing, applied math, visual spatial skills, and motor coordination.

In "Being a Clinical Psychologist at The Lab School of Baltimore," Edwin Oliver writes, "Sally made a significant contribution to my idea of what it means to be a psychologist. She challenged my training, my idea of service delivery, and my overall view of the personhood of the child or adolescent with learning disabilities and/or ADHD. . . . She taught me that if I, as a psychologist, were to truly help children, I was going to have to be in their world and help them to master confusing environments."

Replication of the Lab School Approach

In the "History of the Academy In Manayunk (AIM): Adoption of the Lab School Approach," AIM founders Patricia Morgan Roberts and Nancy Blair tell the story, related here in chapter twenty, of meeting Sally in 2004 and deciding to create a school on the Lab School pattern.

"What worked?" ask Roberts and Blair. "Simply put," they write, "it is the model that works." It was the arts-based learning curriculum, the Academic Club Methodology, the integrated services team, and having partners. Of Sally, they wrote, "She was truly the epitome of *a woman ahead of her time*. What the research is now outlining in the field of learning disabilities, Sally Smith put into practice in 1967."

In "Implementing the Lab School Club Model at the Academy In Manayunk," AIM Clubs Coordinator Chris Herman writes that AIM not only embraced the club methodology but has "made it the crux of our entire program, interweaving thematic concepts throughout our literature, writing, and enrichment activities. . . . Perhaps the most essential notion in substantial and useful historical knowledge is the ability to recognize cause and effect. In traditional history classes, time periods are explored in bubbles, devoid of this concept, and therefore no logical connection between events is developed." Herman touches on an obstacle: "Finding teachers who are willing, creative, and flexible enough to teach in this manner. What works for a group of students one year will not necessarily work for the group to follow. Implementing the Lab School's Club curriculum required the special touch of many talented educators who needed to adjust each aspect of the class for the particular students who would take part in it."

In "Bringing Sally Smith's Vision to Manayunk," Jackie Ford Galbally tells her story of taking part in Roberts' and Blair's launch of AIM. "I feel I have truly realized the total effects of the *Live It, Learn It* methodology. It is an incredibly effective vehicle for delivering content to students who aren't able to access it in traditional ways. The Club system embodies Sally's understanding and dogged insistence for everyone to find and to contribute to others the strengths that are both evident and hidden, waiting to be cultivated." As a PhD and master teacher, Galbally is now a visiting professor at St.

Joseph's University, an urban teaching resident at KIPP: Philadelphia Charter Schools,

and just one example among hundreds of the continuing influence of Sally's former

students.

Twenty-Four — "The Lab School saved my son's life." Sally's Legacy at Fifty Years

With a mist of rain and autumn in the air on a perfect September evening, Karen and I drive past American University and down Foxhall Road's leafy mansions and college campuses. We miss the turn onto Reservoir Road and come to a classic two-story red-brick schoolhouse, looking a bit like a church with its stately white door and bell tower. The sign in front marks it as the Lab School Elementary Campus, including the motto TRANSFORMING LIVES. TRANSFORMING EDUCATION. and the L50 logo, denoting Lab's ongoing celebration which will culminate on September 25, 2017—fifty years since Sally Smith met her first set of students on the sidewalk outside Phelps Place.

In the parking lot, GO DRAGONS and LSW stickers festoon the rear windows of the minivans and Subarus. On the fields below, platoons of red-jerseyed girls work through their soccer drills as parents watch under their umbrellas. At the back end of the parking lot, a well-tended vegetable garden includes a hand-painted sign with rules, starting with BE SAFE. This building was once a DC public school, then a charter school. When it came open for lease a few years ago, the Lab School acquired it.

We get back onto Reservoir Road and quickly arrive at the main Lab School campus, on a rise across from the Georgetown Reservoir. The intermediate and junior high schoolers meet in the red brownstone "castle" that was once the Florence Crittenton Home for Unwed Mothers. We are shown down to the four-story high school building that, even with its angular brick-and-glass façade, blends into the landscape of the campus. The caterers are still setting up for the evening's festivities, the formal dedication of the building, which the high schoolers have occupied since April.

I wander into Beth Porterfield's biology classroom. This is her ninth year at the Lab School. She directs the Tide Turners Program, a summer institute that studies the science and policy behind endangered species and creates small documentaries. The students have been to Chengdu, China, to study giant pandas, the Karen Beasley Sea Turtle Rescue and Rehabilitation Hospital in North Carolina, and the Florida Keys to study various species. Their next destination is a marine lab in Hawaii. Porterfield's bulletin board includes the college lists for the last few years of Lab School students.

Next door the kindly Craig Omerod sits in his environmental/earth science classroom, where he teaches juniors and seniors. He is one of the legions on this campus whose life was changed by Sally Smith. Twenty-five years ago, with his degree in science from Michigan State, he had moved to DC for his wife's job and was looking for work. "What can you teach?" Sally asked. Science, he answered. "She said, 'You're hired,' and told me my starting salary, then asked, 'Can you help out in the PE department too?'" He went through Sally's program at AU and got his MA in learning disabilities, and spent five years as a dean of students without any formal title. "You start doing something and you find you love it," he says. "And I absolutely love it to this day. The students know what their differences are, and they have developed strategies that work for them."

As the guests arrive, we meet former board chair Mimi Dawson and former board member Dane Nichols, who remembers Sally's white legal paper and different colored pens, with which she'd keep track of the different tracks of ideas that would come up in meetings. "All the meetings were held standing up," says Nichols. "That was the whole idea, to keep things quick and to the point." Like many who were involved in the first gala in 1984, she tells her own version of the special bond of friendship that was sparked between Tom Cruise and Cher during their visit to DC.

We meet Mark Jarvis, who subbed as an art teacher for a friend twenty-two years ago and found himself on staff. "When Sally Smith got her hooks in you, that was the end," he says. "Sally was very demanding in a terrific way. You always knew you could run anything by her. She would make it happen. Her passion was infectious."

We sit down at a table and chat with Gary. He says he has read the entire draft of this biography, some chapters more than once. "I like the way you talk about Ben," he says. "She was a second mom."

We meet architect Camilo Bearman of Stantec Architects, whose wiry frame and dark curls would go well in a SoHo gallery. In the three-year process of designing the high school, he talked to the Lab School students about what they wanted. "Students at Lab are special in the way they take ownership of their learning needs," he says. "One said, 'When I read I want to be outside.' It's different from the process that you use to design other schools because the Lab School faculty members are so far ahead in33399 the way they teach. The rest of the world is just catching up. It's project-based learning, passion-based learning. We use this building as a benchmark for our other clients. This would be a great school for all of us."

The formal program for the high school building dedication begins. Head of School Katherine Schantz welcomes the guests and thanks them for their generous support.

Everyone knows it's hard to follow a legend. "In the educational field, it's regarded as professional suicide to take over for a founder," says Schantz. "Sally Smith had a brilliant idea that she made into a reality. After her death, the school needed someone to keep it alive and thriving. It was definitely a compelling challenge for me."

In a unanimous vote of the board of trustees, Schantz was chosen as the second head of school because of her expansive knowledge and experience in educational philosophy and practice, especially in the field of learning differences education. After graduating from Kalamazoo College with a degree in economics, she had worked at the Kildonan School in Amenia, New York, a boarding school for dyslexic children. "My mentor there was Diana King," says Schantz. "She was of the same generation as Sally. Being trained by a founder allowed me to understand the culture I was coming into at the Lab School." After Kildonan, Schantz spent nine years at the Harvard Graduate School of Education, earning her master's degree in counselling and consulting psychology and doing the course work and clinical practice and research in the doctoral program. "Harvard provided me with formative training," she says. "I was working with the top thinkers and researchers on the neuropsychology of dyslexia and learning differences."

Schantz came to the Lab School in 2009 from the Delaware Valley Friends School in Paoli, Pennsylvania. "Quakers are filled with optimism," she says. "And optimism is critical for working in this field, because not all answers are out there waiting for you. In Quaker education, you're always looking for new avenues for students to demonstrate their potential. I've carried that with me."

Schantz found that Lab was a machine that worked well. "The people here knew what to do," she says. "Sally had inculcated so many people on the staff with her gloriously energetic spirit. She had set it up so that her spirit lives on through her successors. Their dedication was inspiring, and they know the mission in their hearts.

"Sally set down a foundation that is time tested. The philosophy and vision of this school have stayed the same. Its reputation had grown even greater as a lot of the ideas that she put into play are now accepted around the country. Sally valued the power of the arts in education before it came into vogue. Now the arts are central to the twenty-first century idea of education and they are coming to the fore again. We're looking at a different kind of learning, a different kind of thinking, that's designed to work creatively, thinking other ways of expressing some of these ideas.

"Generosity with ideas—that is important to the mission of the school. We serve many more children than the ones in our doors through conferences and through the number of people who come through the school. The school has always been seen as a thought leader in this kind of education, partly because we have always chosen to promote those ideas and share them with others.

"Education is much different in the twenty-first century. The Lab School is probably better situated for the twenty-first century. But the playbook that she laid down at the foundation of this school still works. Lab has always been able to adapt because its values reflect the importance of flexibility and innovation."

At the dedication of the new building, Schantz says, "This high school building represents the dreams of our students and the dreams of our faculty. With a focus on mobility and versatility, the building has given our students new and changeable spaces that allow them to unleash the energy, creativity, and brilliance that they bring to school each day. It also nurtures their talents and supports their talents and staff in ways we are now just beginning to grasp. This building symbolizes fifty years of progress, of innovative learning, and kids who learn differently. As we occupy this building for the next fifty years, we will know that this is a Lab facility that matches the Lab philosophy, and the best practices in learning difference education will grow.

"Our next project will be the Sally L. Smith Center for the Arts." Schantz points out Gary and Nick Smith in the crowd and notes that they and Randy have put their support behind the project. "It will be a great tribute to our extraordinary founder," she says, "who must be looking down on us and smiling."

Schantz introduces Hal Malchow, who co-chaired the fund-raising campaign that made the high school building a reality. He comes to the podium and tells a story: "Our

life with the Lab School began when we went to an office on MacArthur Boulevard and learned that our son had learning differences. We asked, 'What can we do?' They answered, 'Try to get him into the Lab School.' We drove straight down to the Lab School. A lot of people here can tell a similar story. On that ride down our car was silent. Both my wife and I were thinking, though we didn't say it out loud, 'Will our son ever go to college?' Today our son is a senior at Denison University. He has a 3.0 grade point average and a job offer after graduation. He walked through the door in fourth grade unable to read a word. The Lab School saved my son's life. Our family owes this school so much that it is a debt that we could never repay. It is the most beautiful work of my life."

The amount that was raised tallied to $12,300,806.

Bill Tennis, the new chair of the board, says, "I am struck by how we got here. These are extraordinary endeavors that are carried out by extraordinary risk takers. They were calculated risks, but they were risks all the same. We had pipe dreams. We made a strategic plan about where this institution was headed. We decided that this was a risk worth taking, to bring this building to fruition. It was a team effort. There were dark nights, early mornings. In the end the budget built the building, along with the group of people who worked to make this happen. We are now marching on to the renovation of the lower school and middle school and the creation of the Sally L. Smith Arts Center."

Sophie Sperduto, a Lab School senior, spoke with passion: "Here's a shout-out to Mr. Camalier, Mr. Malchow, and most importantly our great head of school, Ms. Schantz, for their tireless effort and

Brooks Clark and Nick Smith at the Lab high school building dedication.

leadership to get our new high school built. Thank you. We're also here to celebrate what the new high school symbolizes—fifty years of progress, learning, and transforming the lives of kids who learn differently, and that includes me! Fifty years of the best teachers, the best administrators, the best counselors, and the best specialists—all dedicated to making a difference, and making a difference one kid at a time.

"But the past is past. Lab's past would not mean anything if it did not build a foundation for Lab's future. And what a future those kids will have who enter this building. This building is a state-of-the-art facility that every student, every parent, and every teacher can celebrate. Finally, we have a Lab facility that matches the Lab philosophy! So, in that sense, Lab's mission and Lab's future have only just begun. This building is the seed from which best practices in LD education, and even all education, will grow.

"As members of the class of 2017, the first class to spend an entire year in our great new high school, my classmates and I challenge everyone here tonight to make the next fifty years even more transformative, and even better for LD education. That challenge will honor Sally Smith's vision, Ms. Schantz's incredible cultivation and implementation of that vision, and every single kid who enters through these doors. The class of 2017 says thank you, thank you for building this high school and thank you for constructing the educational challenge of a lifetime."

During the reception, we get a chance to catch up with Nick. We also chat with Sarah and Steve Belson.

When I visited the AU library to go through Sally's papers several years ago, the head of special collections, Susan McElrath, said she was surprised that a biography of Sally had not been done sooner. "I feel as if this will be the first," she said, "and then there will be more after that." I imagine she's right. For example, a person could write a book tracing the teachers who came through Sally's and Sarah Belson's program and the impact they are having on the education world.

Elizabeth Elizardi was in the AU undergraduate program in the nineties. She now directs the Green Trees Early Childhood Village at Isidore Newman School in New Orleans, where Sally's granddaughter Maggie is a middle schooler. At a patron's dinner not long ago, Elizardi chatted with Randy and Diane. She later emailed them, "Sally had such a profound impact on my early career and her spirit has stayed with me as an administrator."

A few days later, Elizardi walked into the dining hall and saw Maggie and her own daughter, Scarlett, sitting side by side. "I walked up and asked Maggie if she had heard about our connection," said Elizardi. "She smiled and said yes. I gave her a big hug and shared with her how special her grandmother was in my life. I hope we can find a way to carry on Sally's spirit through our work at Green Trees, especially with our population of children with special needs."

In spring 2017, Maggie served as a junior teaching artist at Dancing with the Starfish, the New Orleans Jewish Community Center and Southern Repertory Company's joint musical theatre workshop for four- to seven-year-olds. "Maggie has been a wonderful addition to Dancing with the Starfish," wrote program director Shelby Kirby. "She's a both an incredibly hard worker and skilled performer, leading improv games and jumping into her role in the show as Sarah Seaweed with no reserve. She also helps out with less the glamorous tasks of teaching young artists such as chaperoning bathroom breaks, fetching Band-Aids, and re-directing wandering attentions. We're so lucky to have her!"

As noted earlier, Maggie is used to hearing people talk about her grandmother— how she changed their lives and how they are carrying on her work. Maggie is also used to hearing that she takes after Sally, with her blonde hair, bright spirit, and now her creativity in the performing arts and teaching. And Maggie is fine with it. She knows that it is a very nice thing and a special gift to remind people of Sally L. Smith.

Acknowledgements

I am so grateful to my friend since kindergarten Randy Smith for asking me to write this biography and for his cooperation and that of Gary Smith, their cousin Jonathan Low, and my older brother Stocky in their careful reading throughout the process. Special thanks to Sally's sister Hazel Arnett, who patiently provided invaluable information and feedback, and to Sally's dear friends Ruth Lyford Sussler, Kiriki de Metzo, Allegra Fuller Snyder, Tidi King, Sarah Belson, and the late Ben Booz, as well as many others who were so generous in remembering Sally. And thanks to all the Lab School teachers whose words from Sally's books and their own articles bring so much life to her legacy.

Special thanks to Professors Margaret Lazarus Dean, Martin Griffin, and Michael Knight—my Master of Fine Arts in Creative Writing project committee in the University of Tennessee English Department—for their encouragement and advice. Special thanks to my friend and colleague Donna Spencer for generously and skillfully editing the manuscript for publication and to Oliver Munday for generously and elegantly designing the cover. Thanks also to American University Archivist and Head of University Library Special Collections Susan McElrath. And thanks to Marty Cathcart of the Lab School for helping to promote the book.

Bibliography

Biddle, Flora Miller. *The Whitney Women and the Museum They Made: A Family Memoir.* New York: Arcade Publishing, 1999

Birmingham, Stephen. *The Rest of Us.* New York: Little, Brown & Company, 1984. Print.

Borchard, Helen. Two taped interviews with Isaac Liberman. October 26, 1978. Fordham University Oral History Series, Fordham University Library, Lincoln Center Campus, New York, NY 10023.

Frank, Mary and Lawrence K. *How to Help Your Child in School.* New York: Viking Press, 1950.

Friedman, Lawrence J. *The Lives of Erich Fromm: Love's Prophet.* Assisted by Anke M. Schreiber. New York: Columbia University Press, 2013. Print.

Funk, Rainer. *Erich Fromm: His Life and Ideas, an Illustrated Biography.* New York: Continuum, 2000. Print.

Hall, Edward T. *An Anthropology of Everyday Life: An Autobigraphy.* New York: Doubleday, 1992. Print.

Jowitt, Debra. *Time and the Dancing Image.* Berkeley and Los Angeles: University of California Press, 1988. Web. December 2015.

Lacey, Robert. *Model Woman: Eileen Ford and the Business of Beauty.* New York: Harper, 2015. Print.

Leach, William. *Land of Desire: Merchants, Power, and the Rise of a New American Culture.* New York: Vintage Books, 1993. Print

Liberman, Sally. *A Child's Guide to a Parent's Mind.* New York: Henry Schuman, 1951. Print.

Monica McGoldrick, Randy Gerson. *Genograms in Family Assessment.* New York: Norton, 1985.

Rosin, Josef. *Encyclopedia of Jewish Communities in Lithuania.* Translated by Shaul Yannai. Jerusalem: Yad Vashem, 1996. Ramygala pp. 640–641, population 1897–1929, 650 Jews. Web. December 2015 Jewishgen.org www.jewishgen.org/yizkor/pinkas_lita/lit_00640.html

Smith, Richard Norton. *On His Own Terms: A Life of Nelson Rockefeller.* New York: Random House, 2014.

Smith, Sally L.

Different is Not Bad, Different is the World: A Book About Disabilities by Sally L. Smith illustrated by Ben Booz. Longmont, Colorado: Sopris West, 1994. Print.

Live It, Learn It: The Academic Club Methodology for Students with Learning Disabilities and ADHD. Baltimore, London, Sydney: Paul H. Brookes Publishing Co., 2005. Print.

Nobody Said It's Easy: A Practical Guide to Feelings and Relationships for Young People and Their Parents. New York: The MacMillan Company; London: Collier-MacMillan Limited, 1965. Print.

No Easy Answers: The Learning Disabled Child. Rockville, Maryland: U.S. Dept. of HEW, National Institute of Mental Health, 1978. Print.

No Easy Answers: The Learning Disabled Child at Home and at School. New York: Bantam Books, 1995. Print.

The Power of the Arts: Creative Strategies for Teaching Exceptional Learners. Baltimore, London, Toronto, Sydney: Paul H. Brookes Publishing Co., 2001. Print.

Succeeding Against the Odds: Strategies and Insights from the Learning Disabled. Los Angeles: Jeremy P. Tarcher, Inc., 1991. Print

Smith, Solwin. *In Memorium: Robert S. Smith*. New York: Privately Printed, ca. 1935. Tribute by the Hon. Charles G. F. Wahle.

Suskind, Ron. *Life Animated: A Story of Sidekicks, Heroes, and Autism*. New York, Los Angeles: Kingswell, 2014.

Papers and Theses

Liberman, Sally. "Family Biography." 10 April,1950. For "The Family" course. Bennington College, Bennington, Vermont.

Smith, Robert Solwin. *Cultural and Information Programs of Newly Independent Nations as Instruments of Foreign Policy: Case Studies of Egypt, Israel and Pakistan* A thesis submitted to the Harvard Department of Government in partial fulfillment of the requirements for the degree of Doctor of Philosophy in the subject of International Relations Harvard University, Cambridge, Mass., December, 1955.

Magazine, journals, and newspaper articles

Adams, Luanne. "Guest Editor's Note, Special Issue in Honor of Sally L. Smith (1929–2007), The Sally L. Smith Methodology for Infusing the Arts into the Education of Students with Learning Disabilities and ADHD." *Learning Disabilities: A Multidisciplinary Journal* Volume 16, Number 2, Spring/Summer 2010, p. 53.

Alberts, Rebecca. "Discovering Science Through Art-based Activities" *Learning Disabilities: A Multidisciplinary Journal* Volume 16, Number 2, Spring/Summer 2010, p. 79.

Andrews, Robert H. "Cher Among Six Honored as High-Achieving Dyslexics." Associated Press, 31 Oct. 31, 1985. Web.

Bicknell, Noel. "The Academic Clubs: Theory to Practice." *Learning Disabilities: A Multidisciplinary Journal* Vol. 16, No. 2, Spring/Summer 2010: 85.

Booz, Elisabeth Benson. "Who Are You, Elisabeth Benson (Ben) Booz?" *News and Views: The Quarterly Publication of the Geneva Monthly Meeting, Geneva,* Switzerland. Sept. 2013. Print.

Brown, Emma. "Obituary for Sara B. 'Sally' Montanari, teacher, watercolorist." *Washington Post,* 22 Sept, 2010. Web.

Buder, Leonard "Snuffed Cigarette Butts Disclose Human Traits in College Tests." *New York Times* 18 June, 1949. Print.

Chang, Christine. "Memories Are Made of This." *Learning Disabilities: A Multidisciplinary Journal* Vol. 16, No. 2, Spring/Summer 2010: 103.

"Cher's Benefit Costume: It Wasn't By Design." Fashion Notes. *Washington Post* 3 Nov., 985: G3. Web.

Clark, Brooks. "RFK and Remembrance." *Washington Post Sunday Magazine* 6 June, 1993. Print.

Clark, N. Brooks. "Our Moment with Bobby: RFK in the Parrott Library." *The Bulletin,* the St. Albans School alumni magazine. Spring 2008. Print.

Durham, Jennifer. "Sally Smith's Arts-based and Integrated Curricular Approach to Educating Students with Learning Disabilities." *Learning Disabilities: A Multidisciplinary Journal* Vol. 16, No. 2, Spring/Summer 2010: 59.

Edgerton, Mary Ellen "Sally L. Smith: A Genius at Seeing the Potential in People," *Learning Disabilities: A Multidisciplinary Journal* Vol. 16, No. 2, Spring/Summer 2010: 63.

"Ex-Beach Mayor Marcie Liberman Dies." *The Miami News.* April 5, 1966: 1A, 4A. Web.

Ford, Jackie. "Bringing Sally Smith's Vision to Manayunk." *Learning Disabilities: A Multidisciplinary Journal* Vol. 16, No. 2, Spring/Summer 2010: 115.

Green, Susan. "Ralph Ellison's 'Invisible Man': 60 years later theme of racial identity still resonates" BurlingtonTimesFreePress.com Nov. 5, 2012.

Grimes, William. "Edward Hall, Expert on Nonverbal Communication, Is Dead at 95." *New York Times* Aug. 5, 2009. Web.

Herman, Chris. "Implementing the Lab School Club Model at the Academy In Manayunk." *Learning Disabilities: A Multidisciplinary Journal* Vol. 16, No. 2, Spring/Summer 2010: 117.

Holley, Lisa. "Embracing the D." *Learning Disabilities: A Multidisciplinary Journal* Vol. 16, No. 2, Spring/Summer 2010: 81.

Howe, Desson. "Reading the Stars: VIPSs Who Overcame Dyslexia Honored." *Washington Post* 31 Oct., 1985: B12.

"Importance of Non-Resident Term Emphasized by New Committee." *The Beacon,* Bennington College, Bennington, Vermont, 6 Oct., 1949: 1. Web.

Jarvis, Mark. "What Sally Knew and How I Found Out." *Learning Disabilities: A Multidisciplinary Journal* Vol. 16, No. 2, June 2010: 57.

Kernan, Michael. "Winging It." *Washington Post.* 11 Aug., 1982. Web.
https://www.washingtonpost.com/archive/lifestyle/1982/08/11/winging-it/d1554a44-9ad6-4762-bec1-92939a2bd216/

Morgan, Patricia and Blair, Nancy. "History of the Academy In Manayunk (AIM): Adoption of the Lab School Approach." *Learning Disabilities: A Multidisciplinary Journal* Vol. 16, No. 2, Spring/Summer 2010: 109.

Obituary: Marcia Ward Behr (8/22/1916–3/9/2016) Sayles Funeral Home, St. Johnsbury, Vermont. Web.

Obituary: Gerald Olney (G. O.) Herndon *Washington Times*, 24 Nov. 2010. Web.

Obituary: "Mary-Averett Seelye, performance artist" *Washington Post* 10 April, 2013. Web.

Oliver, Edwin. "Being a Clinical Psychologist at The Lab School of Baltimore." *Learning Disabilities: A Multidisciplinary Journal* Vol. 16, No. 2, Spring/Summer 2010: 105

"Profile of Robert Simon Smith." New York Sun. 6 Oct., 1922. Cited in *In Memorium: Robert S. Smith* by Solwin Smith.

Radcliffe, Donnie. "Yes, Chastity Bono is now Chaz." "Washington Ways" *Washington Post* 8 Oct., 1985. Web.

Reynolds, Meredith "Revisiting *No Easy Answers*: Application of Sally Smith's Methods in the Lab School of Washington High School Program," *Learning Disabilities: A Multidisciplinary Journal* Vol. 16, No. 2, Spring/Summer 2010: 67.

Rothschild, John. "When the Shoeshine Boys Talk Stocks It Was a Great Sell Signal in 1929. So What Are the Shoeshine Boys Talking About Now?" *Fortune* 15 April, 1995. Web.

Rowland, Nancy "Becoming a *History Person* or, If Sally Says It's Possible, It Must Be." *Learning Disabilities: A Multidisciplinary Journal* Vol. 16, No. 2, Spring/Summer 2010: 97.

Rozsics, M. Sean. "Sally Smith's Art Methods Applied: Music Education for Adolescents with Learning Disabilities & ADHD" *Learning Disabilities: A Multidisciplinary Journal* Vol. 16, No. 2, Spring/Summer 2010: 73.

"Sally, Kiriki Visit College." *Bennington Weekly* 27 April, 1951.

Selby, Earl and Miriam. "The School That Sally Built" *Reader's Digest* Dec. 1981: 120–125.

Smith, Sally L. "While Getting the Passport . . ." Bennington College *Quadrille* Spring 1971. Vol. 5, No. 2.

Speech and Language Department of the Lab School of Washington. "Speech/Language Pathologists Reflect on Sally Smith and The Lab School of Washington." *Learning Disabilities: A Multidisciplinary Journal* Volume 16, Number 2, Spring/Summer 2010, p. 101.

Tilley, Kim "Understanding the Parent's Perspective *Learning Disabilities: A Multidisciplinary Journal* Vol. 16, No. 2, Spring/Summer 2010, p. 65.

Ushkow, Barbara. "Review of Dance Workshop" *The Beacon* 17 Dec., 1947: 3.

"Winter Work Period Plans." *The Beacon* Bennington College, Bennington, Vermont, 17 Dec., 1947: 1–4. Web.

Wolk, Susan. "An Actor's Role-reading Approach to Reading Fluency with Junior High Students." *Learning Disabilities: A Multidisciplinary Journal* Vol. 16, No. 2, Spring/Summer 2010: 57.

Yang, Zhuang. "School for Learning Disabled Buys Former Crittenden Home." *Washington Post* 8 Sept., 1983 9/8/83. Web.

Zerivitz, Marcia Jo. *Images of American Jews of Greater Miami.* Charleston, S.C.: Arcadia Publishing, 2009.

Notes

Chapter 1 – The Clothes She *Didn't* Wear

3. **Christine Chang**. From her article, "Memories Are Made of This." *Learning Disabilities* Vol. 116, No. 2, June 2010: 103.

5. **Mark Jarvis** from his article, "What Sally Knew and How I Found Out." *Learning Disabilities* Vol. 116, No. 2, June 2010: 57

6. **Luanne Adams**, from her "Guest Editor's Note, Special Issue in Honor of Sally L. Smith (1929–2007), The Sally L. Smith Methodology for Infusing the Arts into the Education of Students with Learning Disabilities and ADHD" *Learning Disabilities* Volume 116, Number 2, June 2010, p. 53.

7. **M. Sean Rozics**, from his article, "Sally Smith's Art Methods Applied: Music Education for Adolescents with Learning Disabilities & ADHD" *Learning Disabilities* Volume 116, Number 2, June 2010, p. 73.

Chapter 2 – Gray Homburg and Spats–and a New Arrival–on West End Avenue

14. **Quotes from Isaac Liberman.** All quotes from Isaac Liberman in this and the next chapter are transcribed from taped interviews by Helen Borchard, October 26, 1978. Fordham University Oral History Series, Fordham University Library, Lincoln Center Campus, New York, NY 10023.

16. **Joseph P. Kennedy** anecdote quoted from John Rothschild, "When the Shoeshine Boys Talk Stocks It Was a Great Sell Signal in 1929. So What Are the Shoeshine Boys Talking About Now?" *Fortune* 15 April 15, 1995. "Taxi drivers told you what to buy. The shoeshine boy could give you a summary of the day's financial news as he worked with rag and polish. An old beggar who regularly patrolled the street in front of my office now gave me tips and, I suppose, spent the money I and others gave him in the market. My cook had a brokerage account and followed the ticker closely. Her paper profits were quickly blown away in the gale of 1929."

16. **Stores like Lord & Taylor, Best & Co., and Abraham & Strauss.** Leach, William. *Land of Desire: Merchants, Power, and the Rise of a New American Culture*, New York: Vintage Books, 1993: 300, citing the reports of vice president Alfred W. Miles of Best & Co.

Chapter 3 – The Rise of Isaac Liberman

19. **About half of Ramygala's 1,326 people were Jews**. Rosin, Josef. *Encyclopedia of Jewish Communities in Lithuania*, Translated by Shaul Yannai. Ramygala: 640-641. Web. Today Ramygala has a population of 1,679. In 1897, a census showed Ramygala with a population of 1,326, of whom 650, or 49 percent were Jews.

20. **No shoes or headscarves in the apartment.** This came from Ruthie Lyford Sussler, who visited the Libermans in their apartment.

23. **The Fifth Avenue Association.** William Leach *Land of Desire: Merchants, Power, and the Rise of a New American Culture New York: Vintage Books,* 1993, p. 174, citing the 1912–17 annual reports of the Fifth Avenue Association.

25. **The work of a matchmaker.** Hazel Arnett is sure that her parents' marriage was arranged by a matchmaker.

25. **Bertha not born in the United States.** Bertha and her twin brother Isadore had been 18 months old in 1897 when their mother Sarah had boarded the boat with her six children to join their father, Samuel, in New York. Over the years the family might have had the impression that the twins were born in the

United States. In his interview with Helen Borchard, Ike Liberman said Bertha had been born in the United States, and Abba Bayer thought the same.

4 – Meet the Bayers, and Ike and Bertha's Life Together

27. **Who was living at No. 8 Eldridge Street in 1900.** These dates come from the Unites States Federal Census, June 5, 1900.

28. **The West Side Jewish Center.** These facts come from Abba Bayer, who notes that "The Jewish Center is still active today and Virginia Bayer, Samuel's great granddaughter, recently served as its president."

30. **Founded the School of Retailing.** Leach 58–59.

30. **Quote on startup meetings on the School of Retailing.** Leach 59.

33. **Merwyn Bayer placed on an executive committee.** *New York Times*, 9 Sept., 1938.

33. **Eileen Ford at Constable, from Lacey's biography.** Lacey, Robert. *Model Woman: Eileen Ford and the Business of Beauty.* New York: Harper, 2015, p. 80-81. Print.

34. "Ex-Beach Mayor Marcie Liberman Dies." *The Miami News* 5 April, 1966: 1A, 4A. Web.

35. **The Bertha and Isaac Liberman Foundation.** As of 2014, the Bertha and Isaac Liberman Foundation had total assets of $5,335,163 and revenues of $232,726.

5 – Young Years on Park Avenue

37. Sally Liberman, "Family Biography," a paper for The Family course at Bennington College, April 10, 1950: 5. All Sally's words and prose poems in this and the next chapter come from that paper.

37. **When Sally was nine.** Sally wrote, "I had a nurse whom I loved deeply for seven years." Hazel Arnett said Anna the nurse was fired when Sally was nine.

37. **"I would love to know that."** Hazel ran into Anna years later in Central Park. Anna was pushing a baby carriage. As is usually the case in these situations, Hazel didn't ask Anna why her parents had fired her, but she wishes she had.

38. **Family systems studies.** I draw mostly from Monica McGoldrick and Randy Gerson in *Genograms in Family Assessment.* New York: Norton, 1985.

41. **Steered $500,000 toward the Whitney Museum in their efforts to keep Calder's Circus.** This comes from Flora Miller Biddle's *The Whitney Women and the Museum They Made: A Family Memoir.* New York: Arcade Publishing, 1999. Web.

47. **Founded to promote the progressive child-centered theories of John Dewey.** Richard Norton Smith. *On His Own Terms: A Life of Nelson Rockefeller* New York: Random House, 2014, p. 47.

48. **Read and wrote numbers backward.** Ibid, p. 46

6 – Modern Dance and Erich Fromm at Bennington

49. Ushkow, Barbara. "Dance Workshop Presented to Enthusiastic Audience." *The Beacon.* Bennington College, Bennington, Vermont, 17 Dec., 1947: 3.

53. Hall, Edward T. *An Anthropology of Everyday Life: An Autobiography.* New York: Doubleday, 1992. Print.

53. **Ned Hall went on to become a pioneer and prolific author in nonverbal and intercultural communication.** After teaching at Bennington, as his *New York Times* obituary summarized, "Mr. Hall directed a program for the Foreign Service Institute in Washington, D.C., designed to help State Department employees negotiate cultural differences when they took overseas assignments. At the same time, he carried out research at the Washington School of Psychiatry that led to his most influential book, *The Silent Language*, (1959), which outlined his theory of explicit versus informal forms of communication." He is remembered for developing the concept of social cohesion, a description of how people behave and react in different types of culturally defined space. He published

The Hidden Dimension in 1966, *Beyond Culture* in 1976 *The Dance of Life: The Other Dimension of* Time in 1983 and his memoir, *An Anthropology of Everyday Life*, in 1992.

Obit: "Edward Hall, Expert on Nonverbal Communication, Is Dead at 95, by William Grimes, August 5, 2009, *The New York Times*.

57. **Prose poem.** Liberman, Sally. "Family Biography," April 10, 1950, a paper for The Family course at Bennington College: 11–12.

57. A satchel full of gourmet edibles. Erich Fromm 's obituary in the Bennington *Quadrille*, March 1980.

57. **Eager for insights into dreams and fairy tales that he could give her.** Jowitt, Debra. *Time and the Dancing Image*. Berkeley and Los Angeles: University of California Press, 1988: 207.

57. **Ralph Ellison wrote much of *Invisible Man* during prolonged visits in an upstairs room reserved for him in their home.** Green, Susan "Ralph Ellison's 'Invisible Man': 60 years later theme of racial identity still resonates." Web. BurlingtonTimesFreePress.com, Nov. 5, 2012. Ellison remained close with his Bennington friends and their offspring and served on the Bennington Board of Trustees from 1970 to 1975.

57. Hall, Edward T. *An Anthropology of Everyday Life: An Autobiography*. New York: Doubleday, 1992: 191. Print.

59. **Commanded a black regiment in Europe and the Philippines.** Grimes, William. "Edward Hall, Expert on Nonverbal Communication, Is Dead at 95." *New York Times* 5 Aug., 2009.

59 Lawrence J. Friedman, assisted by Anke M. Schreiber *The Lives of Erich Fromm: Love's Prophet* New York: Columbia University Press, New York, 2013.

59 **These lectures provided the basis for much of *Man for Himself* (1947) and at least some of *The Forgotten Language* (1951).** Rainer Funk, Rainer. *Erich Fromm: His Life and Ideas, an Illustrated Biography*. New York: Continuum, 2000.

60. **Sally interning at the UN.** "Winter Work Period Plans" December 17, 1947, *The Beacon* Bennington College, Bennington, Vermont, p. 1–4.

60. **Smitty.** From an interview with Carrie McLeod Howson Bennington '56: "Everyone who took his classes just adored him. He also counseled students who needed it. He counseled me. My father was killed in an auto accident when I was a freshman. Smitty helped me through many family issues in those years."

62. Buder, Leonard. "Snuffed Cigarette Butts Disclose Human Traits in College Tests." *New York Times* 18 June, 1949.

64. "Importance of Non-Resident Term Emphasized by New Committee," October 6, 1949, *The Beacon*, Bennington College, Bennington, Vermont, p. 1.

65. Ibid.

7 – Kiriki and *A Child's Guide to a Parent's Mind*

72. Frank, Mary and Lawrence K. *How to Help Your Child in School*. New York: Viking Press, 1950.

74. "Sally, Kiriki Visit College." *Bennington Weekly*, 27 April, 1951.

8 – Paris and Bob Smith

80. **Words used to describe death.** From an Appreciation by Hon. Charles G. F. Wahle. From *In Memorium: Robert S. Smith*.

81. **I had seventy dollars in reserve.** *New York Sun* 6 Oct. 1922, as cited in "In Memorium: Robert S. Smith."

85. Sally L. Smith letter to John Schuman dated July 22, 1953, from the American University Special Collections.

10 — New York, Motherhood, and Geneva

109. **Letter to a *Mademoiselle* editor.** From Sally's papers: Letter to Mademoiselle, Oct. 25, 1954.

108. **From the beginning.** All quotes are from Smith, Sally L. "While Getting the Passport . . ." *Quadrille, the Bennington College Alumnae Magazine*, Vol. 5, No. 2, 1971.

11 – Washington, Themed Parties, and *Nobody Said It's Easy*

117. **As Gary grew older.** All quotes from Sally's article "While Getting the Passport . . ." *Quadrille*, the Bennington College Alumnae Magazine, Vol. 5, No. 2, 1971.

12 – "My child needs a school now!"—The Club Methodology is born.

128. **Gary raised his hand to answer a question about Native American rain dances.** Selby, Earl and Miriam. "The School That Sally Built" *Reader's Digest* Dec. 1981: 120– 125.

133. **Connection between Stoner, Ornston, and Orton.** From a conversation with Stoner's daughter, Caroline Robinson. April 23, 2016.

134. **Ten Million.** Selby p. 122.

134. **Summary from the era.** Ibid. p. 122.

134. **Coping strategies at home.** Smith, Sally L. *The Power of the Arts.* Baltimore: Paul H. Brookes Publishing Co. 2001. p. xiii

135. Ibid.

135. **Mary-Averett Seelye.** Obituary: "Mary-Averett Seelye, performance artist" *Washington Post* 10 April, 2013. Web.

137. **Bert Schmutzhart's glider.** Kernan, Michael "Winging It" *Washington Post* 11 August, 1982. Web. https://www.washingtonpost.com/archive/lifestyle/1982/08/11/winging-it/d1554a44-9ad6-4762-bec1-92939a2bd216/

138. **G. O. Herndon's career.** Obituary: Gerald Olney (G. O.) Herndon, *Washington Times* 24 November, 2010. Web.

138. **Turri Herndon's Film Curricula.** *The Power of the Arts* p. xiii.

138. **Creative Writing at Stoddert.** From the AU Special Collection, Box 11, 1967 – Project 370: The Author Works with the Class (other authors included Russell Baker).

138. **Sally's quotes in this section** are from *The Power of the Arts* pp. xiv, xi, xv.

13 – "I'm Not Stupid. Are You?"—The Lab School Adventure Begins

144. **Quote about financial backers for Lab.** Sally L. Smith "While Getting the Passport . . ." *Quadrille, the Bennington Alumnae Magazine*, Vol. 2, No. 2, 1971, p. 7

144. **Lab named in honor of John Dewey.** Sally L. Smith *The Power of the Arts* p. xvi

145. **Description of Cave Man Club.** Sally L. Smith *The Power of the Arts* p. xii

146. **Anecdote of a dance student.** Earl and Miriam Selby "The School that Sally Built," *Reader's Digest* December 1981, p. 123

149. **Bio notes on Marcia Behr.** Obituary: Marcia Ward Behr (8/22/1916–3/9/2016) Sayles Funeral Home, St. Johnsbury, Vermont. Web.

149. **Bio notes on Sally Montanari.** Brown, Emma. "Obituary of Sara B. 'Sally' Montanari, teacher, watercolorist" *Washington Post*, 22 Sept., 2010. Web.

154. **Sally's quote.** *The Power of the Arts* p. xv.

155. Sally L. Smith "While Getting the Passport . . ." *Quadrille, the Bennington Alumnae Magazine,* Vol. 2, No. 2, 1971, p. 7.

14 – Home Life in the Turbulent Late Sixties

172. **Dinner parties.** Ben Booz said, "She told all her friends, 'If you ever go to a dinner party and they are there, if you don't just walk out, you're not my friend anymore.'"

15 – American University and *No Easy Answers*

175 **Garbled words on the blackboard.** Clifford, Garry. The headline from an interview with Sally in *People* magazine, 28 July, 1980.
171. **Joyous laugh.** Garry Clifford.
177. **Statistics.** 1976–77 The Lab School Handbook, from the AU Special Collections.
178 **Quote from Bertram Brown.** Quoted by Earl and Miriam Selby in "The School that Sally Built" *Reader's Digest,* December 1981, p. 125.
181. **One of NIMH's best-selling titles.** *People*, p. 55.
182. **Ben Booz quotes.** All from her self-biography, "Who are you, Ben Booz?"

16 – Sally the National Advocate; Buying the Castle

182. **Sally filled the journal.** National Education Association Journal *Today's Education*, February–March 1981 (Vol. 70, No. 11).
182. **Sally wrote the forward to** *Drama Integrated Basic Skills: Lessons Plans for the Learning Disabled.* A. Snyder and A. Clopton; Charles C. Thomas and Co., 1979.
186. **Reader's Digest story.** Selby, Earl and Miriam, p. 124
187. **Independence allowed Lab to expand.** Smith, Sally L. *No Easy Answers: The Learning Disabled Child at Home and School.* New York: Bantam Books, 1995. p. x.
185. **$2.4 million.** Yang, Zhuang "School for Learning Disabled Buys Former Crittenden Home" *Washington Post* 8 Sept., 1983. Web.
186. **Night school students had not been previously diagnosed as LD.** Smith, Sally L. *Succeeding Against the Odds*: p. 20–22.
197. **Quickly grew into daylong celebrations.** Ibid, p. xiv.

17 – The Dawn of the Galas

190. **Cher accepted the award to help Chastity.** Radcliffe, Donnie. "Washington Ways: Yes, Chastity Bono is now Chaz." *Washington Post* 8 Oct., 1985.
190. **Quotes from Bruce Jenner.** Howe, Desson. "Reading the Stars: VIPSs Who Overcame Dyslexia Honored" *Washington Post* 31 Oct., 1985, p. B12.
191. **The gala raises $386,000.** Suskind, Ron *Life, Animated: A Story of Sidekicks, Heroes, and Autism* New York, Los Angeles: Kingswell, 2014.
192. **Cher's outfit and hairstyle.** Desson Howe.
193. **Quotes from Cher at the Lab School.** Andrews, Robert M. "Cher Among Six Honored as High-Achieving Dyslexics" AP 31 Oct., 1985. Web.
193. **More quotes from Cher.** Ibid.
193. **Quotes from Tom Cruise.** *The Power of the Arts* p. 135
194. **Quote from review.** Paley, Gissin "Helping Children to Fail," a review of *The Learning Mystique: A Critical Look at LD.* 24 Jan., 1988 *New York Times*.
195. **In her notes.** Sally's notes in reaction to *The Learning Mystique: A Critical Look at LD* by Gerald Coles. Box 8, AU Special Collections.
195. **Reaction to West 57th St. broadcast.** *The Power of the Arts* p. xvii.
196. **Ron Suskind's role in galas.** Suskind, Ron. *Life, Animated: A Story of Sidekicks, Heroes, and Autism.* New York, Los Angeles: Kingswell, 2014: 84–85.

18 – Writing More Books with Ben

204. **The beginning of the Rauschenberg Awards.** Smith, Sally L. *Live It, Learn It: The Academic Club Methodology for Students with Learning Disabilities and ADHD*, p. 94. Remarks by Sally L. Smith at the National Gallery of Art (2003) accessed by LD online. *The Power of the Arts*, p. 135.

205. **Quote from Rauschenberg.** *The Power of the Arts,* p. 135.

206. **What is an art teacher's most important job?** Ibid p .136

206. **Speech at National Gallery.** Remarks by Sally L. Smith at the National Gallery of Art (2003) accessed by LD online.

208. **PEP encouraged Lab to disseminate materials.** *The Power of the Arts* p. xviii.

20 – The Lab School of Baltimore and *Live It, Learn It*

216. **Sally's quote about the Lab School of Baltimore.** *The Power of the Arts,* p. xviii.

217. **Statistics about Baltimore Lab.** Ibid. xvii.

223. **History of the Academy In Manayunk (AIM): Adoption of the Lab School Approach.** Patricia Morgan Roberts and Nancy Blair, from *Learning Disabilities: A Multidisciplinary Journal* Spring/Summer 2010 Vol. 16, No. 2.